Political Economy and Soviet Socialism

Political Economy and Soviet Socialism

Alec Nove

Professor of Economics, University of Glasgow

London
GEORGE ALLEN & UNWIN
Boston   Sydney

First published in 1979

GEORGE ALLEN & UNWIN LTD
40 Museum Street, London WC1A 1LU

© George Allen & Unwin (Publishers) Ltd, 1979

British Library Cataloguing in Publication Data

Nove, Alec
  Political economy and Soviet socialism.
  1. Russia – Social conditions – 1917 – Collected
works
  309.1'47'084   HN523   78-40547

ISBN 0–04–335037–2

Type set in 10 on 11 point Plantin by
Trade Linotype Limited, Birmingham
and printed in Great Britain
by
Billing & Sons Ltd, Guildford, London and Worcester

Contents

Glossary

ASSR	Autonomous soviet socialist republic (national subdivision of a union republic)
Baza (pl. *bazy*)	Supply base, storehouse
Glavk (pl. *glavki*)	Chief department, e.g. of an economic ministry
Gosplan	State Planning Committee (Commission)
Gossnab	State Committee on Material-Technical Supplies
Khozraschet	'Economic' (or 'business') accounting, profit-and-loss accounting
Kolkhoz	Collective farm (literally 'collective enterprise"). The term also covers some fisheries co-operatives
MTS	Machine Tractor Station
Obkom	Party committee of *oblast'* (province)
Obyedineniye (plural: *Obyedineniya*)	(Industrial) association, usually formed by an amalgamation or merger, but sometimes replacing a *glavk*
RSFSR	Russian republic (Russia proper)
Raykom	Party committee of *Rayon* (district)
Snabsbyt	Supply and disposal (organs)
Sbyt	Disposals (organs)
Sovkhoz	State farm (literally 'soviet enterprise')
Sovnarkhoz	(Regional) economic council
Tsentrosoyuz	Central union of (retail) co-operative societies
Valuta	(Foreign) currency, usually 'hard' currency
Zayavka	Request (indent), e.g. for supplies

Notes About Notes

All references to *books* are to author and date of publication of the edition used: e.g. Stalin (1952). Details of title will be found in the list of references at the end of the book.

In the case of *periodical and newspaper articles in Russian*, the reference will be in brackets in the text, usually without the title of the article (for instance: *Pravda*, 21 October 1971). The following abbreviations will be used for periodicals:

EkG	*Ekonomicheskaya gazeta* (as present weekly)
EKO	*Ekonomika i organizatsiya promyshlennogo proizvodstva* (usually six copies a year, Novosibirsk)
EkMM	*Ekonomika i matematicheskiye metody*
Kom	*Kommunist*
MSn	*Material'no-tekhnicheskoye snabzheniye*
MEMO	*Mirovaya ekonomika i mezhdunarodnye otnosheniya*
PEG	*Promyshlenno-ekonomicheskaya gazeta*
PKh	*Planovoye khozyaistvo*
VEk	*Voprosy ekonomiki*

The statistical annual *Narodnoye khozyaistvo SSSR* is abbreviated as *NKh*, followed by the date (e.g. *NKh*, 1973).

Introduction

The papers printed in the present book have in common the fact that they are about Russia, past and present, and/or about socialist theory and practice. They were written at various dates in the past ten years. To my own surprise, there is very little overlap between them. In preparing them for this collection I made a few amendments here and there, brought some statistics up to date, put in some cross-references and mentioned certain relevant books published since the original was written. But with very few exceptions the papers have been reprinted unaltered. I am most grateful that permission to reprint has been so readily given.

Would the papers have been different had I written them today? Of course some would. Thus the long quotation from Rakovsky which I have included in 'Trotsky and the left opposition' *would* have been included in 'Is there a Ruling Class in the USSR?', had I got around to reading Rakovsky in the original at the time the former paper was being written. The article on 'Planners' Preferences' was written at a time when economic reforms were promulgated, and these have been largely frustrated, and so it should be read in conjunction with 'The Politics of Economic Reform'. The paper on Bukharin was written before the appearance of the excellent political biography by Stephen Cohen, and its text would certainly have reflected my reading of this biography. The discussion on 'Market Socialism' would certainly have drawn on important ideas expressed recently by Wlodzimierz Brus and Radoslav Selucky, among others, as well as on subsequent work by Bettelheim himself, but the essentials of the argument would not have been greatly affected.

My 'philosophy' for the study of the Soviet Union and of socialism is set out, by implication at least, in the last article in this collection, on 'Criteria'. It stresses the importance of a realistic approach to the limits of the possible, in the past and in the present. Such limits exist, and to point to them is not to attack either Marxism or any other doctrine. It may be that highly desirable actions, or institutional arrangement, or policy, happen to be impracticable. One is reminded of an old story from the Napoleonic wars. Napoleon ordered that church bells be rung in every town entered by French troops during a campaign in Germany. His troops march into a town and – no bells rang. He called in the Burgomaster. '*Why* no bells?' exclaimed the Emperor. 'Well, your imperial majesty,' replied the Burgomaster, 'there are five reasons. The first is that we have no bells.' '*Stop!*' shouted the Emperor. We too should remember that it is little use discussing whether something would be (or would have been) advisable if, in cold fact, it could not be done. It is also important to note, as

Kolakowski recently had occasion to point out, that certain objectives could prove to be mutually incompatible, which is one reason why the outcome of human effort is so often at variance with the original objectives of the actors.

The author is well aware of the fact that there are many legitimate and opposed viewpoints on many of the questions discussed here. Debate is highly desirable. Out of argument and contradiction comes a closer proximation to understanding – or so we must hope. But we must all avoid the temptation to substitute eloquence or verbiage for hard-headed analysis. Let us cite three assertions which could be made:

(1)   Most of the working class favoured Trotsky in 1923.
(2)   Most of the working class was opposed to Trotsky in 1923.
(3)   Most of the working class was passive and did not care one way or the other in 1923.

All the above statements are 'disqualified' as academic discourse, unless, of course, their author(s) give reasons for their answer. And there could, needless to say, be more than one defensible answer, and some of the evidence may be contradictory.

In the days when I was a student, Professor Laski used to warn repeatedly against analyses in which 'the conclusion is in the premises'. One must not eliminate problems by defining them out of the way. This is not by any means an attack on any one 'ideology'. Thus, as is made clear in the paper on economic thought, illegitimate abstraction from the relevant aspects of reality is a disease to which mainstream 'bourgeois' economics is particularly prone, as are also those Marxist fundamentalists for whom socialism represents (by definition) the elimination of all the perplexing contradictions which beset all existing industrial societies. The planner with perfect foresight and perfectly competitive markets are both impossible, if only because, as Loasby has been pointing out, freedom of choice implies ignorance about what others' choices will be.

Of course it is easy to criticise others, more difficult to live up to one's own academic principles. I can only hope that I have done so.

Finally, I would like to thank Elizabeth Hunter for invaluable help in putting these papers into 'printable' shape.

Part One

History of Russia

I

History, Hierarchy and Nationalities:

Some Observations on the Soviet Social Structure

The notes that follow are essentially a series of hypotheses, discussion points, relevant (in my view) to the origins and nature of the Soviet social structure. It is not my intention to assert that any of the points to be made below represent *the* explanation of a complex phenomenon. For example, the historical past of Russia obviously has *some* bearing on the present, both in forming the ideas of the rulers as to the behaviour appropriate to rulers, and in affecting the willingness of the ruled to accept what others, brought up in another environment, might well regard as intolerable. However, I am well aware that historical tradition is a many-sided thing, that it includes both Peter the Great and Tsarevich Alexei, Bakunin and Pobedonostev, Stenka Razin and Nikon, Dostoevsky and Gorky, to name at random a few personalities unquestionably part of Russia's past and unquestionably different in many essential respects. This being so, no argument is made concerning the *inevitability* of Bolshevism or of any part of the social structure of today, even while its specifically Russian background can hardly be discounted.

Let us begin by discussing the relationship between state and rank, between service to the state (*gosudarstvo*, or *gosudar'*) and status. It is, of course, a commonplace of Russian history that Ivan IV largely destroyed the antonomous territorially based power of the old hereditary nobility, that gradually the descendants of the *boyar* families became merged with the serving-men, the *dvoryane*, who held land on condition of, and as a reward for, service, and that two types of landholding became in effect one, linked formally and informally to the duty of service to the state and to the monarch who embodies the state. Peter the Great finally imposed universal service on all the gentry – if 'gentry' is at this period the right word. (Many of the *dvoryane* in the seventeenth century were still common soldiers and

Reprinted from Soviet Studies, *vol. 21, no. 1, July 1969.*
This paper was written for background discussion purposes in connection with work being done at the Institute of Soviet and East European Studies, University of Glasgow, in the field of Soviet social structure, on a grant from the Social Science Research Council.

petty civil servants.) Peter formalised the gentry's obligations, divided them into fourteen civil and military ranks, with the duty of service for life. The reasons for this stress on universal service, and for the serfdom which was its economic basis, have also been widely discussed by Russian historians: a sparsely populated area, vulnerable to foreign foes and with an open eastern frontier, a weak economy, a low level of culture and of technique, and so the need for great efforts to maintain a viable state. Along with this went a lack of spontaneous social forces: a traditionalist and illiterate merchant class, great shortage of educated officials, virtually no literature. (It is extraordinary how very few works written in Russian in the period up to 1800 can be read with any pleasure or interest at all, save for antiquarian or philological interest, and this in the age of Racine, Corneille, Molière, Shakespeare, Milton, Sheridan.)

In no other European country did the state or the monarch so totally dominate the social scene. Of course, the actions of Ivan against the landed nobility did have parallels elsewhere: Louis XI of France acted similarly a century earlier. In France too the nobility was reduced to courtiers, or to the king's senior civil and military servants. But there was much less total dependence on the king, and the hereditary nobility of France had much wider cultural and political horizons than the *dvoryane*. The French autocracy tolerated, indeed was based upon, a far more developed and more autonomous social life in town and country. In Germany multiple centres of power and prestige developed early, with the emergence of a multitude of independent rulers, large, small and tiny, with a wide variety of internal arrangements (some, as in Prussia, also based on state service and on serfdom). In Poland the *szlachta* (gentry) was exceedingly assertive of its independence of the (elective) monarchy, with some very unfortunate consequences for that country.

However, the really significant point for us is, in my view, that the service-to-the-state idea lasted well into the nineteenth century. The gentry were freed from compulsory service by Peter III (1761), but in practice most of them continued to work in the civil and military spheres for the tsar. Those who did not had no role in society, and were the 'superfluous men' who figured prominently in Russian novels of this period. At the time of Pushkin and later it was still the custom to use the word *sluzhit'* (to serve) as a synonym for being in the service of the state. Only much later did work for some private employer 'qualify' for this designation, from which the modern word *sluzhashchii* (office worker) derives. The legal division into ranks or estates (*sosloviya*) survived until 1917.

The powers of the tsar and of his officials over the everyday life of the gentry even in the nineteenth century were remarkably tight by any standards familiar in the West. To take just a small example,

Count Benkendorff, head of Nicholas I's gendarmeries, was responsible for the behaviour of the gentry in St Petersburg, in the same sense in which the provost-marshal is responsible for the behaviour of officers in the British army. Pushkin's letters contain a reference to some *dvoryane* young men arrested and expelled from the capital for making a noise (*shikanie*) in a theatre. (Pushkin, 1887, vol. 7, p. 42.) Imagine such an occurrence in London, Paris or Vienna in 1830! Pushkin even after his political rehabilitation had to apologise profusely to Benkendorff for leaving Moscow for the country without permission, and he was repeatedly denied the right to travel abroad. One of his biographers chose to emphasise the vital role of rank in Russia in the following words, written fifty years after Pushkin's death: 'Our society is so arranged that the greatest artist without rank appears in official society to be below the lowest clerk', and he went on to assert that Pushkin 'was given the rank of Kammeryunker so that his [beautiful] wife could be invited to balls.' (Vol. 1, p. xvi.) It is worth noting the implication that heredity itself did not convey much status.

In an imaginary conversation, a Spaniard questions the author (Pushkin) and puzzles over the meaning of the word 'aristocracy' in the Russian context. 'It seems that your *dvoryane* are socially equal and there is no restriction on entry into this class. Then on what does your so-called aristocracy rest?' The reply asserts that the ancient Russian *dvoryanstvo* fell and became a kind of third estate. Some of those who lay claim to aristocratic status have recently been ennobled, but 'we are proud not of the glory of our forefathers but the rank held by some silly uncle'. (ibid., vol. 4, pp. 359–60.) Elsewhere Pushkin emphasises that entry into the *dvoryanstvo* 'is accessible to all'. Military and state service and university degrees easily promote into it men of other classes. (ibid., vol. 5, p. 99.) It is interesting that Pushkin took the view that this was a good thing.

'The aristocracy after Peter contemplated limiting the ; but luckily the cleverness of the sovereigns triumphed . . . and the form of government remained untouched. This saved us from monstrous feudalism and so the people were not divided by an unclimbable wall from the *dvoryane* . . . Otherwise [the *dvoryane*] would have eliminated the possibility of freeing the serfs, limited the number of *dvoryane* and closed off access to state rank and honour to members of other estates.' (ibid., p. 12.)

It followed from this that Pushkin regarded the freeing of *dvoryane* from compulsory service in 1761 as a 'disgrace'. Yet he also felt that lack of the hereditary principle was a grave source of weakness. In some of his historical works he wrote (in French) that the lack of *de facto* hereditary nobility represents '*moyens d'entourer le despotisme de stipendiares dévoués et d'étouffer toute opposition et haute indé-*

pendance. L'hérédité de la haute noblesse est une garantie de son indépendance. Le contraire est nécessairement moyen de tyrannie ou plutôt d'un despotisme lâche. (ibid., p. 87.) In some very subtle historical commentary, he traces this to the fact that boyars did not become feudal, that 'they lived at the monarch's court, did not fortify their estates, did not base themselves on the small family, did not fight the monarch, did not sell their services to the towns; they were at once courtiers and comrades, formed factions, counted rank by seniority'. (ibid., pp. 85–6.) The boyars and hereditary seniority (*mestnichestvo*) were liquidated under the pressure of the petty (i.e. non-aristocratic) *dvoryanstivo*, finally by Peter.

So not only was the status of the *dvoryane* originally one of a hereditary service class – though this status could also be acquired by promotion above a certain civil or military rank – but in their social life they were subject to supervision, even tutelage. The emergence of an intelligentsia of non-gentry status must have been a source of annoyance to officialdom, as it did not fit the normal categories. The label attached to them – *raznochintsy* ('other ranks') – expressed this perplexity.

As the nineteenth century wore on, these various class and estate (*soslovie*) distinctions were becoming modified. Thus the close identification between the civil and military service and the *landed* gentry, which was certainly a fact under Catherine, was only very partially the case under, say, Alexander II, when the politically influential *chinovniki* could and did take a view which did not reflect any personal interest in land. Indeed, their *class* nature is something of a puzzle for the analyst. They were not feudal, even more clearly not capitalist. Were they above classes, were they themselves a class?

But it is misleading to look at the gentry and its role *vis-à-vis* the state only from their own point of view or that of the monarch. Equal interest attaches to the folk view of autocracy and gentry. Aware though one is of the danger of generalisation, the following points do seem relevant to our theme and to have some validity.

First, the peasants until the twentieth century recognised the legitimacy and stood in semi-religious awe of the tsar. The many rebellions were directed, supposedly, at the gentlemen-nobles who withheld the truth from the tsar and twisted his will to their own selfish ends. Authority was necessary, otherwise there would be chaos (*chelovek cheloveku volk; homo hominem lupus*) and foreigners would come and seize land and people. In the 1890s, as I recall my father telling me, Russian peasant conscripts sang:

> The Turkish sultan wrote to us,
> He wrote to the Russian Tsar,
> I will invade your lands
> And come myself to live in Russia (*sam v Rossiyu zhit' poidu*).

Instinctively, the bulk of the peasants distrusted the gentry's acquisition of rights. Ivan the Terrible became a folk hero even though (or because?) he shortened the nobility by a head. The 'gentry's liberty' from service was felt to be, and was, a licence to ill-treat the serfs to a greater degree. The tsar could rely, whenever he wished, on support from below against the gentry. Only Peter, by challenging too many of the established traditions, including religious ones (*pravoslavnyi tsar'*, and all that goes with it), evoked substantial personal hostility among many peasants.

The peasants had a duty to those who had a duty to the tsar and the state. This was, after all, the original rationale of serfdom. The continuance of duty to the lord after the freeing of the gentry from the obligation of service was deeply resented. Yet the feeling of some sort of duty to obey constituted authority ran deep, and found expression in two very similar episodes, one in Pushkin's *Captain's Daughter*, the other in Tolstoi's *War and Peace*: rebellious peasants, faced with a determined and bold officer, not only submit but also tie up and hand over their own leaders.

The idea, then, of an autonomous 'gentleman' engaged in his own affairs, and challenging instead of serving constituted authority, ran counter to the folk traditions. A merchant was different. He had the right and duty to buy and sell, and might be regarded as a bold and resolute chap (*molodoi kupets, udaloi molodets* of many folk-songs) in this not very lofty calling. But that educated people should not 'serve' was a new and shocking thought. The unfortunate men of the sixties discovered this, in the course of their heroic and futile 'going to the people'. This attitude may well persist today, since the party conservatives can appeal to the folk against the 'disloyal' literary intelligentsia, and the whole notion of socialist realism can be said to be based less on Marx than on the old idea of universal service to the state, from which writers should be no more exempt than anyone else.

In order to ensure this service, and to fight effectively against subversion from within and from without, the tsar's officials devised controls over expression and movement which, once again, contrasted sharply with what had become normal in Europe in the nineteenth century. I have before me a British passport issued in 1900 (and signed personally, it seems, by Lord Salisbury). Passports were rare in those days, but Russia required one. It bears numerous stamps, showing not only entry and exit (complete with an exit visa) into and out of the empire, but also registration in the appropriate police districts of St Petersburg and Moscow. The parallels between the regulations of the 1840s and those of the 1950s are doubtless familiar to any reader of the reissue of the work of the Marquis de Custine. The system had changed but little by the reign of Nicholas II. The practice of *propiska* (registration, with residence permits) for Russians in Russian cities existed then, and it exists today. The practice of requiring a *kolkhoznik* to obtain a species of leave pass before he leaves his village, which so shocks Western observers, has parallels not only with serfdom but also with the situation after 1861, when the peasant society, the *mir*, had the right and duty of regulating the movement of its members.

Of course, it would be wrong to assert that these or any other restrictions on human behaviour today followed inevitably from the practices of tsarist gendarmes; only that the country was to some extent predisposed or conditioned to such arrangements. Similarly, as a Czech communist once sadly remarked, the behaviour of men in authority, whether communist or no, is always in some degree affected by the memories of how men in authority used to behave in the society in question in the past, 'and the further east you go . . .'.

But let us return to the question of social status and its relationship to service to the state, and for present purposes the party machine and the state can be seen as an integral part of the *gosudarstvo* (and the Politburo as the collegiate head of the real state). Under the tsars, almost until the twentieth century, it could be said that the vast social role of the state was in large part a consequence (and in some degree the cause) of the weakness of autonomous social and economic entities. This was being corrected by industrial advance, by the creation of large Russian limited companies and banks, cartels and peasant co-operatives, the growth of professional and *zemstvo* institutions. The revolution, and ultimately the achievement of 'socialism' in the sense of all-round nationalisation and collectivisation, made of almost everyone either a state employee or a collective peasant (*kolkhoznik*). The practice of allowing only one 'official' professional or artistic association, and of nominating its controllers, further reduced spontaneous activity and the number of organisations within which status could be acquired. The Soviet Union is a country in which the civil and military service can be said to dominate the lives of most men, because they, like the *dvoryane* of Peter's time, are usually in full-time state employment.

This state of affairs carries with it not only certain specifically Russian features, but also the general, universal logic of bureaucracy. The word is not used in a pejorative sense. Bureaucracies are necessary and play a major role in all countries. The point is that in the USSR, despite distinctions between party, government, social organisations etc., there is an important sense in which all are part of one great single hierarchy. The common link is the system of *nomenklatura*. This is the great list of appointments of any importance in any sphere of Soviet life and a list of persons fit to hold them, together with the designation of the party committee in whose patronage the given appointment is. The party's personnel departments assign people to jobs in all the sub-hierarchies. It is as if the establishment division of the British Treasury guided or approved all appointments, from the editorship of a provincial newspaper or a trade union secretaryship in Scotland up to a ministerial appointment and down to a managerial post in the Midlands.

So universal an 'establishment' carries with it certain logical consequences. As in any civil service or army, status becomes very closely linked with rank. Exceptions happen, of course. But rank-consciousness is inevitable, and tends to pervade society to a greater extent if so many are in fact state employees. Inevitably, not only salaries but also material entitlements and 'perks' become attached to rank. A British civil servant who reaches the rank of Assistant Secretary will have his own secretary, a room of defined size, better access to the car pool, a carpet . . . The rules are usually made not only to ensure that promotion receives its due reward, but also so that the reward is not excessive and power is not abused: thus the carpet must not exceed x square feet, and so on. It is quite logical to expect detailed regulation of this character within any bureaucratic hierarchy. If all the society or group is within one hierarchy, a strong tendency develops to carry rank-consciousness and its advantages into family life outside work. One may study this in the peacetime life of a British military garrison overseas. Colin Cross has written of another hierarchical society, that of British India:

'The Simla government issued an elaborate warrant of precedence with 63 ranks – with the Viceroy at the top and a superintendent of telegraph workshops at the bottom. It included military as well as civil ranks, the Archdeacon of Calcutta ranking immediately below a brigadier and immediately above the Tea Controller for India.' (Cross, 1968.)

Peter the Great would have understood. So it is hardly surprising to find tendencies to carry rank-privilege into everyday life, with some resultant abuses, which those in charge of the system may dislike and seek to remedy. These abuses are facilitated by two features of the Soviet scene. One is the strict state monopoly over distribution, accompanied by frequent shortages of goods in demand, which, to an extent hardly possible under private enterprise conditions, facilitates priority allocation to the men of rank and influence in the region (the head of the retail trade network is one of them, or wishes to ingratiate himself with 'them'). Secondly, for familiar reasons, the single-hierarchy situation, in which the local party and state authorities, newspapers, judiciary and so on are run by the same group of people makes it harder to combat petty abuses.

Mention of the army leads to two other thoughts. One concerns the relationship, conceptually, between the army officers and property and so with class in the Marxian sense. In a traditional army in most countries, the officers are drawn in the main from what Marxists would regard not without reason as the ruling class. The army could then be seen as in some degree representative of the class structure of the country, reflecting property relations even while, naturally, the officers did not own the army, and their power over their men had nothing directly to do with property relations. But suppose the whole country were divided into a military and civil service, with ranks and even uniforms. In his later years, Stalin seems to have had such a vision, since he greatly extended the wearing of uniform with rank badges into what is normally civilian life (miners, diplomats etc.). Admittedly this tendency was soon checked and in due course reversed, so it would be quite wrong and misleading to press the military parallel far, even in Stalin's worst years. Yet one could conceive of a 'model' in which everyone did have ranks and owned no means of production at all. Or one could conceive the entire basic capital of the USSR to be in the joint 'ownership' of officialdom, the latter being defined as officials on the establishment list, the *nomenklatura* (*nomenklaturnye rabotniki*), a large hierarchically organised and self-recruiting elite, whose right to suppress any spontaneous social or economic happening outside its own organisation(s) is an essential (*the* essential?) feature of the Soviet system in the Brezhnev as well as the Stalin era. This conception requires us to redefine the word 'ownership' in a way which alters its meaning perhaps too much. Yet somewhere along this line of thought might be found the relationship, if there be any, between property, rank and status in the USSR. (See 'Is there a Ruling Class in the USSR?', p. 195 below, for a further development of these ideas.)

Social mobility and civil and military hierarchy are not, of course, necessarily in contradiction. Peter the Great and even Ivan were quite willing to promote humble men to high office, sometimes to the deep chagrin of the hereditary nobility. (Boris Godunov was described, in a well-known passage, as of slave and Tatar origin, *Vcherashni rab, tatarin*, and his promotion by Ivan led him in due course to the throne.) Much more recently, an examination of the origins of generals and *chinovniki* of Nicholas II suggests that promotion could take men of humble birth well up into the official hierarchy. Officers of the line regiments were more often than not rather simple folk, and were so regarded by the more aristocratic Guards regiments. Well-known World War I generals, such as Ivanov, Denikin and Kornilov, were of very modest origins, and Kornilov was furthermore half a Kalmuk. Research might well show that the Russian imperial service, though based on a hereditary service class, was somewhat more 'democratic' than the British administrative and officer classes of the period. None the less, no one can possibly doubt that the revolution did destroy or drive out the bulk of the old ruling class, including those of its members who had been promoted from the ranks, and substituted a new ruling group. This at first contained a proportion of the old radical intelligentsia. It is a familiar fact of Soviet history that this type of communist, plus the surviving non-party or ex-Menshevik or neo-populist servants of the regime, perished almost to a man in the Great Purge.

The central committee and government organs, and the army, came to be dominated by persons of unmistakable working-class or sometimes peasant origin. The dominance of men promoted from the lower ranks has coloured some important aspects of Soviet life. Upward social mobility and respect for the dignity and wishes of one's subordinates do not necessarily go together. Once again one is tempted to seek parallels in the army. Sergeants are promoted men of the people. In their capacity as sergeants, they traditionally bully and bawl, and their relationship with the private soldiers is not at all sweetened by the fact that they come from the same social milieu. Indeed the bull-necked table-thumping authoritarian party secretaries and other local bosses seemed and sounded the kind of characters of whom tough sergeants are made. The fact that so many of them rose to high position is indeed a sign that the revolution had as one of its consequences a massive promotion of new men from below. But once established, those new men might well be expected to value their hard-won ranks and privileges, and to seek to defend them against their erstwhile comrades. Solzhenitsyn paints a hostile but convincing picture of such an ex-worker–official in the person of Rusanov in his *Cancer Ward*. In another novel, another author commented that, after being promoted from the workers' to the managerial dining-room, a petty cadres-department official came to regard every suggestion to improve the workers' feeding arrangements as personal insult.

It is by no means suggested that *noblesse* always *oblige*, that the interests and comfort of soldiers, workers or peasants were of great concern to the ruling classes of the past. Russian (and other) history is full of examples of the contrary. Yet the intense feeling of hierarchy, the underlining of the superior-inferior relationship in everyday life, numerous instances of crude use of privileged status, seemed particularly offensive in the Soviet context since they appeared to contradict the revolution and all it stood for. As already suggested, there is no contradiction between these abuses and the colossal extent of upward social mobility which was a consequence of the revolution. Indeed, there is a causal connection. The sergeants, so to speak, became the officers. This lead to a marked coarsening of superior-inferior relations, especially at the height of Stalinism. The oppressive severities of the old regime had become markedly softened well before 1917. Referring to the apogee of Stalinism, a Soviet defector of *dvoryanstvo* origin once said to me: 'To understand our human relations, especially between officers and men, you must compare us not with Nicholas II but with Nicholas I.' A similar observation must be made in respect of conditions in prison and in camps. The horrors encountered by the Petrashevsky circle in 1849 were inconceivable in 1900. This greater humanity was typical of the early Soviet period too. The treatment meted out to political suspects in, say, 1922 was similar in many respects to the later-tsarist-decadent-liberal period: most suspects were exiled, wives were allowed to visit and sometimes reside with them, there was no mixing with common criminals, and some exiles, including my own father, were even allowed to leave the country quite legally. This contrasts with the vicious conditions so vividly described by Evgeniya Ginzburg and many others, which became the norm in the thirties. The crudities and petty cruelties were the reflection within the prison system of the often harsh boss-subordinate relations of Stalinist life in general, but also of the uneducated sergeant-type's view of the proper treatment of those suspected of disloyalty, dissident intellectuals in particular. It was complicated by such feelings as the ignorant upstart's revenge on those whom he suspected of feeling superior to him. This, under Stalin, was surely part of the process of producing a smoothly working hierarchial society, in which rank, discipline and obedience would be undisturbed by dissident voices or by persons claiming influence other than through the proper hierarchical channels.

Stalinism was, among other things, the organised rule of men of little education promoted from the ranks. Even after the system became organised and organisationally somewhat ossified, promotion to *nomenklatura* jobs was open to all whose origins, attitudes and working methods appealed to the various cadres and personnel departments. The vast expansion of industry, science and the social services led to an immense upsurge in demand for qualified personnel at all levels, and opportunity knocked at many doors. The Great Purge itself was social mobility on a grand scale: within a largely unchanged hierarchical structure, hundreds of thousands had to be promoted to take the place of the vanished ones.

However, with the passing of time an important change was bound to occur. In the twenties, special preference was deliberately given to working-class youth, to some extent also peasant youth, in access to educational opportunities (*rabfaki* etc.) and (especially) party jobs. In the Stalin period generally, promotion went very often to tough men-of-the-people, whose literary prototype was Ovechkin's Borzov. (*Raionnye budni*, of which the first instalment appeared as early as 1952.) At a higher level, Khrushchev was of this species. But in the fifties and sixties advancement even in the party hierarchy became increasingly confined to those with higher education. This is logical.

Able children of workers had excellent opportunities to get onto the educational ladder thirty years ago and are now in the prime of life. (Something of the kind, following the widening of educational opportunities, is happening in the British Labour party, to the irritation of men like Gunter and others of their generation who left school at 14.) Furthermore, fifty years after the revolution, the party itself has come to represent, and to a great extent consist of, the successful. The *class* contrast between party commissar and 'bourgeois specialist', typical of the early years of Soviet power, has long since vanished. So has the *partmaksimum* insisted upon by Lenin, the rule that party members should earn no more than skilled workers.

This state of affairs has important consequences for our understanding of the changing nature of the party, but this is not the theme of the present essay. The point relevant here is that higher education has become *the* way forward for the vast majority of those who wish to become anybody in the USSR, whether in the intellectual, governmental or party spheres. Observant foreigners have noted that the young official recruited by the party (and perhaps also by the KGB) represents a particular type of student, the species that becomes a secretary of the Komsomol at his higher educational institution. None the less, such a person has been exposed to higher education. In these circumstances, any light which can be thrown on the process of student selection, on the social origins of students, tells us much about social mobility.

Such studies as have been published in the USSR show that a high proportion of the children of persons with degrees make their way into higher education. (For example, see the works of Perevedentsev and others at Novosibirsk.) This is hardly surprising, and it would be quite unreasonable for critics of the USSR to use *this* as proof of the ossification of the social system, of privilege and so on. For reasons familiar in all countries, the children of educated parents have advantages in both the way of help from home and greater interest in learning. Education being free in the USSR, the financial bar to progress up the ladder, in towns at least, is now minimal. Consequently, despite some cases of string-pulling (hardly surprising anywhere, since the population does not consist of angels), it could be argued that the high share taken by the children of the educated of places in higher education is the result of fair competition. Those who criticise this state of affairs would presumably also criticise the kind of measures which used to be taken to combat this trend: special educational privileges for children of proletarians, special difficulties in university entry for children of the intelligentsia. Khrushchev's ill-fated education 'reform' of 1958 was an attempt to redress the balance. Under normal non-revolutionary circumstances, it is bound to appear contrary to sound educational practice and to be a social irritant.

Among the ways up into the technical intelligentsia which ambitious workers do use are evening and correspondence courses, which are highly developed. Many do not make the grade, but there are also plenty of success stories. Concentration in studying in the evenings is doubtless facilitated by the relative absence of distraction, especially in most provincial towns. It is facilitated also by legal provision for time off to take examinations. The USSR publishes many figures of the total number of students divided into day, evening and external (correspondence). It would help our picture of social mobility from the factory floor if there were also figures of actual graduands divided into these three categories.

A much less favourable picture emerges when one examines the situation of the rural population. Of course, in the Soviet Union, as in all other countries, one way of bettering one's lot is to move to town and acquire a trade. The drift of ambitious young men to the bright lights of the city is a universal phenomenon, and it is propaganda and not serious analysis to identify such a trend in the USSR and, without further ado, ascribe it to the collective farm system or to the policies of the government. These have indeed been town oriented in the main, at the least until the most recent years, but before ascribing this to Marxism ideology it is as well to note a very similar trend in most developing countries, even under the authority of rabid anti-Marxists. Nor should it be surprising that the standard of rural schools is below urban levels, or that children of peasants tend to be less academically ambitious than children of many townspeople. I imagine that the educational opportunities in (let us say) Beynac in Dordogne are not equal to those available to the pupils of the great Paris lycées. Egalitarians could argue that, to the credit of the Soviet educational system, it has resisted the temptation to set up anything resembling the great lycées, or to lay any stress on the identity of particular schools, which are usually known only by number and have no distinctive uniforms. Only in the most recent years have we seen a few special schools for high-flying mathematicians and physicists (plus of course musical and ballet schools), which do give their pupils an excellent start in their particular specialisations. But when all is said, the gap between rural and urban schools remains very wide. This was commented upon by the eminent mathematician Kolmogorov recently; he deplored the tiny proportion of villagers who gain entry into universities. The problem is a difficult one. Rural teachers are not well paid, amenities of life are as a rule exceedingly primitive, school rooms are primitive too, being normally built by the village and not by the state. It is hardly surprising that the standard of teaching is comparatively modest, though no doubt there are many thousands of devoted teachers doing their best in often very difficult circumstances.

The gap between the cultural and material level of village and town remains vast. To some extent this is merely the Russian counterpart of the gap one finds in all developing countries: study the contrast between the great cities and the villages in, say, Venezuela, Mexico, Turkey. It has been exacerbated by a generation of neglect under Stalin. It is this gap which helps to explain the existence of legislation which restricts the freedom of the villager to move to town. He needs an internal passport which is, as a rule, issued only to townspeople. He then also needs a police registration certificate (*propiska*). This is exceedingly difficult to obtain in the case of the bigger cities, even for residents of other cities, because there is also a gap in culture and amenities between (say) Leningrad and some smaller town like Tambov or Ufa. These geographical restrictions affect upward social mobility to a quite considerable extent. Rural residents can be denied the right to move to town, and though a number do succeed in circumventing the regulations, some are unable to do so. Thus in Leningrad I once read in a local paper of a village girl who tried to get into a technical college in a city and failed to do so because she 'did not have an urban registration' (*ne bylo gorodskoi propiski*). I also know of a science lecturer whose wish to move from Odessa to Moscow is frustrated by a vicious circle: no job without *propiska*, no housing space without *propiska*, no house or *propiska* without a job, and so on. In an excellent article on this whole subject S. Lisichkin pointed out that one consequence of the regulations was that scientists and lecturers do not dare leave Moscow and Leningrad because of the difficulties they would encounter if they wished to return. (*Novy Mir*, 1967, no. 8.)

The Soviet government very properly takes credit for a great educational advance. Villages have benefited too. There are great practical obstacles in the way of extending secondary education to rural areas, not least of which are distance, lack of roads, lack of adequate premises. The efforts now being made to improve rural life generally will doubtless reduce the gap. But at present the combination of poor schooling, legal restrictions on movement and the general poverty of the cultural milieu combine to place the peasant in a situation where his upward mobility is limited. His hope is to get to town and become a worker. Despite the restrictions many succeed in moving, particularly into construction work.

                                               •

There is ample scope for research on all the topics here referred to, and the present paper does no more than raise questions, scratch the surface and put forward hypotheses. Another area deserving of the closest attention – and getting it in the work of J. A. Newth and others – is social mobility of members of non-Russian nationalities. This above all is an area in which propagandists of both sides have a field day. Books can be written in which all non-Russian nationalities are lumped together into one undifferentiated oppressed whole. Yet quite plainly this approach is far too crude.

Again, a few words of history are in order. Tsarist Russia, despite some foolish attempts at 'russification' in its last decades, gave able men of other nationalities excellent opportunities for advancement and, in many cases, *dvoryanstvo* status too. This was particularly obvious in the case of Baltic German subjects of the empire, as well as immigrants (or sons of immigrants) from West European countries. One has no difficulty in recalling the very large number of German names in the civil and military service right up to 1917. Officers from Malorossiya, as the Ukraine was known, were no more likely to be unfavourably regarded as un-Russian than Anglo-Irish officers of the Ascendancy for being 'Irish'. Cossacks, whether in the Ukraine, the Don, the Urals or elsewhere, were considered to be in a military caste, and men of little education and no family connections could and did rise high in the military hierarchy. The situation of other nationalities varied exceedingly, and it would require a book to trace the full story. Many Poles served in important capacities in many parts of the empire, though after 1863 they held no senior posts in Poland itself. Georgian princes were prominent in the Russian service (Bagration commanded an army against Napoleon). Some of the Muslim mountain races of the Caucasus served as the basis for highland regiments out of which many were promoted to the rank of general (the situation of Muslims in Turkestan was much less favourable). Admiral Kolchak was a Crimean Tatar, and so on. The Russian empire was known as *Rossiiskaya imperiya*; the word *Rossiikaya* was distinguished from the plain and ordinary *Russkaya* by implying a multi-national state, under a Russian Orthodox monarch, of course. The relationship between 'British' and 'English' under Queen Victoria would be a parallel. Here too the Scots and the Irish had ample opportunities for promotion, in the sense of being accepted into the largely English establishment in London and into the armed forces. With the exception of Irish Catholics, the obstacles were of class and wealth, not nationality. Much the same obtained in Russia, except for the Jews and some other *inorodtsy* (aliens), and even they could shed their disabilities by changing their religion. So the tsarist empire was in some degree multi-national, and the career advantages of being 'Russian' were open to most people of most nationalities if they chose to talk, act and feel as members of the Russian service.

However, the national cultures and languages of the non-Russian nationalities were neglected when they were not actively discouraged. While some of the present area of Soviet Central Asia was ruled by emirs, and tribal forms survived in parts of the Caucasus, there was a rule no local native government or native hierarchies. (After 1863,

Russian Poland was divided up into ordinary Russian-style *guberniyas*; Finland remained unique throughout.) Economic and cultural development in the south and east was extremely slight. In the Baltic states there were German, Russian and Yiddish cultures, while the Estonian and Latvian languages were thought of as primary forms of peasant speech, as was the Ukrainian 'dialect'.

The Russian republic (RSFSR) set up after the revolution retained the 'multi-national' term *Rossiiskaya*, which still forms part of the RSFSR of today. But from 1922 the 'USSR' is officially no longer 'Russian'. Union and autonomous republics were set up in which the non-Russian language was encouraged, and national-republican political hierarchies were created. One could rise in one's national capacity and speaking one's own language. Thus I once met in a train in Baku an Azerbaijani woman wearing the badge of membership of the Supreme Soviet of that republic, but she could not speak Russian. In some periods there were excesses, insisting upon the local language under conditions somewhat reminiscent of the status of Irish in present-day Ireland. There were also swings towards russianisation, especially under postwar Stalinism.

This is not the place for a discussion of all the complicated aspects of nationality policy in the USSR. I will therefore confine myself to matters bearing directly upon the role of nationality in the social structure and in social mobility, abstracting from real or alleged 'bourgeois nationalism', 'great-power chauvinism', the mythical right of succession, the extent of republican powers and other eminently discussable matters.

No one, in view of the careers of Stalin, Beria, Mikoyan, Kaganovich, would presumably care to deny that non-Russians could rise high in politics in the USSR. Nor could it be seriously maintained that the rank and career of Timoshenko and Bagramyan were adversely affected by Ukrainian and Armenian nationality. Within a national republic, membership of the titular nationality usually confers a definite advantage, in obtaining official positions and places in higher educational institutions. (Indeed, one reason for the unsatisfactory position of Jews is that they are not the titular nationality in any republic, except for the autonomous region of Birobijan, in which very few Jews live.) Examples of pro-native discrimination may be encountered in literature and in statistics. Thus Solzhenitsyn in his *Cancer Ward*, wrote that a Kara-Kalpak, by reason of his nationality, was quickly promoted in the medical service. Statistics of students show that, for instance, in Uzbekistan and in Moldavia the proportion of day students in the total number of students is notably higher for Uzbeks and Moldavians. (Since all persons qualified to become students can be assumed to wish to be day students, i.e. to study full-time with a stipend, this can be said to measure a certain favouritism to one's own nationality in choosing among those qualified.) There are also statistics showing that expenditure on schools in Central Asia is above the all-union average. (Cited in Nove and Newth, 1967, p. 84.) Since per capita income is lower there, this suggests a conscious effort to redress the balance, to pull up the backward.

The careers open to the talents in the national republics are an integral part of the *nomenklatura* system. Thus the jobs of, let us say, minister of local industry or editor of a daily newspaper in Turkmenistan are almost certainly subject to decision by the personnel department of the all-union central committee of the party. But, though power of decision may often rest in Moscow, membership of the republic's own nationality confers advantage, provided there is no suspicion of disloyalty, of course.

Statistics show that in Central Asia the majority of the republic's nationality tend to be peasants, and European immigrants are predominantly urban – though there are descendants of Russian peasant settlers in several of the republics; I visited Russian *kolkhozy* near Alma Ata, for instance. Russians can be shown to occupy a high proportion of technical and managerial posts in Central Asia. Members of Central Asian nationalities tend to study to be teachers and doctors, rather than engineer-technologists. New industrial employment opportunities in the region are still rather frequently taken by Russians or Ukrainians, not because of a plan to 'colonise' the area, but because of the reluctance of the native inhabitants to move into an alien industrial environment out of traditional village life. In fact, a fascinating survey of undesired and unplanned labour mobility from Siberia to Central Asia documents the evident dismay of the authorities at this turn of events; this study analyses the reasons for the local inhabitants' lack of interest in industrial employment, which, after all, could provide and was intended to provide an opportunity to move out of peasant and into worker status. It turns out that industry is taken to be 'Russian', or anyway requires a knowledge of the Russian language, simply because so many of the industrial workers and engineers *are* Russian and do not know Uzbek, Tajik etc. (Perevedentsev, 1966.) Furthermore, in higher education most scientific textbooks and much of the instruction are in Russian.

So an attachment to a native way of village life, and an inability or reluctantce to learn and speak Russian at work, would appear to affect the social mobility of Central Asians, in so far as technical and industrial work is concerned. To a considerable extent this is a matter of choice for the individuals concerned. If Ahmed is offered the opportunity to learn the trade of instrument mechanic and prefers to pick cotton, this is not to be ascribed to the nature of the Soviet system. But of course if Ahmed has serious difficulties with an alien language and culture, that is a factor that cannot be ignored. (After all, the

Portuguese claimed that any Angolan could have become a Portuguese if he had made the effort . . .)

The desire of people to live among their own kind also affects the geographical mobility of the nationalities. This is subject to the same restrictions (passport, *propiska*) as apply to all Soviet citizens desirous of changing their location. However, there is absolutely no evidence that a non-Russian who wants to live outside 'his' republic encounters any special problems for that reason. Again, the chief variant seems to be individual preference. Thus 98 per cent of all Georgians, and 95 per cent of all Georgian graduates, reside in Georgia. Armenians, on the other hand, may be found all over the Soviet Union: only 51 per cent of their graduates live in Armenia. (Calculated from census data and from *Vysshee obrazovanie v SSSR*, 1961, pp. 70–1.) Since there is no evidence that the rules are differently applied to these two nationalities, it follows that Georgians seem to prefer to achieve *their* social climbing among Georgians in Georgia, whereas Armenians wander far. It would appear that the citizens of the Baltic republics also show a marked predilection to stay at home. As for the Ukrainians and Belorussians, it may be argued that, just as in tsarist times, their careers within the *nomenklatura* jobs are almost indistinguishable from those of the Russians. Rural inhabitants of these and many other nationalities, often with very poor Russian, may have little chance of advancement, but this may be a special case of the general handicaps of being a peasant. Of course, if suspected of nationalism, anyone's career prospects become very dim.

It is this last factor which sometimes confuses 'committed' commentators. Nationalism, other than Russian nationalism, is the subject of police attention. Ukrainian, Lithuanian or Turkic intellectuals get into trouble, the KGB may arrest alleged Zionists, all for the crime of disloyalty to the multi-national USSR, within which, as has been repeatedly stated, Russians are the elder brothers, numerically and culturally dominant. This, however, is *not* the same as asserting that preferment is given to Russian nationals for official jobs. An Uzbek suspected of pan-Turkism has no more and no less chance of advancement than a Russian who goes to church. Russians do hold some key posts in the national republics, though this varies a good deal: thus Georgians dominate their own republican hierarchy to a much greater extent than the Turkmens or Tajiks dominate theirs. This could be a by-product simply of different levels of cultural development (certainly it is not due to fears of nationalist deviation, since nationalist feelings in Georgia happen to be exceedingly strong).

Anyway, once considered loyal and 'Soviet' in spirit, persons of all nationalities can and do get on to the all-union *nomenklatura*, and once they get there promotion is little affected by nationality, with some exceptions which need to be carefully qualified. The first concerns the

Jews, who, for reasons which cannot be examined here, are kept out of certain categories of jobs (diplomacy, foreign trade, some military posts) and appear to find special difficulties in others. The second is a by-product of a conscious aim to balance numbers of nationalities in categories of jobs in which such a balance is deemed desirable: this could benefit or harm an individual depending on the given circumstances ('we need another Central Asian'; or 'we already have enough Balts'). However, it is not an unfair generalisation to assert that upward social mobility is seldom actively impeded by national origin alone, provided the individual adopts Soviet ideology and – save in some republican hierarchies – the Russian language. Thus, to take an entirely random example, a recent debate on economic planning elicited contributions from all-union officials of various planning agencies whose names included virtually every union-republican nationality, except that Central Asians were notably under-represented. (Examples: a deputy chairman of Gosplan is Armenian, a deputy head of Gossnab a Ukrainian, a deputy minister of non-ferrous metals has a Lithuanian-sounding name, and so on.)

The above needs some careful qualification, and no doubt will get it in more specialised and lengthier work on the subject. Thus there is a possible correlation between russification and promotion (except that for the thoroughly russianised Jews this is of little help). Furthermore, at the very top the dominance of Russians has been reinforced of late, as a glance at the list of Politburo members and ministers would confirm. It is significant too that, according to Khrushchev, Molotov raised objections to Mukhitdinov's membership of the Politburo because Central Asians should not be in a position to decide all-union policy. True, Molotov was defeated in 1957, but shortly afterwards Mukhitdinov was demoted, and by 1963 Khrushchev himself was placing Russian party overlords in charge of the four Central Asian republics (Brezhnev abandoned this arrangement, which must have been resented by the local nationalities). There may well be some tendency to regard Russians as somehow more reliable, in cases of doubt, because they are Russians.

Thus we have a multi-national elite, and within the overall *nomenklatura* there are national ladders to climb. But the Russian language is an important qualification for many species of advancement. *Russian* nationalist sentiment does not seem to contradict the official 'Soviet patriotism' whereas other nationalisms are held so to do. Stalin himself, Georgian though he was, enforced a russianisation policy, but used large numbers of non-Russians in the task of carrying it out.

It would be fascinating to compare the situation of Soviet nationalities with that of other minority groups in other countries. Thus, for instance, the knowledge that the adoption of the majority language gives career advantages drives many parents quite voluntarily to send their children to Russian-language schools, especially in the less nationally conscious autonomous republics (e.g. the Udmurt, Komi, Mari and perhaps Tatar ASSRs), but also among those who live out-side their own national republic (e.g. a Ukrainian in Latvia or a Latvian in Uzbekistan will go to Russian schools). There is a parallel in such a country as Canada, where to the chagrin of the supporters of French culture, immigrants from Europe of the most diverse origins opt for English-language schooling. Gaelic-speaking Scots have for generations been switching to English as part of a voluntary process. In other words, quite apart from any state policy or official pressure, we must see that, simply because Russians and Russian culture are predominant within the USSR, there must be a tendency to spon-taneous russification.

It is tempting to regard the USSR as *Rossiiskaya* in the old imperial sense, but it is misleading because the differences are so great. Though Soviet federal republics have very little power compared with the all-union organs, the theoretically multi-national nature of the Soviet state does have real significance, for social mobility and for the existence of nationality-hierarchies. It plainly matters that there are Georgian and Uzbek ministers, school administrators, academicians, heads of research institutes and party secretaries, whose functions and careers relate to Georgia and Uzbekistan, despite what we have already said about the process by which they are appointed.

Yet the *nomenklatura* system within which they rise is, in the last resort, Russian-dominated. It is, at all-union level, perhaps close to being *Rossiiskaya*. I would end by recalling a conversation in Rostov. A local citizen was extolling the bravery and self-sacrifice of Russians in the war. A friend said: 'What about the other nationalities?' To which the reply was: '*Ya vsekh ikh russkimi schitayu*' (I consider them all Russian).

Where does communist ideology come into the picture? Does it affect – and if so, how – the structure and evolution of Soviet society in respect of social inequalities and social mobility? Can Marxism be used to describe the Soviet social scene?

The ideology looks forward to the elimination of differences be-tween town and country, between physical and mental labour, between the more advanced and the backward nationalities and regions. Uni-versal education is to lead to an increasing inter-job mobility. Engels used to imagine people taking turns at different jobs and hobbies, and no doubt the othodox Marxist, like Lenin, should look forward to the elimination of bureaucracy in the sense of a *professional* official class when every cook can take her turn as an official – and presumably the official will take a turn at cooking, which is a rather alarming prospect for the digestion. Some of this may appear a little utopian. The idea that education gives to all men some special aptitude for administrative tasks surely cannot survive a year's experience on a university senate. The *practice* of the Soviet system has, as we have seen, tended to hierarchy and discipline, and, at least under Stalin, the country-dwellers were neglected in the interests of industrialisation. Furthermore, socialist and Russian-peasant traditions of egalitarianism were disregarded and, under Stalin especially, wage and salary differentials rose to great heights, as part of the search to stimulate effort in the course of the great industrialisation drive. This was given priority over virtually all other considerations. However, ideology undoubtedly predisposed the authorities to make great efforts in the field of education, and also to favour the less developed nationalities of the south and east.

The ideology, in the sense of the letter and spirit of Marx, Engels and Lenin, is, of course, hardly consistent with ranks, hierarchy, *nomenklatura* and the rest. This, I realise, raises the question of the meaning of the word 'ideology'. After all, for some the essence of Soviet ideology *is* party control through ranks, hierarchy, *nomenklatura* and the rest. These, like party control over the state, or a scarcely disguised Russian nationalism, are indeed integral parts of the Soviet scene. If generalised practice *is* ideology, then of course it cannot fail to be consistent with it. Yet it seems to me to be meaningful to insist on the words of the founding fathers. Christianity's emphasis on poverty and humility did not, after all, prevent the emergence of worldly aristocratic prelates, but this did not turn the ideology or theology of the Church into an apologia for worldly aristocracy; it created a contradiction. So also in the Soviet Union the generalised practice of Soviet power does at times contradict its own professed ideology, and argument can be and sometimes is based on such contradiction. Thus Stalin's introduction of tuition fees for secondary and higher education, and of many civilian uniforms, was out of line with what was seen or felt as fundamental belief and these particular distortions were in due course brought to an end. However, no one is at present allowed to question, or even generalise about, the hierarchical nature of Soviet society in the Soviet Union itself (though sociological surveys are beginning to describe some aspects of the real situation). This is one of the main obstacles to the study of the social system. In most other countries various theories contend and arguments abound. In the Soviet Union the official version alone can be expounded, and in this version there are two friendly classes, workers and peasants, with a stratum (*prosloika*) of intelligentsia, in process of evolution towards the classless society of communism. Needless to say, all kinds of detailed deficiencies are admitted and explored: bureaucratic indifference, petty abuses, overcrowded schools and so on. Certainly it would be wrong to argue or imply that the Soviet press and literature are confined to glorifying successes. What is lacking is any attempt, in print, at critical historical and social generalisation. The censorship would undoubtedly refuse to allow it.

So let us end by examining some possible or plausible generalisations.

Engels said somewhere that, if socialism meant only the state ownership of the means of production, then the first socialist institution was the regimental tailor. This suggests that he at least knew that property relations, however important they may be, are not the sole determinants of class relations in a sense relevant to the meaning of the word 'socialism'. A regimental tailor undertakes a form of manufacturing, and his relation to his colonel is not a property relation. The Soviet Union evolved out of a Russian empire which itself evolved, amid many external enemies, in the form of a service state, in which rank and even property were thought to be related to the duty one owed to the sovereign. Though this might remind some Western historians of feudal tenure (and some Russians speak of feudalism in connection with late tsarism), the Russian gentry lacked the *de facto* independence and authority of the West European feudal lords, and the differences seem greater than the similarities.

The revolution interrupted a process of change in economic and social organisation which was already quite far advanced; indeed it was the speed of change, and the failure of political reform to keep pace with it, which underlay many of the strains and stresses which led through social breakdown to the Bolshevik seizure of power. While denouncing hierarchy and bureaucratism, the new rulers quickly found that both were essential for survival. The party operated amid what was then described as the 'petty-bourgeois elemental flood', i.e. among a peasant majority indifferent or hostile. To preserve its own rule, and later to impose collectivisation and the sacrifice of rapid industrialisation, and to prepare and fight a destructive war, there developed a form of organisation designed to enforce a revolution from above and to plan economic development, while firmly suppressing dissent. It seemed necessary to place in the party's hands control over not only the political-governmental but also the economic, social, cultural, scientific organisations and hierarchies. At first this took the form of the selection and supervision of non-party specialists by specially selected commissar-supervisors whose loyalty to the party, rather than efficiency or training, was their principal qualification.

This form of government became institutionalised and developed strong vested interests in its continuance. It could appeal, as we have seen, to national tradition, to patriotism. It is decidedly convenient for men in authority to decide who can be promoted up the social and rank ladder, to have the power to decide what kind of criticism can be permitted and to punish transgressors, to forbid the setting up of any association which the official hierarchy does not approve or control.

What can we call such a society and its ruling stratum? Is it a Russian semi-oriental empire in new clothes, with an eleven-headed emperor-politburo, which in the last analysis decides who shall hold what rank? Or is it a modern industrial or industrialising corporation, with the politburo as its board of directors, deciding, as directors do, who should be promoted within the corporation? Is it a neo-oligarchy open to talent through promotion? The *nomenklatura* can be seen as an appointments and promotion list, such as is kept by the adjutant-general's department in the British army, where it is decided that Colonel de Vere should occupy the post of chief of operations staff of the 2nd Division. By now, it could be argued, those responsible for operating the *nomenklatura* look less for a politically reliable than for an efficient appointee.

This is still a list of questions rather than an answer. What *is* the nature of Soviet society? We seem to need new categories of thought to describe it. The ruling stratum could be identified as co-extensive with the holders of all positions on the *nomenklatura*. These men, acting through the departments of appropriate party units, in effect recruit their own successors, and control all other organisations. A self-perpetuating, industrialising oligarchy, perhaps, or a kind of meritocracy, who decide on the use of the socially owned basic capital, and who provide – through an ambitious and far-going educational programme – the means by which upward social mobility is possible for ambitious people of all the strata of society, though peasants do suffer from some handicaps and obstacles. 'A non-hereditary caste system', as an East European once said in conversation.

Marx might well have identified the interests of the ruling stratum in the continuance of an arrangement from which it benefits in both material and non-material terms, and it might have seemed to him that the power of the state is used to preserve and further the interests of the rulers, in the Soviet as in other societies. He would also have noted that able persons of non-*nomenklatura* origin are recruited by promotion into the ruling stratum, that the real as well as formal ideology is strongly against any inheritance of *nomenklatura* status, even while parental string-pulling does give certain alvantages: as we used to say in the army, 'it's not what you know but *who* you know'.

We are witnessing at present a growing impatience of especially the younger generation with the social-cultural controls of the system, controls originally devised to cope with revolutions, emergencies, crash-programme industrialisation and military dangers, which, unless such good reasons exist, become intolerably restrictive. In terms of the present discussion, the 'liberal' opposition is seeking the right to set up organisations outside the strait-jacket of party and *nomenklatura*, and thereby provide means of advancement and influence outside the official hierarchy, one and indivisible. It seeks the means to give expression to unorthodox opinions, including theories on the nature of Soviet society and literary works questioning the myths as to the past as well as some of the claims of the present. Officialdom resists. This is not a class struggle in any conventional terms. In military language, 'they' see it as mutiny.

2

Russia as an Emergent Country

I did not invent the title of this paper: the organisers of the conference at which it was originally presented did. It is challenging, but opens boundless vistas. A book on the economic history of Russia, reinforced by long commentaries on various historical interpretations of Russian development, might meet the bill – 700 pages, say. Time is a scarce commodity, however, and the patience of conference participants and author alike wears thin. So what I have done is discussed a few selected aspects of Russian history which bear on the theme represented by the title.

By age-old tradition, Russia was a country of potential anarchy and relatively weak spontaneous social forces, and so the state had to be strong and to some extent to act as a substitute for weak or non-existent enterprise. The state and territory of Russia were exposed to powerful enemies: Tatars in the south and east, Poland and other culturally and economically more developed powers to the west. In 1571 the Crimean khan burnt Moscow and took away great numbers of people to sell as slaves. In that same period Ivan the Terrible was raging a hard and generally unsuccessful war against the Poles. Like many Russian rulers after him, he saw the underdevelopment of his country primarily in military terms – scattered population, low level of literacy and know-how, inability (despite the magnificent 'tsar cannon' still to be seen in the Kremlin) to produce adequate supplies of what were then modern weapons. Ivan also saw the threat to stability posed by the power of the landed nobility, and did much to weaken it by the organised terror of the *Oprichnina*, a special body of servants to whom he transferred land confiscated from the nobility. His centralising and military policies increased the burdens on the peasants, who sought to evade these burdens by migration into the open spaces to the north and east.

People in such a situation cannot easily be 'exploited' by conventional economic means, a point noted recently by Samuelson: 'But actually this [exploitation] hypothesis is absurd in the context of Smith's early and rude state. What hold does the capitalist there have on the worker? . . . What that is useful can the employer withhold

Reprinted from A. J. Youngson (ed.), Economic Development in the Long Run, *London, Allen & Unwin, 1972.*

from the rude worker, who hunts where he pleases on superabundant acres . . . ?' What indeed except slavery, as Samuelson also notes, can enable a surplus to be exacted? (Samuelson, 1971, p. 406.) Substituting the state for the capitalist, there is here the rationale of state serfdom in a sparsely populated and vast land with an open frontier. So the strengthening of central autocratic power was accompanied by the gradual attachment of the peasants to the land, land mostly held by the tsar's servants on condition of service. It is hard to consider Ivan as a moderniser, in that he was superstitious, cruel, barbarous. He had about as many wives as Henry VIII, but, unlike Henry, he executed none of them, since he could obtain annulment by sending them to a nunnery. In this respect at least he was *less* barbarous than some of his contemporaries. Yet Stalin was surely right to treat him as one of his great precursors. One sees in him some key elements of a repetitive theme: forced development by the state, the 'hypertrophy of the state' (to use a phrase of the philosopher Berdyaev), the great importance of military *raison d'état* as a motive for development, and finally the close association of the growth of state power with enserfment.

Ivan's autocratic rule was followed by a period of confusion and anarchy, establishing in the minds of people another element of their consciousness: the danger of anarchy; the need for a strong centralised autocracy to prevent chaos. This is still an important factor in the political culture of the country. Of course, order, as against disorder, facilitates economic development in all times and places, not least in developing countries of the twentieth century. Or the nineteenth, for that matter: the unification of Germany has evident developmental consequences, for instance, and Prussian and German governments took military questions very seriously indeed. There are, no doubt, parallels elsewhere for many features of Russian history. However, it is still arguable that the interlinkage between autocracy, the state as an agency of change, fear of anarchy, serfdom (or forced labour), and military-strategic questions, were peculiarly and even uniquely important in understanding Russia, from the sixteenth century to the twentieth century.

The seventeenth century saw the restoration of order under a new dynasty, the Romanovs, the further regularisation of serfdom, a series of wars with Poland, expansion eastwards to the Pacific Ocean across sparsely peopled Siberian wastes undertaken by relatively small groups of cossacks and adventurers. Some advanced statesmen were deeply concerned at the cultural and economic gap separating Russia from the rest of Europe, but it was not until Peter the Great's reign that a leap forward was attempted.

Russian industry was at this time based on scattered and mainly rural handicraftsmen, with few urban workshops, and no guilds. Merchants played a vital role in linking these mini-producers with the market. In his classic work on *The Russian Factory*, Tugan-Baranovsky emphasises the role of merchant capital, some of it very large scale, in contrast with the small scale, unorganised and poor producers. 'Our first capitalist class, the merchants, showed no propensity to take production of goods into its hands. Controlling the market, the merchant preferred to buy the goods made by the petty producer and keep the latter dependent upon him, without turning him into a hired labourer.' (Tugan-Baronovsky, 1934.)

Some traditionally minded Russian economists in the latter half of the nineteenth century 'blamed' Peter for not using the comparative advantage of small-scale handicraft industry, and forcing instead an 'unnatural' growth of factories. Tugan-Baronovsky rejects the category 'unnatural' (or 'artificial'), and points out, very properly, that the kind of products Peter needed could not be made by petty handicraftsmen: iron, guns, broadcloth, sailcloth, and the like. Nor could the small producers hire foreign experts or purchase instruments abroad. What the handicraftsmen could not do, and the richer merchants would not do of their own volition, was done by the state. Peter ordered the construction of manufactories. Some were built by the state, and then handed over to private entrepreneurs. In other cases the state subsidised would-be manufacturers, granted them interest-free loans, exempted them from taxes; but Tugan showed that much of the capital came from the rich merchants as well as from the state. The main customer was the state itself. The new entrepreneurs came, in the main, from the merchant class. Some of the factories were large indeed: examples cited include one employing 1,162 persons in making sailcloth. At this stage foreign entrepreneurs were relatively few, but of course imported specialists and know-how were of the highest importance. Peter also sent Russians to study abroad, and himself learn about shipbuilding in Holland and England.

Peter's motives in speeding development were predominantly military. Early Western commentators on Russia, such as Scherer (1788) and Herman (1822), in referring to Peter's policies, attributed them to 'Peter's need for a regular army, artillery, a fleet', and his unwillingness to be dependent on other countries for soldiers' uniforms, firearms, powder, ships.

These policies of technological westernisation might have been accompanied by some move towards social westernisation, in the sense of greater freedom of movement and the relaxation of serfdom. It is one of the paradoxes of Russian history that what actually occurred was the exact reverse: Peter's policies reinforced serfdom. True, the upper classes now wore 'German' clothes and learnt to speak French, but they were also mobilised to serve the state for life. This can be explained in several ways. Firstly, the strain of waging war, setting up factories, building ships, greatly added to tax burdens and also required the mobilisation of society, from the gentry to the common people, for the purposes of the state. Far from relaxing serfdom, it was necessary to strengthen it as a means of providing a supply of forced labour, and also to sustain the gentry in the service of the tsar. Secondly, the new factories themselves could only be manned by serfs, for there was no free labour force on which to draw. The population of whole villages was turned over for compulsory factory labour, along with rogues and vagabonds, and even 'public women'.

Tugan-Baronovsky contrasts this situation with West European factory work, where skilled workers and old guild tradition provided a reservoir of relatively well-trained labour, and of course people could move more or less freely from the villages. Russia had serfdom, and a grave shortage of labour of any kind of skill, and so forced labour seemed inescapable. But only the *dvoryane* (gentry) were allowed to keep serfs, and few of the gentry were operating factories at this time. Hence a decree by Peter (January 1721) allowing merchants to own and purchase serfs, 'under the condition that these villages will always be attached to the factories'. So, quoting Tugan again, 'instead of capitalist industry which was then developing in the West, we had large-scale production based on forced labour'. By 1736, decrees issued by Peter's successors bound even the hitherto free factory workers 'for ever' to their factories. Factory owners were allowed to punish their workers, and those who proved difficult could be handed over to the state (the *Kommertskollegium*) for deportation to remote areas 'so as to cause fear in others' (ibid., pp. 23, 24, 25) (the words are in the decree).

Indeed it is a feature of early Russian economic thought, especially that of the pioneer thinker I. Pososhkov (1670–1726), that they believed in the necessity of the whip rather than the carrot. Pososhkov advocated flogging as a cure for overcharging, for malfeasances by state officials, and for idleness by common people.

Much space is sometimes devoted to the existence or non-existence of feudalism in Russia. It all depends on definitions. There was in Peter's Russia a unique kind of universal service state, with lands and sometimes factories held on condition of service. As in feudal Europe, the obligation to serve gradually disappeared (in Russia 'the freedom of the gentry' was decreed in 1762). However, the differences are profound. The Russian hereditary aristocracy did not have regional power centres, had no private armies of retainers, no fortifications. Peter merged them with the untitled serving-men in the civil and military service, and long after 1762 they still owed everything to the tsar: status, influence, rank. In this sense it was possible for the great poet (and excellent historian) Pushkin to assert in 1830 that the Russians had no hereditary aristocracy in the European sense. He deplored what he considered to be the resultant 'slavish obedience' to the monarch. So an important qualitative difference was the lack of countervailing forces, the more so as the towns remained poorly developed, with little corporate and guild life. (Novgorod, which had such life in association with the Hanseatic League, was almost destroyed by Ivan III and Ivan the Terrible.) The autocracy, the state, had perforce to play the decisive role in economic development, and the specific interests of the state and its administrative machine deeply affected the policies adopted, in ways to be further discussed below.

Another feature of Russian life distinguished it from Europe (and still does so). This is the control exercised by the state over movement of people. It is extraordinary to read that, as early as 1734, a resident of a small provincial town was registered as a merchant and then 'his passport was endorsed for Moscow' where he worked in a factory, 'with his passport endorsed every year'. He then left his employment, and the factory owner claimed that he was attached to his work 'for ever'. The case went to the Senate (which acted as a kind of administrative high court) for decision, on the issue of whether, as a registered merchant, he was exempted from the law binding factory labour to their factories. The point of interest here is the passport. (Tugan-Baranovsky, 1934, p. 24).) In the nineteenth century it was still common practice to deny even gentry the right to reside where they pleased, or to travel. Pushkin was reprimanded for travelling to the Caucasus without the permission of the chief of the gendarmes. The right to reside in cities is limited by police regulation to this day, and the citizens need to have their passports endorsed for change of residence. This affected, and still affects labour mobility. It can be an economic nuisance, but seems administratively convenient.

However, to return to the eighteenth century, in the second half of that century there was a most unusual politico-economic conflict, which can have no Western parallel. The gentry (*dvoryanstvo*) began to see advantages in setting up factories, and a challenge to themselves in the rise of rich factory- and serf-owning merchants. So they petitioned the monarch to stop merchants who had become manufacturers buying serfs. They wished to confine factory owners of the merchant class to the hiring of wage-labourers, partly to maintain the gentry's monopoly of serf ownership, partly because the employment of their serfs as wage-earners might give them (the gentry) money via quit-rents, and finally to give themselves an advantage as factory owners using slave labour. For the same reason (quit-rents), the gentry wished to encourage handicrafts and also trading activities by their peasants, while the merchants complained bitterly of peasant competition, asking the state to forbid peasant enterprises which competed with the hereditary functions of the merchant estate. There was a very Russian tendency to appeal to the state, to the monarch, to determine such issues. There was also widespread resentment at the monopolist privileges granted to big factory owners, to some of the merchant class, and also to some foreigners. Many products made by unfree labour were of very poor quality, despite many decrees and orders defining what ought to be produced.

Catherine II came to the throne with the help of gentlemen guards officers (who murdered her emperor husband for her), and during her reign the interests of the gentry estate were furthered. Serfs lost such vestigial rights as they had held to appeal against their masters. The ideas of the physiocrats suited the landed interest, and so official statements (for example, the famous *Nakaz*, or legislative instructions) extolled agriculture and encouraged handicrafts. There is a reference in the *Nakaz* to the danger that machines (*makhiny*, in the antique Russian) would threaten employment. Their use was recognised, how-ever, in exporting industries, where competition requires costs to be kept low. (1768 edn. Two Russian graduates of the University of Glasgow, Desnitsky and Tretyakov, may have had some influence in the drafting of this document. They had attended Adam Smith's lectures.)

Catherine stopped the merchant estate acquiring serfs by purchase, but, interestingly enough, by a decree of 1763, allowed foreigners to do so if they set up factories in Russia.

The net effect of Catherine's measures was to increase not only handicraft production but also the number of factories, the latter being due largely to the lifting of restrictions which had protected the monopoly position of large establishments set up under Peter. A decree of 1775 authorised the setting up of industrial establishments by anyone. The supply of wage-labour increased, many of the labourers being serfs who left the village on paying their masters a quit-rent (*obrok*). Under Catherine there was a little more scope for free enterprise. Peter's system involved minute regulation of the factories, justified no doubt both by their monopoly privileges and by the fact that their products were made to the orders and requirements of the state. Indeed, the operation of a factory was regarded as a species of state service, under close supervision undertaken by various *kollegia* (ministries). Catherine eliminated some of these controls and controllers, though the state continued to be the principal customer of the large factories, and in her reign, too, there were many examples of obligations imposed on factories to deliver specified types of product (e.g. cloth) to the state, with a ban on sales to anyone but the state.

When Catherine died, her son Paul took steps against the privileges of the gentry, and authorised merchant factory owners once again to buy serfs, though this was not done on a large scale, no doubt because of the growing advantages of employing wage-earners. (Paul was assassinated in 1801, by a conspiracy of the gentry.)

Russia's mining and manufacturing in the first years of the nineteenth century was part slave and part free (the latter category including wage-earners of serf status paying quit-rent). The large factories primarily supplying the needs of the state were predominantly slave; the smaller-scale workshops supplying the needs of the market were mainly free. There were many intermediate situations in practice.

The growth of capitalist enterprise conflicted with serfdom, and a variety of expedients were devised to get round it. Tugan-Baranovsky cites the remarkable case of the textile town, Ivanovo-Voznesensk. Factories were set up there by serfs, who began as handicraftsmen and accumulated large profits, paying their 'owner', Count Sheremetev, a share of their earnings. Some of these serf capitalists bought serfs for themselves (theoretically they were the count's serfs) and employed hundreds of other serfs and some free men as wage-earners. This was so profitable for the count that he demanded a very high price when these now rich capitalists wished to buy themselves their freedom: 20,000 roubles was not untypical, and only a very rich man indeed could raise such a sum. Other capitalists were former artisans of non-serf status, as well as merchants and, less often, gentry.

By the 1820s there came to an end the purchase of serfs to work in so-called 'possessional factories', i.e. those operated with forced labour; but the existing forced labourers and their progeny were still bound to factory work. A series of decrees sought to regulate their status. They included provisions for limiting hours of work on a scale laid down, an obligation to provide work and also medical services; in addition rates of pay and holidays were determined. The fact that these were 'possessional' factories entitled the state to interfere also in determining what these factories should produce. They were not allowed to change their product mix without permission. The result of all this was greatly to diminish the advantages of forced labour, which was anyway unsuitable for work with machines. Factory owners tried to evade their obligations. A decree adopted in 1840 gave the right to entrepreneurs to let their 'possessional' (i.e. serf) workers go, with compensation if they had paid for them, and to go over to production with free wage-earners. Many took advantage of this. An ex-serf-worker, now freed, had the choice of registering as a state peasant or as townsman (*meshchanin*). Some workers preferred to stay in their factories and there were cases of their having to be expelled from their homes there by force. Some had to be flogged to persuade them to go and be free men; they had a paid job and some sort of security and housing at the factory, and had nowhere else to go.

Was the use of slave labour profitable? Adam Smith's *Wealth of Nations* was translated into Russian on the orders of the minister of finance (typically this too was a state initiative!), and his ideas were used to strengthen the case for a free labour force. Despite this, serfdom survived unaffected in the villages. As for industry, in 1825, of the 210,568 workers in factories, 114,515 were wage-earners, the others virtually slaves. The slaves still prodominated in industries supplying the state (primarily the army); thus, in manufacturing wool cloth for uniforms, the slaves outnumbered the free by five to one, in metallurgy by four to one. (Figures cited by Tugan-Baranovsky, 1934, p. 73, from an industrial census.) By contrast the new and rapidly growing cotton industry was almost totally 'free'. It is the 'free' industries which grew in the period 1800–60, while metallurgy, notably, stagnated. Tugan-Baranovsky argues that this was due in large part to the fact that the state provided privileges and forced labour, and thereby removed any incentive to improve technique and productivity. This is a stimulating paradoxical idea: the interest of the state in metallurgy was itself the cause of its failure to grow. One must add other reasons, especially remoteness and lack of communications, and cost reductions abroad. The lag in metals production set Russia very far behind the West, not least in the military sphere: the Russian navy in the Crimean War had neither steam nor ironclads, and could only be scuttled to prevent the Allies from sailing into Sebastopol harbour.

In this war, Russia had to sustain her army in the Crimea by bullock cart, which explains why sufficient forces could not be deployed. In 1854 the only railway of consequence completed was from St Petersburg to Moscow.

Why so little progress between 1815 and 1860? Russia seemed so strong at the end of the Napoleonic wars. Did the emperors not know that military strength required economic modernisation.

They were certainly told of this. Histories of economic thought ought to pay some attention to the Russian statesman and economist, Count S. N. Mordvinov, admirer of Adam Smith, who corresponded with Bentham. Years before Friedrich List he put forward ideas of national economic development, and (despite his admiration for Smith) he argued for protection to defend Russian industry against British competition. (He argued in vain: low tariffs were then the rule.) He looked forward to Russian economic penetration of Asia. He urged the spread of education and saw that 'the brains and hands of slaves cannot bring riches to a nation', though he also saw the need for caution in liberating the serfs. One of his works, *Some considerations on Manufacturing in Russia and on Tariffs* (Russian edition, 1815), was translated into French.

Then why so little progress? Two reasons suggest themselves. One is the survival of serfdom, a survival partly due to the reliance of the state on the land-owning gentry (which provided the civil service, army officers, local government, and which gathered the taxes), partly to fears of what might happen if serfs were set free – the belief that peasants were children who might wreak havoc unless told what to do. Serfdom stood in the way of labour mobility and removed incentives to efficiency, productivity, mechanisation. The other reason is the intense conservatism of Nicholas I (especially) and his ministers. They were real reactionaries, genuinely taking pride in preventing progress and change, considering these as undesirable in themselves. Kankrin, the tsar's minister of finance, knew about railways and thought that they were bad: they concentrated large numbers of potential rioters in one place, and helped people to move about in uncontrolled ways, as well as 'increasing equality among social estates'. Industry itself was a potential source of trouble and commotion. The Western commercial spirit was alien to the tsarist bureaucracy, as it was alien also to the gradually emerging radical opposition to auto-cracy. The landed gentry were interested in cheap imports from the West, and were hardly likely to be a pressure group in favour of industrial development. Nicholas I was no Peter the Great, and showed no will to enforce industrialisation upon his minister-bureaucrats. In any case, Russia's immediate neighbours (Prussia, Austria, Turkey) were not then in the throes of an industrial revolution. The dominant industrial power, Great Britain, was far away. There was also military over-confidence.

The shock of the Crimean War changed this situation. It is tempting to say simply that the abolition of serfdom in 1861, and the other reforms of that decade, showed that the government became committed to rapid industrial development, and that serfdom was abolished because it stood in the way. This is tempting – but over-simple (though the government did learn that railways *were* necessary). The liberation of the peasantry was accomplished in a manner not in the least conducive to industrialisation. The peasants remained in effect bound to the land, with a communal system of land tenure reinforced by a joint responsibility for taxes and redemption dues, with no right for the individual to sell his land and get out, and indeed with severe restriction on movement out of the village. The form in which the landowners were compensated (state bonds) did not help them to raise capital which might be invested in industry.

Why was such a policy followed? Because the stability of the state and its administration had top priority. The liberation of the serfs was a complex and risky undertaking. State revenues needed safe-guarding. Fear of peasant revolt, itself a major cause of the liberation, led to much concern about minimising the social disruption of so major a change in human relations. The peasants felt dissatisfied by what they regarded as an inàdequate share of the land. Their folk memories saw all land as theirs, with serfdom as part of a universal obligation of service to the tsar. But since for a hundred years the gentry had held no obligation to serve, were they still entitled to own any land? Rapid population growth caused increasing pressure on the peasants' land in the decades that followed. Many landlords found it difficult to readjust to the new situation, and financial difficulties were common. Thus the poet Nekrasov was right:

> The great chain burst asunder, and one end hit the master, the other – the peasant.

Alexander II must have felt he had little room for manoeuvre, that fiscal and police reasons stood in the way of assuring full mobility of labour and giving the right for the peasants to own and sell their land as private property; he may not have understood that such policies were desirable anyway.

Industrialisation was discussed, but opinion was very mixed. The followers of free trade doctrine, already strong earlier in the century, still reasoned against protectionism, urging that Russia's comparative advantage lay in agriculture. The internal market for industrial products was weak because the peasantry was poor. Some argued that to raise agricultural production was a precondition for a healthy development of Russian industry. Others pointed to the horrors of Western capitalism, and saw in the village commune the precursor of a Russian road to socialism. A relatively liberal tariff policy was followed until the end of the 1880s with little opposition from influential groups. The Russian industrial bourgeoisie was still a feeble and dependent infant.

The real industrialisation boom did not begin until 1890. It was preceded by state-supported railway building, which greatly increased demand for rails and other equipment, at first imported from the West, and for mobile labour. There was also much naval and military investment. The imposition of heavy tariffs on imports in 1891, and the role of the railways both as consumer of industrial goods and linking together products and markets, was of key importance in the process. The government, especially the ministry of finance under Witte, became conscious at this period of the need to stimulate industry, not least on grounds of national defence. Witte's many writings and speeches show clearly that he was an economic nationalist, and indeed he was the author of a work on Friedrich List. The lack of entrepreneurial ability and of capital was recognised, as also was the need for a modern banking system. Witte, particularly, did his utmost to make Russia attractive for foreign investors. Witte, and also his predecessor Vyshnegradsky, must be seen as pursuing a vigorous and conscious policy of industrialisation, with a strong bias towards heavy industry. All this was doubtless facilitated, or made possible, by the abolition of serfdom. But Gerschenkron is surely right in stating that it did not stand high on the list of the conscious motives of those who carried out the liberation in 1861. (See his contribution to the *Cambridge Economic History of Europe*, vol. 6, part 2.) (Habakkuk, 1965.)

By the 1890s Russia was launched on the road of capitalist indust-rialisation. True, in the launching and in much of the navigation, the state had to play a major role. In the words of Portal,

'Spontaneous growth of national consumption . . . could not have provided its industrialists with customers enough, had it not been for the orders for military equipment and the works undertaken or guaranteed by the state. Railway construction stimulated the economy generally, not only by ending the isolation of a great many regions of the immense empire, but also by bringing about a sudden increase in metal production and coal mining, which until then had been negligible.' (*The Industrialisation of Russia*, Habakkuk, 1965, vol. 6, part 2.)

(At the end of the eighteenth century Russia had been one of the world's largest producers of iron, but by 1860 had fallen very far behind.)

The state had constant financial troubles, and its ability to finance development directly was limited; and Witte's tariff policy was designed to create profitable opportunities for domestic and foreign capital. This no doubt partly explains the gradual withdrawal of the state from *direct* involvement in industrialisation, in the sense of leaving actual management and entrepreneurship increasingly in capitalist hands (though foreigners in Russia in the second half of the century complain repeatedly of petty regulations of various kinds.) Adam Smith and free trade may have been fashionable in 1820, but the needs of the state seemed plainly to require serfdom, forced labour in factories, and a close link between these factories and the state as consumer of the bulk of their products. It could easily be shown that the evils of serfdom, social and economic evils, were known not only to Mordvinov or to the Decembrist rebels, but also to both Alexander I and Nicholas I, but they did not feel able to dispense with it. The internal market was exceedingly small: the upper classes used mainly imported manufactures; and at first it was only the cotton industry which supplied goods primarily to the market rather than to the state, the other needs of ordinary people being met by handicraftsmen and artisans. By the end of the century 'national economics' had replaced belief in free trade, but direct activity by the state was declining relatively. Under shelter of protective duties, sometimes with state guarantees and credits, domestic and foreign owned capitalist enter-prises grew rapidly.

One institutional obstacle remained. The restrictions on peasant mobility were somewhat eased in the last years of the century, and migration to Siberia was even encouraged when the great Trans-Siberian railway was begun in 1893. But the communal forms of tenure remained, and were an obstacle to growth. Evidently the preservation of medieval-type strip-cultivation, with (in many areas) periodic redistribution of the land, was not conducive to land improvements and productivity. If the holdings could be consolidated, if the poorer peasants could sell out to their more efficient and ambitious neighbours, it would greatly stimulate the development of commercial agriculture among the peasants, lead to the emergence of a peasant bourgeoisie who would be conservative supporters of political stability, and speed up migration from villages to town. Witte favoured such measures, which were certainly a logical part of the spread of capitalism in Russia.

They were opposed by the conservatives, who still saw the peasantry as in need of special 'parental' supervision. They were opposed by slavophils of radical hues, because the communal institutions were a Russian road to a Russian species of socialism. They were opposed even by the political party closest to representing the urban bourgeoisie, the Constitutional Democrats, when the proposals reached the stage of legislation, for reasons hard to fathom. Marxist socialists opposed them too, because of their total opposition to tsarism, and because political stability and a peasant bourgeoisie hardly suited their interests. So it was not until after the shock of another defeat, in the war against Japan (1904–5), and major land riots in villages (1905–6), that a shaken monarchy finally resolved to support the able prime minister, Stolypin, and to reform rural land tenure. At long last, in 1906–11, laws were passed making it possible for peasants to opt out of the commune, to sell their land, to consolidate their holdings. The process of change speeded up, to be interrupted all too soon by war and revolution.

So, within a relatively short time, Russia moved from an economy dominated by serfdom and the state to something which was visibly taking the capitalist road to development. Until almost the end of the nineteenth century the growth of Russia as a great power was closely associated with serfdom and slavery. The state mobilised scarce resources in a poor country to keep up with Europe, and so peasants were enserfed; the gentry were largely confined to the service of the state (after 1762 they could also vegetate on their estates if they chose); the first factories were run for the state if not by the state, by men who could hardly be called entrepreneurs without stretching the meaning of words. Russia entered the capitalist road with a political structure left over from the earlier autocratic-bureaucratic stage, with the masses' psychology still deeply affected by serfdom ('We are squeezing the slave out of ourselves drop by drop', wrote Chekhov), and with a bourgeoisie lacking numbers, confidence, political influence, and a sense of independence *vis-à-vis* the state bureaucracy on which it was so long dependent. Perhaps somewhere here can be found some of the principal causes for the contrasts between Russian and Japanese patterns of modernisation. It is important to note how strong were the currents of opinion hostile to the logic of European capitalism: the intelligentsia of almost all hues was opposed to it from various socialist points of view; the gentry was divided; the bureaucracy was unimaginative and often highly conservative, as poor Witte found to his cost. The peasants still wanted the landlords' land, resented heavy taxation; many clung to the old communal forms and opposed the Stolypin reform, as may be seen by the speed with which they reversed it during the revolutionary chaos of 1917–18. The workers in factories were largely composed of uprooted ex-peasants, living in slum conditions and prone to angry riot and strike. It was an explosive mixture, which, under stress, duly exploded. It was not the absence of industrialisation, but the strain of industrialisation which, along with the war, brought down the empire.

The 'Witte' period of industrialisation brought some interesting problems to the surface.

One of these was the role played in industrialisation by the peasant masses in a predominantly agricultural country. In the eyes of many economists it was the low purchasing power of the peasants which held back industrial growth, because the internal market was too small. But Witte's policy greatly increased Russia's import bill (first for railway equipment, then for many other capital goods), and foreign investors and bondholders had to be paid. The government's own expenditures required increased taxes. This policy required a large increase in sales of farm produce, and the burdens on the peasants were designed to force them to sell grain. In the words of Tugan-Baranovsky, exports were based on 'the *muzhik* not eating his fill'. So paradoxically, deliberately sponsored industrialisation actually tended to impoverish the peasants, and this contributed to political instability. No adequate statistics exist to show whether or how far their incomes actually fell, but it seems clear that official policy was not concerned with enlarging the market for industrial goods among the peasants; but was very concerned indeed with the balance of payments. Stalin in the 1930s also collected food for export while the peasants tightened their belts. It must be added that the reforms of 1906–11 gave a powerful impetus to agricultural productivity; a marked upward trend was interrupted by the war, with peasants buying not only more industrial consumers' goods but also farm equipment in rapidly increasing quantities.

The second feature of the period was a highly marked contrast between the old and the new, between modern large-scale manufacture and antique workshops and handicrafts. Why was the modern sector so modern, so capital-intensive? There is a considerable literature on the subject of labour-intensive investments, and it is there frequently implied that the existence of abundant labour and scarce capital in developing countries proves the irrationality of labour-saving investment. If in a 'dual economy' such investments are made in the modern sector, this is often ascribed to unreasoning preference for having the latest equipment, or to protective labour legislation which artificially increases labour cost. Indeed, it is pointed out that within the modern sector itself many tasks (e.g. materials handling) are carried out by medieval methods, and this too is taken to be evidence of irrationality.

It is therefore important to note that in Russia under Witte it was found advantageous to instal the latest machines, although this was not a consciously pursued policy, and although labour legislation was rudimentary and wages were very low. The reasons have been pointed out not only by Gerschenkron but also Tugan-Baranovsky, Hexthausen and others: Russia had plenty of unskilled peasants, but reliable factory labour was scarce, inefficient, and, despite the poor wages, *expensive*. Even if it were technically feasible, it would not have paid to substitute labour for modern metallurgical equipment. But where there were opportunities for the 'Volga boatmen' type of mass physical labour, these opportunities were often taken, even in the modern factories themselves. The irrationality is only apparent, and the appearance is due to wrongly treating labour as homogeneous.

The 'dual economy' in Russia, as elsewhere, must be seen as part of the process of change, since it is plainly impossible to alter methods, organisation, equipment, or human attitudes, within a very few years. By 1913 it could be argued that Russia was moving towards a European-type economy, though with still a long way to go. Despite the interruption due to depression and disorder in 1903–6, Russia's industrial growth rates in the period were impressive, 5 per cent per annum in 1888–1913 according to Raymond Goldsmith's computations. There is much controversy as to whether she was in fact catching up with the West. Such authors as Grinevetsky and Prokopovich, writing fifty and more years ago, argued that progress was insufficient and that Russia was not keeping pace with Germany, which was very far ahead and drawing away. Others have pointed out that growth rates on the scale of 1890–1913, if continued over thirty to forty years, would have brought Russia to a high level of industrial development (which is no doubt true, but assumes that the social-political breakdown and the First World War had not taken place). Still others point to the heavy Russian dependence on foreign capital, and the difficulty which would have been encountered in keeping up the flow. Let us not pursue these 'what-might-have-beens' of history. Let us simply assert that Russia was on the capitalist road, that this caused strain, that the tsarist regime was slow to adjust, that the opposition to the tsar was also, in the main, opposed to the capitalist road, and that industrial and social weaknesses led to disaster when the challenge of the war was faced. Despite Witte's industrialisation strategy, Russian industry could not sustain an army in modern war, and in fact was greatly dependent on Germany for machinery. The revolution was caused by, indeed itself was, a social breakdown. With no faith any longer in the divine attributes of tsardom, the masses had no faith either in the middle-class liberal and moderate-socialist alternative.

The breakdown having occurred, Lenin and the Bolsheviks succeeded, after a bitter civil war and much anarchy, in re-establishing order. They faced the problem of continuing the industrialisation of Russia, a problem complicated by the rural revolution, which destroyed not only the landlords but most of the consolidated 'Stolypin' peasant holdings also, thrusting the villages back into the era of medieval strip and communal tenure from which they had begun to emerge. Russia could not now depend on private enterprise, since the entrepreneurs were destroyed and driven out by revolution (the petty 'NEPmen' of the New Economic Policy period were very petty indeed, and played no part in large-scale modern industry). So once again, as in the distant days of Peter the Great, modernisation and factory building were to be the responsibility of the state. No one else could do it.

'Peter the Great was the first Bolshevik': thus wrote a poet, Maximilian Voloshin, early in the 1920s. They were to be despotic modernisers. Addressing Lenin's successors, another poet, Sergei Yesenin, exclaimed, in 1924:

> Oh you, whose task it is to tame the wild waters
> of Russia between banks of concrete.

Stalin himself understood the parallel well, and insisted on Peter (as well as Ivan) being presented favourably in history books. Gerschenkron, too, has argued: 'The resemblance between Soviet and Petrine Russia was striking indeed.'

Is all this far-fetched? I do not think so. Stalin's collectivisation, with forcible deliveries at nominal prices, was the imposition of a kind of developmental serfdom. Those who went to town to work in the new industries could be said to be paying quit-rent (*obrok*) to the state in the form of turnover tax. Forced labour was widespread. The managers of state enterprises, producing largely to the orders and for the purposes of the state, bore some relationship to the factory managers of Peter's time, who also were ordered what to produce in a kind of primitive version of a planned economy. The universal service state was re-established under Lenin and Stalin, with the hierarchical establishments structure run by the party (the *nomenklatura*) replacing

Peter's 'table of ranks'. Stalin of the 1930s was as concerned as was Peter with the military aspects of economic development. Stalin mobilised society to create the basis of a modern war industry, and so justified the high tempos he imposed. Terror was used by both to maintain order and discipline. The revolution had destroyed the classes capable of autonomous economic and social initiative; and collectivisation ended the peasants' control over land and produce. 'Lenin destroyed the factory owners and merchants. But the nature of Russian history caused Lenin . . . to retain the curse of Russia: the association between its development and unfreedom, serfdom.' Thus wrote Vasili Grossman, Soviet novelist and publicist, in an unpublished and unpublishable analysis of the post-revolutionary era. Stalin was, from his standpoint, a logical follower of Lenin and of Peter. Just as Stalin's penal system had nothing in common with the comparative liberalism of the last tsars, and was a throwback to earlier and more barbarous ages, so the state resumed under him the task of modernisation which, under Witte and his successors, it was sharing with private enterprise. Foreign know-how and technicians were imported by Stalin, as by Peter, but in the form of imports by the state itself, rather than direct investments by foreigners.

There is much else that could be written on this subject of 'emergent' Russia. Bolshevik economic strategy could be analysed. So could the concept of primitive socialist accumulation. The fascinating arguments about development in the 1920s can be, and have been presented as pioneering the doctrines of development economics. (See Collette, 1968, and Erlich, 1961.) Centralised planning, its use in a period of rapid change, and its limitations in a modern industrial society, could also be discussed. People have written books and articles about the relevance of the Soviet model to other countries. I have deliberately taken another and more 'historical' road – not because this is the only way to look at things, or necessarily the most useful, but because it is less frequently attempted.

Surely there are insights to be gained from observing the role of slavery in early Russian industrialisation, and the role of the state as organiser and customer of industrial production. It may well be that the problems faced by the development of capitalism in Russia were a function of this unhappy past association of industry, state and serfdom, in a way and on a scale unknown elsewhere in Europe, and very different from Japan also. Some sceptics may ask: what has all this to do with the behaviour of economic men in the twentieth century? Is this not an overstress on historical continuity, or national character? I do not think so. Culture and tradition affect what happens and how it happens. It does so through the behaviour pattern of the leaders, and also through what ordinary people consider right or are prepared or accustomed to accept. Who can doubt that Japan's present-day industrial performance is influenced in some important degree by Japan's social-historical traditions, altered though they have been by the passage of time? Or that it is easier for Soviet leaders to impose an internal passport system and police registration because control over free movement has existed in Russia for centuries?'

Stalin has been dead for eighteen years; Russia's industrialisation has made great progress; the mass terror is no more. Yet would-be reformers make little headway; political-cultural controls are as tight as ever, and the economy remains centralised. Political or economic pluralism remains unacceptable. Change towards market socialism is resisted for a number of reasons, practical as well as political-ideological. However, among the latter one should include as a factor the specifically Russian political climate and her traditional way of organising the economy and society for the pursuit of state purposes. So while life has become easier, and the use of such emotive terms as 'state serfdom' increasingly misleading, the heritage of historical experience remains a factor highly relevant to an understanding of contemporary Soviet economic and political reality.

Russia's past is in many ways more relevant than Marxism to an understanding of Soviet political and economic structure. This is certainly the case in the field of politics. The phraseology is Marxist, but the one-party state, the bureaucratic controls over movement and the printed word, and much else besides, owe nothing to Marx's ideas. Indeed, even Lenin put forward no theory of the one-party state either before or during 1917. The economy too is encompassed by the party-state system. It is surely the case that under any government capable of establishing and maintaining order Russia would have been a major 'emergent' country in the present century. Development plans as such were devised also by non-Bolsheviks: thus a far-reaching set of ideas on industrial growth was put forward by the talented Grinevetsky in 1917–18, and he was strongly opposed to Lenin. Lenin knew of his work, and used it, and that of other experts, in his own first ideas on the reconstruction and electrification of Russia: the so-called GOELRO plan put forward in 1920. Grinevetsky also envisaged an active role for the state, but in his mind there would also be a market and capitalist entrepreneurs. The fact that it was the Bolsheviks who imposed order on anarchy made a difference to the pace and direction of industrial development, and the successive destruction of the land-lords, bourgeoisie and a landowning peasantry obviously owed much to the Leninist ideology. However, once they were destroyed, the state organs alone could be agencies of economic growth, and the traditions of Russian statehood soon gave to Marxism a distinctly Russian translation. Naturally the state planned production and invest-ment, for no one else could do so. This made politics of economics, or rather linked the two indivisibly together. Russian political culture thus became a vital factor in economic organisation, and this political culture certainly owes more to Peter the Great than to Karl Marx.

N.B. The statistics quoted above on the proportion of free to slave labour in the factories are challenged by some scholars. For example, some quite different figures have been quoted by Strumilin and others. Apart from the statistical inadequacies there are complex conceptual problems. Thus some adscripted peasants spent only a part of the year at factories and the rest on the land, and some workers who were treated by their employers as free wage-earners were in fact the serfs of a distant master to whom they paid a quit-rent.

3

A Note on Trotsky and the 'Left' Opposition, 1929-31

This Note is based upon a reading of two years' issues of *Byulleten'* *oppozitsii*, published first in Paris and then in Berlin by a group of Trotskyists, and containing a great many articles written by Trotsky himself during the first years of his forced exile from Russia. Also of importance are the occasional contributions from oppositionists smuggled out of the USSR, especially the thoughtful and intelligent ideas of Khristian Rakovsky.

I set myself, in reading through the journal, the following question. What light does it shed on how Trotsky and his friends understood what was happening in Russia, and in the Comintern, during these dramatic years? Of course, it is easy to criticise with the evidence of hindsight, and naturally there could and would be errors of interpretation, especially when they were cut off from systematic communication with one another and with what was happening in the Soviet Union. However, it would still be proper to comment critically on their basic approach to the reality of the time. As we shall see, there were some points on which they showed acute understanding of events and trends. There were others where there seemed to be fundamental misunderstanding. Or so it seems to me. The whole subject is very *diskussionnyi*, to use the Russian word for 'controversial'.

A few words are needed to set the scene. The first issue of the *Byulleten'* was dated July 1929. Trotsky had been exiled to Alma-Ata at the beginning of 1928, and expelled (to Turkey) in February 1929. In these years (and until he was killed) he was chief editor of the journal, his son Leon Sedov the working editor. His fellow-oppositionists were arrested and exiled in large numbers during 1928. However, during that same year, having destroyed the 'lefts', Stalin himself turned left. He broke his alliance with Bukharin by adopting a policy of forcible procurements of grain and other measures increasingly inconsistent with the NEP (mass collectivisation had not yet begun). Successive drafts of the five-year plan of industrial development became more and more ambitious. In the Comintern,

Reprinted from Soviet Studies, *vol. 29, no. 4, October 1977. An Italian translation of this article appeared in* Studi Storici (Rome), *and thanks are due to its editors for permission to re-use it.*

the politics of comparative moderation (symbolised in Trotsky's eyes by the alliance with the Kuomintang in China, and the 'Anglo-Russian committee', with its apparent collaboration with the British trade union leadership) were followed by a drastic left turn in strategy and tactics. All this had led some of Trotsky's former supporters, notably Radek, Preobrazhensky and Smilga, to reapply for membership of the party from which they had been expelled, and in various degrees to renounce their oppositionist views (this did not prevent them, or the far more craven Zinoviev and Kamenev, from sharing the fate of the stauncher oppositionists when killing time came).

During the period covered by these notes, collectivisation and the deportation of the kulaks occurred, as did an even greater speed-up in the tempos of industrialisation. Abroad there were the rise of the Nazis in Germany, the beginnings of the Great Depression, political crisis in Spain, while Trotsky tried to find himself a home, and also political allies among left communists. Stalinist repression meanwhile intensified.

The first subject to be discussed was the reason for Trotsky's exile. There was a quotation from Stalin's speech at the Politburo, allegedly from the stenographic report: the object was to discredit Trotsky and the opposition, as he would inevitably appear to have gone over to the bourgeoisie, and 'if Trotsky attacks and exposes the leadership, then we can present him as a traitor'. Bukharin, Rykov and Tomsky – not yet expelled – were shown as voting against deportation. Alas, this never seemed to have lessened Trotsky's animus against these so-called 'rights'.

Trotsky saw what was taking place as what he called 'bonapartist usurpation', and that Stalin was already trying to 'link the opposition with plots and the preparation of an armed uprising' the better to repress it, to 'draw a line of blood between the official party and the opposition' (no. 1–2, pp. 2–3).

In his 'Letter to the workers of the USSR', Trotsky indignantly denied reports that he left Russia of his own volition. No, he asked instead to be imprisoned. To leave Russia (voluntarily) would represent an admission that the situation was hopeless. Trotsky vigorously attacks the 'capitulationists' (i.e. Radek, Preobrazhensky etc.). What, then, was his own understanding of Stalin's 'left turn'?

First, there is stress on the role of the left opposition in forcing or pushing the Stalinist majority leftwards. They are repeatedly labelled 'centrists', between left and right, manoeuvring under stress of circumstances. 'Finding themselves in an economic cul-de-sac, the Stalinist cadres, against their will, are undertaking a leftward zigzag, which in the process of struggle took them further left than they wished. Nine-tenths of these cadres dream of returning as soon as possible to a more "sound", "normal", "national" line, and hate us precisely because, by our implacable stand, we prevent them from doing this' (Trotsky, no. 1–2, p. 9). 'For a serious Marxist it is clear that the centrists' left turn was ensured exclusively by our struggle' (Trotsky, no. 3–4, p. 33).

The 'centrists' were seen as allies, until 1928, of the 'right' of Bukharin and co. Bukharin and his friends represented the kulak interest, the 'centrists' that of the bureaucracy, much of it of non-proletarian origin or non-Bolshevik, and this tended of its nature to unite with the 'right'. 'Thermidor' and its Russian implications (and applicability of the parallel) were much discussed. In a long piece written in September 1929, Trotsky refers repeatedly to the *dangers* of Thermidor, but rejects the view that it had already occurred, since, if so, the USSR must have a bourgeois government, which is a proposition he finds unacceptable, since he believed the system could be reformed (no. 5, pp. 9, 11, 12). In retrospect, much of the analysis was not only wide of the mark but too schematic, too wedded to dogmatic Marxian categories of class, into which individual policy positions were too neatly fitted. We shall see how this led to further misunderstanding.

Another and more 'objectively' based explanation of the left turn in domestic politics is the economic problem, especially what was seen by Trotsky as a kulak strike, the withholding of grain in the winter of 1927–8. This forced Stalin to recognise the danger of the kulaks, for so long denied by him and his faction, and the emergency action which this strike rendered necessary led to a breach with Bukharin and the 'right'. Trotsky and his friends had also urged higher industrialisation tempos and they had been criticised for this, but now in 1928 the urgency of more investments, especially in heavy industry, became apparent. On this view, Stalin, 'clinging to unlimited apparatus-absolutism', and after having politically destroyed the left opposition, found himself under the necessity of adopting their policies. However, this was done in an adventurist-bureaucratic way, so that in fact he went much further, both in industrial and peasant policies, than the opposition wished or the real situation warranted.

A key element in the criticism, understandably, was the regime in the party, the persecution of the opposition, the suppression of free discussion at all levels. But, at this early stage, the chief fear seems to have been that Stalin and his bureaucrats, owing to the position they occupied in the opposition's 'class' analysis, and their irresponsibility to the workers, would swing back to the right. Among Trotsky's ablest and most eloquent supporters was Rakovsky. Writing in April 1929, he noted that the leadership had been 'compelled to appropriate for its own use many elements from the opposition's platform, was compelled to repeat after us that every concession to the kulaks or other hostile classes would lead to their strengthening ' (and so on), but 'all this is but words. Still faithful to its centrist position, which consists of uttering left phrases and committing Right deeds . . . , asserting in words the existence of a right danger, announcing that any concessions to the kulak must be eliminated, the party leadership in practice made concession after concession. Thus in June [1928] it raised grain prices' (no. 3–4, p. 13).

Similar views were expressed by others (for instance, Sosnovsky). Even when kulaks were being deported, the expectation was that the strata of kulaks would rise again, within the collective farms, this being based on the fact that these farms were being created before the necessary machinery could be supplied; therefore the peasants would work in the main with their own equipment, therefore differentiation among the peasantry would revive, giving rise to kulaks yet again. As we shall see, Trotsky and his friends had some very acute things to say about agriculture, but this was certainly not one of them.

What of the international left turn? Here, Trotsky points to the transference to the International of the typical Stalinist tactics.

'Centrism is a midpoint between reformism and communism. It does not and cannot have its own line . . . It zigzags from one extreme to the other . . . It is wholly bureaucratised and wholly subordinate to the commands of the top of the Stalinist fraction. This gives to each zigzag of the leadership an international aspect, regardless of the real situation of the labour movement in the given country. As a result world communism loses ground' (Trotsky, no. 3–4, p. 29).

Here, of course, the opposition is on solid ground, and there appear many bitter and well-documented denunciations of the extremist tactics of the period, 'social fascism' among them. As in the case of industrial and peasant policy inside the USSR, the leadership is blamed for first refusing to listen to 'left' criticism (e.g. of the disastrous Chinese policy of 1926–7) and then for a rush to ultra-left excesses, which was combined with the elimination of any leaders who might question Stalin's infallibility.

Let us now proceed to analyse the views expressed in the *Byulleten'* by subject, as the situation developed, beginning with internal affairs and with agriculture, i.e. essentially the issue of *forcible collectivisation*.

Trotsky analysed the problem clearly enough. Agriculture was backward and fragmented. In conditions of isolation, i.e. without support from more developed socialist countries, there was bound to be difficulty. Peasants gained in land, and the abolition of rent. They lost through prices: high-cost state industry had to raise additional resources for investment through prices. Trotsky himself coined the term 'price scissors' in 1923. He repeated that the peasantry had to pay 'tribute', but seemed also to agree that the 'scissors' of 1923 had opened too wide, i.e. the peasants were too greatly overcharged. He also continued to argue *both* that the condition of the working class ought to be more rapidly improved, *and* that much greater efforts to industrialise should have begun much earlier, say, in 1924. This combination of arguments suggests certain inconsistencies. Of course, it is easy to say that if industry grew faster exchanges with the villages could take place on an expanded basis which would have encouraged more marketed production, more of which could have been exported to buy more foreign machines and other goods. It was indeed part of the 'left' case that the leaders were going too slowly. Trotsky quotes mockingly and repeatedly Bukharin's phrase about going at 'the pace of a tortoise'. But why did Bukharin use these words? Surely not because this was a pace he preferred, but because, within the constraints of NEP, there was little room for manoeuvre. At no point does Trotsky quantify: *what* additional measures, which would not antagonise the peasantry and cause the blades of the price scissors to widen, could in fact have been taken in 1924–6, say? More could have been done, no doubt, but how much more, and what difference would it have made? Matters are not helped by repeated accusations, directed at Bukharin and Stalin, of having been too soft on the kulak for too long. Surely, sterner measures against the more prosperous peasants would have had adverse effects on production and marketing? More collectives? But Trotsky himself argued that this depended on new techniques, not yet available, and on the willingness of the peasants to join, as he did not advocate coercion (except to restrain the exploitative tendencies of kulaks).

Trotsky rightly points out that the speed up of industrialisation in 1928–9 inevitably led to shortages, queues, these being 'the most vivid argument against socialism in a separate country' (no. 7, p. 2). He showed no sign of understanding the connection between shortages and prices, however, or at least not yet.

As already mentioned, Trotsky viewed the grain procurement crisis of the winter 1927–8 as a manifestation of kulak power, and regarded the belated (and too small) price rise of mid-1928 as an intolerable concession to market forces. It follows that he favoured the 'extraordinary measures' taken by Stalin, though perhaps not the crudity with which he collected the grain. Indeed, he and some of his correspondents alleged that, in the course of these exactions, the kulak was still somewhat favoured. This, I suppose, followed from his mistaken picture of the nature of Stalinist 'centrism': the bureaucracy just *had* to be kulak-influenced (and no doubt some of the bureaucrats were!).

Eventually, Trotsky recognised that the anti-kulak campaign was real. But, of course,

'the kulak is not separated from the middle peasant by any impenetrable wall. Under conditions of commodity production, the middle peasants automatically produce kulaks from among themselves. The hail of administrative blows on the kulaks, unco-ordinated and panicky, which hit not only kulaks, put a barrier to the development of the upper strata of the middle peasantry . . . The peasants started to rush around looking for another way forward. Thus "total collectivisation" arose'. (Trotsky, no. 9, p. 3, written in February 1930.)

Here and elsewhere, he showed that at first he thought that the leadership had been taken unawares by the peasants' rush to join the collectives, a rush due to the state's actions in closing markets and enforcing compulsory deliveries. 'The gates of the market were locked. After waiting in fear outside them, the peasantry rushed into the only gates that were open, the collectivisation gates' (no. 9, p. 4). But then 'the collective farm can become a new form of disguise for the kulak' (ibid., p. 5). (How wrong this was!)

By June 1930 two things had become apparent, in messages received from Russia. The first was the extent of administrative coercion, against both the kulaks and ordinary peasants, coercion which had the result of causing even the poorest peasants to take a negative view of collectivisation. The other was Stalin's notorious 'dizzy with success' article, which laid the blame for excesses on local officials, and which led to a rush of peasants to get out of collectives (into which they were compelled to return in subsequent years).

An article by F. Dingelshtedt refers to 'wholesale collectivisation, carried out by crudely violent methods (*metodam Prishibeevykh*, from the Chekhov story, *Unter Prishibeev*) has caused unparalleled disruption to the national economy'; huge losses in livestock, utter confusion in the minds of officialdom, precipitate retreat, all are noted and justly so (no. 12–13, p. 18).

'We are for industrialisation and collectivisation', but 'against bureaucratic charlatanism'. Yes, but in November 1930 the error is repeated: 'Collective farms without the necessary industrial base will inevitably secrete kulaks. To call wholesale collectivisation based on peasant tools socialist amounts to reviving the Bukharinist theory of the growing into socialism of the kulaks, but in an administratively disguised and so more malignant form' (no. 17–18, p. 25).

Apart from this tendency to expect the Stalinist 'centrism' to swing right, Trotsky's other error in respect of agriculture appears to me to have been derived from a gross overestimation of the advantages of large-scale mechanised cultivation. In this he followed Lenin ('If we had 100,000 tractors . . . then the peasants would say, "We are for communism"'). He was thus able to argue *both* that collectivisation was necessary *and* that it could be carried out voluntarily as the necessary machinery became available. Subsequent experience (in Poland, to go no further) suggests that this view was wrong. Stalin, brutal though he was, seemed to have been more realistic about peasant attitudes.

This brings one to Trotsky's views on tempos of industrialisation and accumulation. As already mentioned, he repeatedly asserted that the troubles of 1928–30 would have been avoided, the need for drastic action would have been far smaller, if only the policies he advocated in 1923–5 had been followed. True enough, he was able to show that Stalin had denounced his proposals as adventurist and super-industrialising, before adopting wildly extravagant and unreal tempos in successively more ambitious versions of the first five-year plan. True also that the official forecasts of industrial growth for the period 1924–8 were exceeded in practice, and this could be presented as proof that they were too low. But Trotsky nowhere compares these actual growth rates with those he advocated: in these five years industrial output more than trebled. True, he urged more for heavy industry, including the tractor industry. But at the cost of what? Workers? Consumer-goods industries? Peasants? One could hardly get far by just increasing taxes on kulaks! What *was* the room for manoeuvre available within NEP? In his article in *Vestnik Kommunisticheskoi akademii*, 1927, no. 22, Trotsky's former comrade Preobrazhensky vividly described the dilemmas and the constraints, which, in his judgement, followed inexorably from Russia's backwardness and isolation. Trotsky himself on occasion used similar arguments, when denouncing the Stalinist concept of socialism in one country and stressing the need for revolution in advanced capitalist countries. But, given that these revolutions had not occurred, this reader at least is left with the impression that Trotsky (like so many other oppositionists the world over) had not worked out the 'feasibilities' of his alternative policy.

But, this said, his and his comrades' denunciations of Stalinist excesses were quick, sharp and very much to the point.

True enough, as Trotsky said, in 1928–9 there was a violent change in official policy.

'All arguments against "super-industrialisation" were suddenly rejected. The apparatus, working for years in the spirit of economic Menshevism, received orders to regard as heretical all that had previously been holy writ, and to turn into official figures those heresies which yesterday had been called "Trotskyist". The apparatus – communists and specialists alike – were quite unprepared for this task. Attempts to resist or timidly to seek explanations led to immediate and severe punishment. Planning officials accepted that it was better to *stand* for high tempos than to *sit* (in prison) for lower ones' (Trotsky, no. 7, November–December 1929, p. 3.)

Trotsky followed with a vigorous article, entitled 'On economic adventurism and its dangers' (no. 9, February–March 1930), referring again to the swing from over-caution to extremism:

'Now the slogan is: full speed ahead, regardless of anything. The plan is repeatedly revised upwards. From passive possibilism [*sic*] the opportunists have gone over to unbridled subjectivism. If a manager or worker refers to objective obstacles, such as poor-quality equipment, lack of raw materials . . . , this is treated as treason to the revolution.'

From time to time Trotsky uses the evidence of high tempos actually achieved (or claimed) both as evidence of the correctness of the earlier criticisms by the left opposition *and* as proof of the advantages of a 'centralised state economy' (for instance, see no. 10, p. 16). However, he returns again and again – and quite rightly – to criticising unsound extremism, 'prize-gallop industrialisation', which he contrasted with his own policy, which was not 'the general line of the bureaucrats', but which 'flowed from an assessment of the real and dynamic equilibrium of economic and class factors, including international ones'. And again, on the same page he notes the tendency to ignore material constraints on industrialisation tempos, which lead to 'breaches of all economic and therefore also social equilibria' (letter dated 20 December 1929, in no. 10, p. 16). Note the use, twice on one page, of the word 'equilibrium'. There are some who imagine that this was a word used only by Bukharin and the 'rightists'.

Trotsky (unlike some naive contemporary 'Trotskyists') did not ignore the existence of interest groups during the period of socialist construction, and indeed advocated them: conflict 'would greatly increase on a new basis. There would be fractions of "electrifiers", "oil-men", "peat-men", "tractorists", "collectivisers" etc., and the struggle of these in a framework of industrial democracy would be one of the important ways of regulating industrial development'. The elimination of these open conflicts was, in his view, a very important reason for unbalanced extremism (ibid., p. 17).

Then perhaps Bukharin was right in warning the party against unbalanced extremism in his well-known article, '*Zametki ekonomista*' (September 1928)? Apparently not. At the time, and subsequently, Trotsky regarded it as evidence of right-wing deviation. He remained obstinately unable to see any virtues in the 'right' position. 'We have nothing in common with them,' particularly as they had by then capitulated to Stalin. 'The rightists are as "correct" on questions of industrialisation as the French social-democrats are right in saying, contrary to Molotov, that there is no revolutionary situation in France.' In other words, while facts are facts, those who point them out can (in this case should) be regarded as enemies, though, of course, for other reasons.

Rakovsky too denounced adventurism, failure to take account of social-economic constraints and lack of resources, which led to heavy losses in agriculture and to acute disproportions in industry, fall in quality, inflation, reduction in living standards in town and country etc. Writing from his place of exile (in July–August 1930), he followed his very solidly argued and highly critical analysis with the conclusion that a retreat from extremism was essential, but he too attacked the 'rightists', who also are supposed to be counselling retreat: 'The difference between us and rightists is the difference between an army in orderly retreat and fleeing deserters: the apparent similarity on the surface arises from the fact that the army and the deserters are proceeding for a time in the same direction' (no. 25–26, p. 30).

Trotsky several times attacked Stalin's policy as being excessively autarkic. That is to say, not enough attention was paid to the possibilities opened up by world trade. Russia's economic weakness could be somewhat mitigated by utilising the international division of labour. As the Great Depression developed, he also saw clear political as well as economic advantages in barter agreements with Western countries: the USSR could gain materially, and also demonstrate to the numerous unemployed the superiority of a planned economy (e.g. no. 15–16, pp. 30–34). However, on the evidence of these issues of his journal it is hardly possible to assert that Trotsky believed that socialism *could* be built in a Russia integrated more closely into the world trade system, as seems to be argued by Day in his already cited book. Mocking, negative comments on 'socialism in one country' continue throughout these two years.

Trotsky and his friends complained with wholly understandable and growing bitterness about the repression from which his fraction suffered in the Soviet Union. These were still the first years in which the GPU (forerunner of the NKVD and of today's KGB) turned its coercive power upon *communist* oppositionists. Trotsky learnt with evident horror of the shooting of Blyumkin (the ex-left-SR assassin of Count Mirbach in 1918, who had become a communist GPU official), apparently for making unauthorised contact with Trotsky in Constantinople. Shooting of oppositionists was not practised at this period, so this case was unique. Others were in exile and prison, communicating with increasing difficulty with one another and with the outside world, and often in bad health in climatically harsh places. False accusations were made, about their alleged counter-revolutionary acts and beliefs, calling forth a long series of spirited denials from them and from Trotsky, to whom (at least until 1932) they were still able occasionally to smuggle letters. It seems as if the *Byulleten'* itself found its way into Russia, probably by the same route: via the journeys of Soviet officials to and from Europe. Possibly this helps to explain why Stalin was to massacre so high a proportion of Soviet diplomats a few years later.

Trotsky, Rakovsky and their comrades could therefore have had few illusions about their enemy, Stalin, and his system of 'justice'. All the more astonishing is their credulity with regard to false accusations, made about others than themselves, by this very same GPU.

Thus, in an article (unsigned) about the 'trial of the wreckers' of the so-called 'Industrial party' (Prompartiya) in 1930, Trotsky's journal accepted all the accusations and confessions as true, and used the evidence about the anti-industrialisation activities of Ramzin and the other 'wreckers' to attack the Stalin–Bukharin line. 'In 1923–28, i.e. during the assault against the left opposition, the central committee was unconsciously acting with wrecker-specialists who, in their turn, were paid agents of foreign imperialists . . .' Of course, these specialists had occupied leading positions in the planning and managerial mechanism in those years. All this was proved 'by undeniable juridical proofs' (! ?) (no. 17–18, p. 21). Well, well. No wonder these very same specialists hated and feared the left opposition, as may be seen from evidence in the valuable book by N. Valentinov (1971), a reprint of memoirs written in 1956 in Paris.

More striking still was the reaction of Trotsky (or perhaps of his son Sedov who acted as editor; the article is unsigned) to the so-called trial of the Mensheviks in 1931. Again, the accusations are believed, although they were even more far-fetched than those directed at the (non-existent) Prompartiya, and were vigorously denied by the 'implicated' émigré Mensheviks. They were alleged to have made clandestine journeys to Russia at dates at which they were attending conferences in the West, and were supposed to have plotted to invade the Soviet Union with the aid of the imperialists and of such notoriously warlike figures as MacDonald and Blum. Yet these stories were eagerly swallowed by the Trotskyists of the period: the ex-Mensheviks (men like Groman, Bazarov, Ginzburg etc.) worked willingly in Stalin's economic apparatus so long as the Stalin line was against the left opposition, but when Stalin turned left – the Mensheviks – turned to plotting. 'The links of the Mensheviks with wreckers on the one hand, with the imperialist bourgeoisie on the other, represent nothing unexpected.' The 'incontrovertible evidence' showed that it was impossible to advocate 'pure democracy' without advocating 'capitalism', and, in turn, 'one cannot move towards capitalism without becoming agents of the international bourgeoisie. In its class content the role of the Mensheviks in the USSR differs not at all from the role of the Labour party in Britain, the social-democrats in Germany. The form is different . . . , but the essence is the same. The struggle against the social-democrats is the struggle with the democratic wing of imperialism' (no. 21–2, p. 35).

Yet here again the evidence, the confessions, the trial, did not merely contain lies but what the Russians call *vran'yo*: totally invented fantastical rubbish, all of it written to order in the procurator's office. So blinded was Trotsky by his 'class' analysis of the role that social-democrats *ought* to be playing, that it did not occur to him to question the 'evidence'. Yet when a communist ideologist of repute, Ryazanov, was expelled from the party and accused of plotting with the Mensheviks, Trotsky exploded with indignation about these Stalinist slanders (no. 21–2, p. 20). In this instance he could see that the GPU chiefs, Menzhinsky and Yagoda, would accuse Ryazanov of 'anything, if so ordered' (ibid., p. 22). So how does it happen that the same Trotsky is so credulous if those accused happen to be politically alien to him?

Perhaps part of this blindness may be connected with his refusal to discern the real nature of Stalinism for too long. Or, rather, he saw only part of the truth. The word 'centrism' was used, along with 'Thermidor' and, on occasion, 'Bonapartism'. He could see that the old party was being destroyed, that something despotic was taking its place, and he denounced these tendencies eloquently. Yet it was still somehow his party, he sent appeals to it. The 'Stalinist bureaucracy' was to him an alien growth, he looked for links with the old ruling classes, with kulaks, with bourgeois specialists. That the party could actually degenerate from within its own working-class core he found hard to admit. In extenuation it might be said that, though the party members were indeed cowed into obedience, they were not yet the disciplined servants whom Stalin wanted; he had to kill many of them a few years afterwards. None the less, Trotsky cannot be said to have understood, at this stage, just what forces were betraying, or digging the grave of, the revolution be believed in.

It was not Trotsky but Rakovsky who had the honesty to raise the key issues. Rakovsky, on the evidence of these volumes, was a man of courage and intelligence who is worthy of much more thorough study. A translation of his 'letter on the causes of the degeneration of the party and state apparatus', written in exile in Astrakhan' on 2 August 1928 (published in no. 6, pp. 14–20) may be found in Howe (1976). He noted the passive indifference of the working class, including party members, in the face of growing arbitrariness and appalling abuses of power. He then tackles the problem of the changes that take place when the working class becomes a *ruling* class. This situation is full of danger. *This would exist if there were no non-proletarian classes and no hostile capitalist environment.* It is the *'professional risk'* of power. One must, he wrote, look at the relations which the seizure of power creates within the working class. 'When this class seizes power, a certain part of this class turns into agents of authority (*agentov . . . vlasti*). In this way bureaucracy arises. In a proletarian state, in which capitalist accumulation is forbidden for the ruling party, the above-mentioned differentiation is at first functional, but later becomes social.' Rakovsky lists various material privileges distinguishing the ex-worker official from ordinary workers. 'The unity . . . which was formerly the consequence of revolutionary class struggle can now be preserved only through a whole system of influences, designed to preserve equilibrium between various groups of the same class and of the same party, to subordinate them to the basic goal.' Individual rights are meaningless unless there is the necessary 'political ability' to use them. He went on to cite Robespierre's warnings against becoming 'drunk with power'. In the USSR, 'the party and the working class neither physically nor morally resemble what they were ten years earlier . . . A party member of 1917 would scarcely recognise himself in a party member of 1928'. He urged careful study of these changes 'in substance and in function, including the composition of the working class itself and its experience'. He draws attention both to the miserable lower strata ('living on the borderlands on the tiny government doles, beggary, robbery and prostitution') and to the effect on the psychology of former workers of their rise to leading governmental and managerial positions. 'For instance, an administrator-*Derzhimorda* [police-sergeant-type], though a communist, though of proletarian origin, though maybe only a few years ago actually working at a lathe, will not now embody, in his relations with the workers, the best qualities of the proletariat.' And, of course, the party also contains non-proletarian elements (though Rakovsky had the ruthless honesty not to lay stress on this, nor, as we have seen, on the capitalist environment and the petty-bourgeois peasantry, as basic explanatory factors of the phenomena he was analysing).

'Soviet and party bureaucracy [he went on] is a phenomenon of a new order . . . , a new sociological category to which a whole dissertation should be devoted.' But why, he asks, are the workers, in and out of the party, so passive? Some comrades regarded 'grain procurements and self-criticism' as due to the resistance of the proletarian elements of the party (to the alleged right-wing course of Stalin and Bukharin), but this was false, the policy change in these respects being decided at the top. Pressure from the workers was quite insufficient to prevent the expulsion of the opposition. The vast majority of workers who joined the party in the twenties had no idea of what the party had once been like, they lacked a sense of class solidarity, they needed a 'long and difficult' period of being taught (*vospitanie*). Lenin saw the need to protect the party and the working class from 'the decomposing effects of privilege, preferment and petty advantage', which was associated with power in the past, avoiding the influence of NEP and of bourgeois habits of mind. The party leadership was to have created a genuinely worker-peasant administrative apparatus, and it failed.

A powerful analysis, but its conclusion raises a question: if the worker-members of the party, who were often semi-literate, were raised to positions of authority and were prone to abuse their position, becoming separated by their essential functions from the masses whence they came, *who* is to carry out the 'long and difficult' *vospitanie* of the workers and peasants in the apparatus? Honest intellectuals like Rakovsky? But was it not inevitable that they would be thrust aside? Was this not a predictable tragedy?

Rakovsky was co-author (with V. Kossior, N. Muralov and V. Kasparova) of a declaration which was sent to the Sixteenth Party Congress in April 1930, and was published in no. 17–18 (pp. 11–19). After a vigorous criticism of agricultural and industrial policies, and of falling living standards, the authors return to the theme of the style of party rule and of bureaucracy.

'From *a workers' state with bureaucratic deformations*, Lenin's definition of our form of government, we are developing into a *bureaucratic state with proletarian-communist relics*. Before our very eyes there has been and is being formed a large *class of rulers*, with its own inner subdivisions, growing through calculated co-option . . . (through bureaucratic appointments or fictional elections). What unites this peculiar (*svoeobraznyi*) sort of class is the peculiar sort of private property, namely, state power.' 'The bureaucracy possesses the state as private property,' said Marx in the 'Critique of Hegel's state law' [emphasis in original].

They go on: 'it is not hard to guess how attractive for the bureaucracy are wholesale collectivisation and extremely rapid industrialisation tempos. They enlarge the army of bureaucrats, its share in the national income, its power over the masses.' Rakovsky and his friends also attack the leadership's national policy, the weakening of the power of the republics, the growth of bureaucratic centralism, a theme which had brought Rakovsky into conflict with Stalin in earlier years also. It is interesting how the words 'class of rulers' are used, rather than 'ruling class'. This must have been the subject of heated debate among the oppositionists. (It still is!)

Rakovsky's analysis led to a lively discussion among exiled oppositionists, and several discussion documents from Russia were printed in no. 15–16. 'What is the bureaucracy, a class or not a class? A group or person named XYZ wrote:

'Up to the moment when the bureaucracy can be seen as a group or a caste, its domination, however despotic, did not deprive the state of its proletarian character. But once it became a class, which you [Rakovsky] assert it has become, the Soviet state at once shed its proletarian clothing . . . One must choose: either the ruling bureau-

cracy is a class, in which case the dictatorship of the proletariat is no
more, or else it is a group or a caste . . . '

The critics note that bureaucracies have grown up everywhere, control
the state in many countries, but 'Marx never defined the bureaucracy
as a class'. So

'in our view the bureaucracy is not a class and will never become one
. . . It will degenerate, it is a nucleus of a class which will not be
bureaucracy but another hitherto unknown one; its appearance will
mean that the working class will become another oppressed class. The
bureaucracy is the nucleus of some kind of capitalist class, controlling
the state and collectively owning the means of production.' (No. 15–16,
p. 63.)

How 'modern' all this sounds! Marxists are still puzzling over these
perplexing questions.

How significant in this entire analysis is Russian backwardness? It
seems to me to underlie much of Rakovsky's analysis, though he refers
to it only by implication. Trotsky himself was, at least at this period,
less forthright in analysing the *proletarian* origins of the Stalinist
'bureaucracy', but showed very clear awareness of the importance of
the 'historical peculiarities of Russia', to cite the title of his own article
published in 1921. This contrasts with the schematic ahistoricism of
many who now call themselves Trotskyists. Attacking Stalin's crude
assertion that all communists should base their policies on 'the general
features of capitalism' which are 'basically identical in all countries',
Trotsky argued thus:

'National peculiarities are the most general, so to speak summary
product of the unevenness of historical development. This must be
correctly understood as a whole, including the pre-capitalist past. The
more rapid or slower development of productive forces; the gradual
or rapid way in which whole historical epochs are passed through,
e.g. medievalism, craft guilds, enlightened absolution, parliamentarism;
the unevenness of economic development, of various classes and social
institutions and of culture . . . , all these things lie at the basis of
national 'peculiarities'. The October revolution was the most grandiose
of all the manifestations of uneven historical development. The theory
of permanent revolution, which gave the prognosis of the October
revolution, was based on the law of unevenness . . . not in its abstract
but in its material manifestation, in the form of social and political
peculiarities of Russia.' (No. 12–13, p. 32.)

Trotsky then contrasts his analysis with Stalin's 'messianic inter-
nationalism accompanied by bureaucratic-abstract inter-nationalism':

socialism in one country, which positively exaggerates the pecularities of Russia ('permitting the building of socialism regardless of what happens with the rest of humanity'), plus the disregard of the specific features of all other countries and parties. (ibid.)

Trotsky again refers with emphasis to Russia's backwardness in another article (no. 17–18, p. 29), but then, in assessing the role of the party in this situation, he loses his way. 'If we admit for a moment that economic officials and the ruling stratum of workers cease altogether to be under party discipline . . . , then the road to socialism will be barred.' He imagined the trusts becoming more autonomous, weakening planning and giving rise to a struggle between the management and workers. He went on: 'Does the present party regime, despite economic successes, threaten the collapse of party lines and discipline? Certainly.' Immediately afterwards he wrote that 'the party as a party does not exist today', and again there seems something wrong with his analysis: it was not the weakening of party discipline which was barring the road to socialism! Indeed, later in the same article he was speculating on possible 'counter-revolutionary regimes . . . , with elements of Thermidor and Bonapartism, i.e. a greater or lesser role will be played by the Bolshevik-Soviet bureaucracy, civil and military, and at the same time this regime will be the dictatorship of the sword over society in the interests of the bourgeoisie against the people' (ibid., p. 30). Yes, but a year earlier he wrote to Souvarine: 'The problem of Thermidor and Bonapartism is in its essence the problem of the kulak' (no. 1–2, p. 22). It seems to me that Rakovsky understood it all better.

Finally, a brief, a too brief, look at foreign affairs.

There is no need here to repeat Trotsky's frequent and well-known criticisms of the disastrous China policy of 1927. He drew the conclusion that there should only be a 'dictatorship of the proletariat', *not* 'the democratic dictatorship of the proletariat and peasantry' (no. 3–4, p. 9). Where, one wonders, would Mao Tse-tung's strategy fit in, which was already then in the process of development?

Trotsky devoted much space to *supporting* the Soviet stand on the Chinese Eastern Railway against Chiang Kai-shek. For him it was an essential test: those oppositionists abroad who saw no point in defending Stalin's Russia against what was, after all, an attempt by China to eliminate extra-territorial rights received short shrift (no. 3–4, pp. 1–4, no. 8, p. 5 etc.).

Trotsky devoted several effective articles (notably in no. 8) to the errors and follies of the Comintern. The 'left turn' of 1928–9 was based on no solid evidence: the party was everywhere in decline. The unreal assessment of the situation, the extremist tactics advocated ('general strike', 'class against class', 'Soviet power', and so on), the lack of attention to local conditions, the total subordination of the foreign parties to the Comintern and so to Moscow, and the expulsion of any leaders who had independent ideas, all these tendencies were very properly denounced. All this was largely written by Trotsky himself. Understandably, oppositionists in Russia wrote primarily about the internal situation.

This Note is already too long, and it has deliberately concentrated on Soviet internal affairs. I will therefore be brief in referring to two other 'international' matters: Trotsky's relations with other oppositionists, and 'social fascism'.

Trotsky tried, of course, to maintain links with other leftists in various countries. There are letters to the Italian opposition, following the expulsion in 1929 of many of the old leaders, and the firm establishment of the leadership of Ercoli (Togliatti). There were correspondence with and articles about members of the Leninbund and other German oppositionist groups, those around the periodical *Vérité* (France), even with some survivors in Shanghai. He criticised the small Belgian 'left' group, led by Van Overstraten, for not supporting the USSR over the Chinese railway. He wrote to the Austrian opposition, and to Hungarian émigrés urging them to work together against Stalinism and Bela-Kunism. There is even a proclamation 'to the communists of China and all the world' (no. 15–16). Yet how weak and insignificant were all these forces! There he was, writing at length about the dictatorship of the proletariat as the only alternative to Italian fascism, or on what to do in Spain, or the ideological errors of Brandler and Thalheimer in Germany, or the slogan of the constituent assembly in China. Of course, he also wrote about uniting the various opposition fractions, or fragments. But, as Deutscher and others have noted long ago, how few were his followers, how politically ineffective, even meaningless, were his eloquent, if sometimes dogmatic, words.

On the issue of 'social fascism', the dogmatic ultra-left-turn of the Comintern gave Trotsky an opportunity for eloquent attacks on a basically absurd official line. It must be stressed that Trotsky was bitterly hostile to the social-democratic leadership. Many of his words can be cited to show 'that he denounced them unmercifully as bourgeois and counter-revolutionary by nature'. Thus 'Müller and MacDonald grovel disgustingly' trying to prop up capitalism (no. 10, p. 5), etc. etc. His attacks on the Anglo-Russian committee also showed how he regarded moderate Labour and trade union elements. However, he was quick to see how absurd was the slogan of 'social fascism', and quick also to stress the danger of fascism in Germany. This danger, in Trotsky's eyes, was enhanced by 'the conservative role of social-democracy', as well as by the weaknesses and errors of the communists. Trotsky treated social-democracy as a 'powerful enemy', but as one which 'cannot be fought by incantations'. Most workers and trade unionists still followed the social-democrats, in Germany, France,

Britain, Austria etc. One must plainly avoid offending and repulsing them, and the abusive 'social-fascist' nonsense which the Stalinist leadership of the Comintern was perpetrating was, Trotsky rightly insisted, stupid and harmful. The chosen tactic helped the social-democratic leadership: 'In those countries where fascism is a powerful force . . . , it is easy for the social-democrats to show not only the difference but also the hostility between them and fascism . . . A barrier is erected between the communists and the social-democratic workers . . .' (no. 10, p. 4), and these arguments are repeated and developed in other articles. In retrospect, it is astonishing to read the official communist literature of the time. Trotsky's intransigent attitude to anyone to the 'right' of him was notorious, but he saw clearly the ultra-stupidities of the Comintern (and Stalin) line. It was, indeed, suicidal.

I hope that this survey, though incomplete, may help the reader to appreciate how the Soviet 'left opposition' saw the world, and above all their own country, at a critical time.

NOTE

See also the article of Richard Day (*New Left Review*, January 1977), which recounts Trotsky's dispute with Kondratiev about 'long-wave cycles', and in which the concept 'equilibrium' plays a major role. See also Day's book (*Leon Trotsky and the Politics of Economic Isolation*, Cambridge, 1973) for evidence of Trotsky's view of the market as against bureaucratic centralisation in subsequent years. This article was published before the appearance of the excellent book by B. Knei-Paz: *The Social and Political Thought of Leon Trotsky* (Oxford, 1978).

Part Two
Political Economy

4
Lenin as Economist

This paper is not intended as a survey of Lenin's economic *policies*. Such a survey would require an examination of the history of the Russian revolution, of War Communism and of NEP, which would not be justified in the present context. An attempt will be made below to consider Lenin's qualities as an economic theorist, and to some limited extent also to examine the theories implied by the manner in which Lenin tackled practical issues. The latter approach is justified in his last years, when he was evidently much too busy to set down much of significance on theory as such.

But was Lenin an economist at all?

1 *Early Period*

In the introduction to the volume of his works which contains – indeed, consists of – the famous *Development of Capitalism in Russia*, the Institute of Marxism–Leninism describes it as 'a remarkable example of the unity of revolutionary theory and practice'. Yet this is the most considerable work of Lenin the economist, in length, depth and scope. In other works, the connection with contemporary politics is even more direct, the subordination of economic science to the exigencies of the moment more obvious. Some may conclude that our study therefore has no point. Lenin was not an economist – and that's that.

Such a view, however, would be altogether too narrow. No one disputes that Lenin was primarily a politician. Even so, some supposedly orthodox economists have also had strong political views, and their motives in devising various economic theories have included a wish to prove the desirability of some policies, the undesirability of others. Marx, too, was a fighter, a committed revolutionary; yet few would argue that this displaces him from his position in the history of economic thought, for all that his economic theories were deeply influenced by his political programme and objectives. Lenin produced no *Das Kapital*, it is true. He was much more concerned with everyday politics than was Marx. His economic interests were undoubtedly one-sided. There was no micro-economics at all. Yet it can certainly be shown that he understood a good deal of economics, that he handled

Reprinted from L. B. Schapiro and P. Reddaway, eds, Lenin After Fifty Years, *London, Pall Mall Press, 1967.*

statistics with enviable dexterity, that he knew well what Marx meant and how to interpret him, and that he was highly skilled in argument about economic structure and policy. He concentrated a great deal of attention on class analysis, on 'the relations of production', on seeking the determinants of change and growth. He was, in fact, a political economist in a sense that might have appealed to Adam Smith as well as to Marx. (In his young days he had very carefully read Adam Smith and frequently quoted him.)

It is true that late in life he wrote, rather surprisingly: 'Politics cannot but have dominance over economics. To argue otherwise is to forget the ABC of Marxism.' (*Pol. sob. soch.*, vol. 42, 1963, p. 278.) This would seem to be a somewhat un-Marxist overemphasis on voluntarism as against determinism. However, no serious Marxist has doubted that economic circumstances can be affected by political action, and the over-emphasis in the above quotation reflected Lenin's concentration on the political struggle, and on the party's grip over society and over economic strategy at the time when he was chairman of the Council of People's Commissars. This is not a very unusual *déformation professionelle*. Harold Wilson once taught economics but he doubtless saw things from a rather different angle from No. 10 Downing Street.

Lenin's early works show a preoccupation with the evolution of Russian society and of market relations within Russian society in particular. Rapid changes were in progress, and it was a matter of dispute among the intellectual left wing just what these changes meant, and what kind of policies ought to be devised to deal with the situation. Great industries were being set up, and the forces of change were beginning to affect the traditional forms of organisation in agriculture too. What was Russia's likely pattern of development? What role would be played in the future by large-scale factory industry as against handicrafts, by commercialised landlord and peasant agriculture as against peasant communal institutions? Would Russia travel the road of Western European capitalism? How far along this road had it already travelled? How could the rather inadequate and fragmentary statistics which were then available best be used to show up the existing trends and to provide answers to some of the above questions? One feels that Adam Smith would have understood the relevance of these matters to his own concepts and to the wealth of the nation in question. Western orthodox economics had, however, by then taken a turn towards marginal analysis, largely static in character and based on the concept of equilibrium and the best allocation of scarce resources. It is not altogether surprising that Lenin had no time for this. Sixty years after Lenin's early writings, development economists are still struggling with some of the problems that he raised, and most of those who have anything interesting to say about them are not concerned with marginal analysis. An outstanding contributor to modern growth theory, Luigi Pasinetti, has recently reminded us that

a typical marginalist scheme of general equilibrium . . . presupposes the existence of given natural resources in fixed quantities and of a given number of individuals (owning the resources) with well-defined utility preferences . . . They have to find those prices (equilibrium prices) which bring about the optimum allocation of the given resources relatively to their original ownership distribution . . . I have thought that it may be not altogether useless, after a century of marginal economic analysis, to go back and explore the possibilities . . . inherent in the other approach to economic reality, which has been left in oblivion since the time of the classics . . . All commodities are produced, and could be made in practically whatever quantity may be wanted, provided there is devoted to their production the amount of effort which they technically require.' (Pasinetti, 1965, pp. 577–8.)

Pasinetti also finds it convenient to divide the product into producers' goods and consumers' goods. Equally apt would be the following quotation from a 'moderate' American development economist, Benjamin Higgins:

'For a short time the present writer was engaged in wartime planning, and he has been struck since by the similarity between the *nature* of the problem confronting economic planners during the war and in underdeveloped countries . . . "Total war", like planning development of poor and stagnant economies, involves marked and discontinuous structural changes, and resource allocation without reference to the market.' (Higgins, 1959, p. 453.)

One can hardly blame Lenin, given his preoccupations, for neglecting even to bother much with the neo-classical school.

The Development of Capitalism in Russia (1899) had an avowed object, that of proving that the narodniks (populists) were wrong, because the traditional Russia of subsistence economy peasants and handicrafts workers had already been permeated with commercial and capitalist relations, and that the tendency towards the break-up of patriarchal and village community institutions had gone far and was now irreversible. To prove his point Lenin deployed an impressive battery of statistics. He did not deny that the old existed side by side with the new, or that traditional institutions or subsistence agriculture were not widespread phenomena in the 1890s. Subjecting to vigorous criticism the ideas especially of Daniel'son (Nikolai-on), Lenin not only poured scorn on their hopes for the development of a specifically Russian socialism by and through traditional institutions, but also asserted that the destruction of these institutions was progressive. Capitalism was destroying the separateness and isolation, the fragmentation of the petty producers, binding them to the market, creating new contradictions in the process. The narodniks were thus not only wrong in underestimating these trends, they were also wrong in deploring them. In arguing thus he was in line with other Russian Marxists, including the future Mensheviks, but he went somewhat further than his colleagues of that time in seeking to prove that capitalism was already established. It is true that some of Marx's writings, notably his letter of 1881 to Vera Zasulich, could be cited in favour of the proposition that Russia might go forward to socialism through its traditional communal institutions. However, the letter to Zasulich remained unpublished, and was apparently unknown, even to Lenin, until it was unearthed in the early twenties (it was first published in Russia in 1924). In any case, Lenin could argue that other statements of Marx on this point related to the past, and that the developments since 1883 had altered the situation. (There was a great industrialisation boom in the years following 1891.)

Recent research has tended to show that Lenin overestimated the extent and speed of the capitalist transformation of Russian agriculture. The Stolypin reforms were still over a decade away when Lenin wrote *The Development of Capitalism in Russia*, and the Russian peasantry was to demonstrate its attachment to the traditional communal forms even in the first ten years of bolshevik rule. It is not that Lenin's statistics were 'wrong'. The point is simply that he had to adapt and arrange fragmentary data, and it would have been possible for an able opponent to adapt and arrange other fragmentary data to modify somewhat his picture of the 1890s. However, Lenin was surely right in his assessment of trends. Either Russia was already on capitalist rails, or the combined efforts of Witte and Stolypin were going to put it there, with the help of winds of change which were already blowing strong and which Lenin correctly identified. Capitalism, as Lenin saw it, was ensuring 'exceedingly rapid' growth in comparison with the pre-capitalist epoch, but he maintained that this was slower than was possible 'with the contemporary level of development of technique and culture'. Slower, because

'in no capitalist country have there survived in such profusion the institutions of a bygone age, inconsistent with capitalism, holding back its development, vastly worsening the position of the producers who suffered both from capitalism and from the inefficient development of capitalism.' (*Pol. sob. soch.*, 1958, p. 601.) (The last words are a quotation from Marx's *Kapital*.)

In this and his other early works, Lenin showed skill in using statistics, and also great ability in interpreting Marx in answering some of his critics. In later years his argument became increasingly disfigured with polemic zeal – one can almost see him spluttering with indignation – with the result that the academic value of what he said was greatly reduced. In his early years, however, he still argued as an economist as well as a politician. It must be admitted that the narodnik theoreticians were a relatively easy target for his criticism, since their economics were often rather naive. In their oversimplifield criticisms of capitalism Lenin sensed, not only theoretical inaccuracy, but also an attack damaging to his own position, in so far as he appeared at this time, in common with most other Marxists, to be advocating capitalism at the next stage of Russian development. Consequently, in several works of the early period, he appeared to be defending capitalism from some exaggerated accusations. The narodniks had been putting forward a crude underconsumption theory which, according to Lenin, they had derived indirectly from Sismondi. In its crudest form this theory asserted that, since capitalism impoverishes people and at the same time causes output to increase, there is no one to buy this extra output, and therefore either one has economic crises or the surplus goods have to be exported to other countries. Lenin poured scorn on this. In doing so he traced the error back to Adam Smith. Smith divided up the national product into three kinds of income, accruing respectively as wages, rent and income from capital. This, wrote Lenin, is misleading. It is not true, he argued, that the tendency of capitalism to depress incomes and the purchasing power and absorptive capacity of the internal market is a direct cause of crises and the export of capital. This is because, under capitalism, as the economy grows so does the proportion of goods devoted to the production of other goods. Adam Smith, Sismondi and other economists, so Marx as well as Lenin asserted, failed to see that some goods in fact serve as capital, and are not reduceable into anybody's income. As a simple example Lenin cited seed grain. This led him into a restatement and extension of Marx's theory of simple and expanded reproduction, and so to the all too well-known assertion concerning the priority of the rate of growth of department I over that of department II.

The basic concepts are probably familiar: producers' goods output must grow faster than consumers' goods output. Department I produces goods which are consumed in the course of production. The capitalists and workers engaged in making these goods obtain consumers' goods by exchanging them for the products of department II. This department in turn requires producers' goods (raw materials, fuel, machinery parts etc.) to keep production going. The theory further distinguishes between 'constant capital' (represented by goods, including fixed capital, used up in production) and 'variable capital' (represented by payments to labour). 'Surplus value' is obtained by capitalists in both departments. Constant capital and variable capital are, naturally, required both in department I and department II. Lenin summarises his theory as follows.

'Let us first assume simple reproduction, i.e., the repetition of the process of production on its previous scale, the absence of accumulation. Obviously, the variable capital and the surplus value in department II (which exists in the form of articles of consumption) are realised by the personal consumption of the workers and capitalists of this department (for simple reproduction assumes that the whole of the surplus value is consumed and that no portion of it is converted into capital). Further, the variable capital and surplus value which exist in the form of means of production (department I) must, in order to be realised, be exchanged for articles of consumption for the capitalists and workers engaged in the making of means of production. On the other hand, the constant capital existing in the form of articles of consumption (department II) cannot be realised except by an exchange for means of production, in order to be put back again into production in the following year. Thus we get variable capital and surplus value in means of production exchanged for constant capital in articles of consumption; the workers and the capitalists (in the means of production department) in this way obtain means of subsistence, while the capitalists (in the articles of consumption department) dispose of their product and obtain constant capital for further production. Under simple reproduction the parts exchanged must be equal: the sum of the variable capital and surplus value in the means of production must be equal to the constant capital in articles of consumption. On the other hand, if we assume reproduction on a progressively increasing scale, i.e., accumulation, the first magnitude must be greater than the second, because there must be available a surplus of means of production with which to begin further production' (*Pol. sob. soch.*, vol. 3, 1958, p. 52.)

This leaves out constant capital in means of production, which is 'realised partly by exchange among capitalists of the same department' such as, for example, when coal is exchanged for iron; and partly by re-use in the same economic sector, as, for example, seed grain, or coal used for the production of more coal. 'As for accumulation, its starting point as we have seen is a surplus of means of production (taken from the surplus value of the capitalists in the department), a surplus that also calls for the conversion into capital of part of the surplus value in articles of consumption.' Lenin draws the following conclusion:

'Capitalist production, and consequently the home market, grow not so much on account of articles of consumption as on account of means of production. In other words, the increase in the means of production outstrips the increase in articles of consumption. Indeed, we have seen that constant capital in the articles of consumption (department II) is exchanged for variable capital plus surplus value in means of production (department I). According, however, to the general law of capitalist production, *constant capital grows faster than variable capital.* Hence constant capital in articles of consumption has to increase faster than variable capital and surplus value in articles of consumption, while constant capital in means of production has to increase fastest of all, outstripping both the increase in variable capital plus surplus value in means of production and the increase in constant capital in articles of consumption.' (ibid., p. 54.) [Italics in original, as throughout this chapter.]

He therefore concludes that for capitalism . . . the growth of the home market is to a certain extent independent of the growth of personal consumption, and takes place mostly on account of productive consumption'. True, this does not mean that 'productive consumption is entirely divorced from personal consumption'. However, 'the former can and must increase faster than the latter'. He goes on to say:

'This larger consumption of constant capital is nothing but a higher level of the development of the productive forces, one expressed in terms of exchange value, because the rapidly developing means of production consist in the main of materials, machines, instruments, buildings and all sorts of other accessories for large-scale and especially machine production. It is quite natural, therefore, that capitalist production, which develops the productive forces of society and creates large-scale production in machine industry, is also distinguished by a particular expansion of that department of social wealth which consists of means of production.' (ibid., p. 55.)

This theory of Lenin's concerning the necessarily more rapid growth of producers' goods as against consumers' goods has played a considerable role in theoretical and practical discussions in the Soviet Union long since his death. Thus one finds Pashkov quoting Lenin to prove the inadmissible heresy of such an orthodox Marxist as the Polish economist B. Minc. (Pashkov, 1958, p. 198.) To the mind of the scholastic Soviet theoretician, the matter has been resolved by the appropriate quotation. What did Lenin mean, and to what extent can he be said to have been right?

One possible answer for a Soviet Marxist, and this answer has been made, is that Lenin was talking about a capitalist society, and trying to explain how it is that production can go on increasing while consumption does not increase. It might be said that Lenin was trying to show in this way an undesirable feature of capital society, which socialism could overcome. However, since his theory concentrated on goods rather than on income, and appeared to be derived from technical rather than class considerations, these objections did not seem to have very much force. In any case, Lenin's analysis seemed all too apt to describe the Stalinist model of industrialisation, in which spectacular increases in the gross national product and in industrial production were accompanied by a very moderate, in some years negative, rise in personal consumption. What can we say about Lenin's theoretical formulation?

Two phrases that he used require emphasis, particularly the second of them. He speaks of 'reproduction on a progressively increasing scale, i.e. accumulation'. What do the words 'progressively increasing scale' mean? Why not just say 'accumulation'? Did he have in mind an *increasing* rate of growth? If he did, then, other things being equal, it is clear that in each year a larger proportion of the product would have to be laid aside for future use, and so the share of consumption would fall. On the other hand, this process can only go on for a limited period of time, since it is clear that otherwise we would reach the absurd conclusion that all output would consist of producers' goods and the consumers would all starve to death.

More to the point is Lenin's other assertion, which was certainly implied by Marx, although it was Lenin and not Marx who drew the conclusion which is here being discussed. The phrase reads: 'According to the general law of capital production, constant capital grows faster than variable capital.' If this is so, then it would follow that even if one were to assume a constant rate of growth, there would still have to be relatively more producers' goods compared with articles of final consumption. In terms of the labour theory of value, a relatively larger number of persons have to be engaged in making 'materials, machines, instruments, buildings and all sorts of other accessories'. But is this necessarily so? Was it necessarily so at the time that Lenin wrote?

We are accustomed nowadays to think in terms of capital-saving as well as labour-saving investments. A capital-saving investment would enable a given volume of end products to be made using less capital, less materials. It would enable the capital-output ratio to fall. It might save more capital than labour. In these instances, Lenin's theory would be plainly untrue, whether one assumes capitalist or socialist productive relations. But, written in 1896, Lenin's views did broadly correspond to observable reality. Many Western commentators – for example, Colin Clark – would date a change in respect to the capital-output ratio round about 1920, with the development of new materials and new techniques. Therefore Lenin's point did have some validity at the time at which it was made. It must also not be forgotten why it was made. He was combating a much sillier narodnik theory.

Lenin made a significant step forward in developing Marx's theories of simple and expanded reproduction. Those who engaged with him in matters of interpretation – for instance, Struve – came out very plainly on the losing side of the argument. Whether the theory was of any use or not is quite another question. Some students of the Soviet scene are fond of quoting with approval the words of Popov, the author of the first balance of the national economy in 1925. Popov found that it was impossible to apply the Marxian categories to the statistics of production in Russia. The reason was that the available statistics merely related to the output of goods, and many of the same goods were used for a great many different purposes, in department I as well as in department II, for accumulation as well as consumption. The point is a valid one, and the difficulty still faces anyone endeavouring to make input-output tables in Russia or any other East European country. It seems to me that, while Popov and his colleagues were entirely right in so far as practical calculations were concerned, this does not affect the validity or otherwise of the theoretical construction. No one has seen in real life either an indifference curve or a demand function. As already pointed out, the most promising and most ingenious of recently devised growth models – that of Pasinetti – is rather closer to Marx and Lenin than to the neo-classical marginal utility school.

It is interesting to note, in view of his own later work on imperialism, how impatiently Lenin dismisses the idea that foreign trade is the means by which unsalable surpluses are, so to speak, eliminated from the capitalist system. Struve attacked Marx's and Lenin's theory of realisation on the grounds that foreign trade had been omitted from it. Lenin counter-attacked vigorously. For purposes of theoretical analysis, what difference would it make if we took several countries instead of one? If goods are sold abroad, then other goods are bought. In most countries and in most periods, payments are balanced. If some goods are realised in the world market, then other goods made in other countries are realised within the country in question. It is not customary to give goods away. Therefore, said Lenin, Struve was wrong, and the narodniks were wrong earlier when they too brought up the question of the external market in this context. (*Pol. sob. soch.*, vol. 4, 1959, p. 79.)

2 *Imperialism and Capitalism*

Lenin in subsequent years plunged more and more into the everyday life of politics, and his theoretical contributions did not have much to do with economic theory. It therefore seems proper to jump forward twenty years and consider Lenin's theory of imperialism.

As is well known, Lenin derived many of his ideas from the works of J. A. Hobson and of Hilferding. (Though never admitting it, he may also have been influenced by Bukharin, who had been writing on the same theme.) Living in Switzerland in the middle of the First World War, Lenin had both the time and the facilities to use many statistical sources and to rise above the everyday exigencies of politics. The first part of *Imperialism: The Highest Stage of Capitalism* (1916) documented the concentration of capital and the growth of monopolies. Lenin quoted Hilferding approvingly concerning the new relations between the banks and finance capital on the one hand, and the manufacturers on the other. All this is reasonably familiar. He went on to contrast the 'old capitalism, when free competition held undivided sway', with the latest stage of capitalism. In the former there was export of goods; typical of the latter is the export of capital. He emphasised the unevenness of development of different countries, and the existence of what he described as an enormous surplus of capital in the advanced countries. To avoid a decline in profits which would take place if capitalists continued to invest only in their own countries, capital is exported to backward countries where 'profits are usually high, for capital is scarce, the price of land is relatively low, wages are low, raw materials are cheap'. (As a communist student song once had it: 'The rapidly declining profit rate is rough on the colonial boys.') Just as monopoly capitalist associations divide up the domestic market among themselves, in the interests of ensuring a regular outlet for their products, so they also endeavour to divide up the world's markets. This leads to a struggle for spheres of influence and for colonial possessions as a means of giving advantages to one's own capitalists. Whereas 'in the most flourishing period of free competition in Great Britain, i.e. between 1840 and 1860, the leading British bourgeois politicians were opposed to colonial policy and were of the opinion that the liberation of the colonies and their complete separation from Britain was inevitable and desirable' (Lenin, *Collected Works*, vol. 22, 1961, p. 256), by the end of the century opinions had altered. Cecil Rhodes and Joseph Chamberlain were typical of the new era. Cecil Rhodes is quoted as advocating imperialism as a means for finding lands to settle the surplus population, to provide new markets. He went on: 'The empire, as I have always said, is a bread and butter question. If you want to avoid civil war, you must become imperialists.' (ibid., p. 257.) It is perhaps noteworthy that at several points in this book, and also in his statistical tables, Lenin identifies the Asian territories of tsarist Russia as 'colonies'. Thus the British capitalists are said to be exerting every effort to develop cotton growing in their colony, Egypt, while the Russians are doing the same in their colony, Turkestan. (ibid., p. 262.)

Lenin quoted Kautsky's definition of imperialism: 'Imperialism is a product of highly developed industrial capitalism. It consists in the striving of every industrial capitalist nation to bring under its control or to annex all large areas of agrarian territory irrespective of what nations inhabit it.' Lenin disapproved of the emphasis on 'industrial' capital, and also of the emphasis on agrarian territory. He cited with approval, against Kautsky, Hobson's definition of the new imperialism as being above all 'the theory and practice of competing empires, each motivated by similar lusts of political aggrandisement and commercial gain; secondly . . . the dominance of financial or investing over mercantile interests'. (Hobson, 1902.) (Lenin had been very impressed with Hobson's book when he had read it twelve years earlier and he had tried to translate it into Russian.) He also poured scorn on Kautsky's idea of some kind of ultra-imperialism, in which the various imperialist interests joined together to divide up the world. Lenin treated this as a piece of unrealistic reformist apologetics.

Lenin endorsed Hobson's vision of a largely idle parasitic class of 'wealthy financial aristocrats' drawing a vast tribute from the backward parts of the world, and employing others as 'retainers and tradesmen', while industry withers away, since all but the 'final stages of production of the more perishable goods' could occur in what we now call underdeveloped countries. Goods would be sent to the imperialist powers in the form of tribute, i.e. as interest and profit remittances, while the imperialists would form themselves into 'a larger alliance of Western states' for the purpose of the more efficient exploitation of the backward world. Hobson thought that countervailing forces would make this outcome improbable, and Lenin agreed with this, as well as with the view that existing trends pointed in the direction indicated above. Lenin wrote: 'An increasing proportion of land in England is being taken out of cultivation for the diversion of the rich. As for Scotland – the most aristocratic place for hunting and other sports – it is said that "it lives on its past and on Mr Carnegie".' (Lenin *Collected Works*, vol. 22, 1961, p. 282.) Though there was (and is) some truth in these assertions, it is clear that the general trend was not towards still more playgrounds for the rich, still more servants and retainers. By hindsight we can see how wrong both Hobson and Lenin were. The Common Market would seem to fit the prophecy about a union of European states, but far from drawing industrial production from overseas as tribute, the industrialised countries have vastly expanded their own production, and they have expanded their export of goods more rapidly than that of capital. Lenin's vision of imperialism as the last stage of a dying capitalism was evidently mistaken. Capital has, indeed, been exported, but not much of it has had the aim or effect of increasing the industrial output of Asia, Africa and Latin America, as communist and other critics are constantly reminding us. It is also important to note that the bulk of capital exports from developed, capitalist countries have gone to other developed capitalist countries, which must affect one's interpretation of the economic motives and consequences of imperialism.

It is true that Lenin did not go so far as to say that capitalist countries were doomed to immediate decline. In his *Imperialism* he wrote: 'It would be a mistake to believe that this tendency to decay precludes the rapid growth of capitalism'. (ibid., p. 300.) He therefore did see that very considerable investment opportunities still existed in capitalist countries. He never quite reconciled this with his support for some of Hobson's ideas. Nor it is clear how this assertion can be made consistent with his view, in the same book, that imperialism is 'moribund capitalism'. His one model of an allegedly decaying capitalism was Britain, with its very slow rate of growth and its falling share in world industrial production and world trade. This, as he pointed out, was due to effective competition from younger and more vigorous imperialisms, such as that of Germany. However, the rise or fall of one particular capitalist or imperialist country does not seem logically to lead to any conclusions concerning the allegedly moribund nature of the entire system.

Lenin and Hobson had grievously underestimated the developmental potential and profitability of so-called monopoly capitalism. Private capital tends to flow to developed rather than to underdeveloped countries, as the latter are pointing out. Industrial output has risen in the developed countries; the numbers employed in serving the aristocracy (whether the old or the new financial one) have declined; the service industries have become part of a mass consumption society which Lenin could not begin to contemplate, since he believed in the dogma of the absolute and relative impoverishment of the proletariat and the increasing proletarianisation of the middle class. True, in *Imperialism* he noted and commented upon the rise of an upper stratum of the proletariat. In fact, he quoted approvingly a letter Engels wrote to Marx as long ago as 1858 to the effect that 'the English proletariat is actually becoming more and more bourgeois'. But an Engels wrote in that same letter that this was only possible 'in a nation which exploits the whole world', Lenin was able to argue that part of the proletariat of an imperialist country could be bribed by the proceeds of the very high profits arising from colonial exploitation. Recent history shows that this view was also mistaken. In one of his last works, Varga pointed out that such countries as the Netherlands actually became more prosperous *after* they lost an immense colonial empire (and no one can claim that Indonesia has been an example of neo-colonialism!). Varga also reminded his readers that the evident failure of communist parties to make headway in Western Europe is scarcely consistent with the literal interpretation of the law of ever increasing misery.

What contribution, if any, did Lenin make to economic thought in his *Imperialism*? The growth of monopoly, of cartelisation, of the increasing role of banking and what he called finance capital, of inter-imperialist rivalry, had been described by others, and Lenin was not in any sense original in pointing to these phenomena. Hobson and Hilferding had written about these matters, and so had Rosa Luxemburg and Bukharin. Many of Lenin's points were no more than a vigorous formulation of views already current. Some of his formulations were reasonable enough. No doubt 'the struggle for sources of raw materials, for the export of capital', and so on, did contribute to a propensity for territorial expansion. Lenin noted that this was an addition to what he called 'the numerous old motives for seizing other people's territory'. So far so good. However, he has practically nothing to say about the relative importance of the various motives. Expansionist policies of the tsar's or the kaiser's government may well have been due to some mixture between 'old motives' and the new commercial ones. If various autocracies have waged aggressive wars for reasons which have very little to do with monopoly capitalism, might not states that fly the Red Flag and claim allegiance to the principles of socialism also launch aggressive wars? Might they not do so for economic reasons too? If monopoly capitalists wish to safeguard their sources of raw materials and their markets, why should not planners, in their capacity of 'state-capitalist' monopolists, do the same? Lenin does not even contemplate such a possibility.

3 *Socialist Economics*

What of Lenin's economic ideas on the eve of the revolution? By this time he had to consider the possibility that he might soon be ruling Russia. For such practical purposes, models of expanded reproduction and ideas on the development of capitalism in Russia had little more relevance than equilibrium economics or models of pure capitalism would have had. How could or should a victorious socialism manage the economy?

One can distinguish several strands to Lenin's thinking at this point of time.

First: the German war economy, or the Rathenau model. Lenin had plenty of opportunity in Switzerland to contemplate this. Germany already before the 1914–18 war had been *par excellence* the country of trusts and syndicates. With the coming of the war, these had been effectively absorbed into the war machine, subordinated to the state. Lenin drew the conclusion that, if one took over the state, then one would achieve effective control over the cartelised industries. One sees this line of thought in a number of his speeches on the eve of the revolution, and also after the revolution. The various divisions of the Supreme Council of the National Economy after December 1917 closely corresponded to the controls devised by the imperial Russian government for wartime exigencies, and the names and personnel were similar to those of the Russian syndicates. Lenin also spoke a great deal about workers' control, but his behaviour after the seizure of power suggests that he regarded it very largely as a means of disorganising the enemy, rather than as a serious form of socialist economic organisation. In much the same way, slogans urging the election of officers and the ending of severe discipline in the army were primarily intended to disorganise the army before a revolution. Lenin became a very firm believer in discipline, once the Bolshevik party was in control of the state.

Secondly, there was Lenin's view of the peasants and the peasant question. A great deal could be, and has been, written on the whole subject, but it has little direct bearing on issues of economic theory. It is not for nothing that Zinoviev said: 'The question of the role of the peasantry is the basic issue of Bolshevism, of Leninism' (in a speech in 1924, shortly after Lenin's death). We have already seen the importance which Lenin attached to this whole question in *The Development of Capitalism in Russia*. In the early years of this century, Lenin evolved a number of ideas concerning the stratification of the peasantry and the relationship of various peasant strata to socialism. While all this is of the very greatest importance in assessing the role of Lenin as the adaptor of Marxism to a relatively underdeveloped country, one can hardly go into these matters in this essay. One must just mention that the stratification was both arbitrary and imprecise, and that Lenin's successors, even more than Lenin himself, found themselves prisoners of undefinable categories. The debates of the twenties were full of futile efforts to identify middle peasants, poor peasants, kulaks. Lenin himself, when asked what a kulak was, replied impatiently: 'They will know on the spot who is a kulak.' This cannot be said to be a scientifically precise definition.

Thirdly, Lenin held a semi-utopian belief in the simplicity of economic administration. Micro-economic problems seemed not to exist for him, or were concerned only with accounting. Just as in *State and Revolution* (written in August–September 1917) the need for a professional bureaucracy was largely ignored, so the task of planning was neither properly defined nor understood. It is this strand in his thinking that made him misunderstand the essence of the German war economy. Everything would be simple if only the strings were in the right hands. In an extreme propagandist form, his argument came to the following:

'Make the profits of the capitalists public, arrest fifty or a hundred of the biggest millionaires. Just keep them in custody for a few weeks . . . for the simple purpose of making them reveal the hidden springs, the fraudulent practices, the filth and the greed which even under the new government are costing our country thousands and millions every day. That is the chief cause of our anarchy and ruin.' (Lenin, vol. 25, 1964, p. 21.)

It is true that this demagogic statement was made in a speech to a mass meeting, the First Congress of Soviets. However he returns to similar kinds of thoughts in his less impassioned moments.

In *State and Revolution* one finds the following:

'All that is required is that all [citizens] should work equally, do their proper share of work, get equally paid. The accounting and control necessary for this has been *simplified* by the capitalists to the utmost and reduced to an extraordinarily simple operation, which any literate person can perform, of supervising and accounting . . .' (ibid., p. 473.)

This thought pattern continues in his well-known *Can the Bolsheviks Retain State Power?* (written in early October 1917). The following is an example:

'Capitalism has created an accounting apparatus in the shape of the banks, syndicates, postal services, consumer societies and office employees' unions. Without big banks socialism would be impossible . . . A single state bank, the biggest of the big, with branches in every rural district, in every factory, would constitute as much as nine-tenths of the socialist apparatus. There will be country-wide *book-keeping*, country-wide *accounting* of the production and distribution of goods; this will be so to speak something in the nature of the skeleton of socialist society . . . The actual work of book-keeping, control, registering, accounting is performed by *employees*, the majority of whom themselves lead a proletarian or semi-proletarian existence. By simple decrees of the proletarian government, these employees can and must be transferred to the status of state employees, in the same way as the watchdogs of capitalism, like Briand and other bourgeois ministers, by a simple decree transfer railwaymen on strike to the status of state employees . . . Capitalism has simplified the work of accounting and control, has reduced it to a comparatively simple system of *book-keeping* which any literate person can do.' (Lenin, vol. 26, 1964, p. 106.)

He is thus conscious of problems of technique and of problems of accountancy. Economics as such disappears. The complexities of economic administration are not understood.

4 *War Communism and NEP*

For reasons explained at the beginning of this chapter, I do not think that Lenin's behaviour as a political leader fits very well into this survey; the period of war communism provides striking examples of economic policy rather than of economic theory. In an emergency situation people do not usually act in accordance with their doctrines. It would be wrong, for example, to deduce a theory from the behaviour of Lord Robbins in the British government service in wartime. Such key elements of the war communism period as the virtual confiscation of peasant produce cannot be ascribed to any abstract principle or ideology, since no one in his senses, and certainly not Lenin, intended to base the relationships between agriculture and the urban community on forcible confiscations, save as a purely emergency measure. However, we can deduce certain very general attitudes, and perhaps an underlying theoretical pattern, from some of Lenin's behaviour in 1918–21. Thus, he was deeply suspicious of syndicalism and basically against workers' control once power had been won. He was not well disposed to egalitarianism, and one finds him advocating wage differentials, bonuses and other material inducements. He was very ready to equate the search for profit in trade with criminal speculation, though part of this might be ascribed to the emergency and therefore to the inevitable association of free trade with the black market. He showed a predisposition towards goods exchange rather than trade as the basis for commodity relations between town and village. While on the morrow of the revolution he was advocating state capitalism, involving the survival of some capitalists, he appears to have favoured wholesale nationalisation in 1919–20. His analysis of peasant stratification led him into over-sanguine hopes as to the effectiveness of class war in the villages. He looked forward to the implementation of great plans of reconstruction, and in particular showed faith in electrification. Finally, he may well have been among those who, in the words of Lisichkin, had before them a model of a 'super-concern', i.e. the operation of at least the state sector of the economy as one single firm. (Lisichkin, 1966.) (Lisichkin himself does not name Lenin as one of those who had such illusions, but neither does he say that he had not.)

In 1921, having long resisted criticism of war communism from the Mensheviks and others, Lenin at last decided to launch the New Economic Policy (NEP). In terms of the objective needs of the situation his decision was belated. However, he seems to have been ahead of the large majority of his own followers. To end this study, we must consider what theoretical conclusions he may have drawn from the experiences of war communism. It is only realistic to assume that the terrible events of these years did make some impact upon Lenin's mind.

As we know, he described the decision to launch NEP in a variety of not always consistent ways. Sometimes it was a forced retreat, 'like Brest', a forced and temporary compromise. But at other times NEP was defined as a return to the correct position, indeed to the position which Lenin was beginning to occupy early in 1918 and which he had to abandon under the temporary stress of war emergency. But in that case the system as it existed early in 1921 was wrong for the then existing circumstances, and a recognition of this fact was not a retreat. No doubt these and other somewhat inconsistent formulations were due to the exigencies of current politics. However, in Lenin's attitude during the period 1921–3 one can identify a number of common features. One finds him repeatedly using such phrases as the following: 'We must learn to trade'; 'Matters must be looked at commercially'; 'Enterprises must cover their costs.' He advocated credits for capital investment; the leaving to the market of supplies to, and disposals by, state enterprises; the need to study the market; the importance of gold and of the gold standard. The following is a quotation from a note by Lenin to the then commissar of finance, Sokol'nikov:

'In connection with our talk of yesterday, I beg of you as quickly as possible to take the following steps: to set down on paper your proposals concerning the free circulation of gold (the ten points you made yesterday), and to send one copy of them to me and the other to Krzhizhanovsky for Gosplan.' (*Pol. sob. soch.*, vol. 54, 1965, p. 139.)

Sokol'nikov was aiming at the convertibility of the rouble, and Lenin knew of this and approved.

What kind of a policy was Lenin now advocating? What kind of an economic theory of socialism was beginning to emerge from his mind when he was struck by paralysis? Naturally, he had no time to write any major theoretical work, and we can only reconstruct his pattern of thought from very fragmentary evidence. We can put the question in the words of Lisichkin:

'It may be asked, was the then existing economic system in the socialist sector an exceptional and temporary one, inevitably bearing the stamp of capitalistic methods of management which it was necessary to abandon as soon as successes in the construction of socialism made this possible? Or, on the contrary, was this the system organically in the nature of socialism, the only one which could be described as normal under conditions where abundance did not yet exist?' (Lisichkin, 1966, p. 45.)

In other words, did Lenin accept the necessity and desirability of market relations between and within the socialist enterprises as a long-term prospect, covering the entire transition period to the dim and distant future of full communism? Or did he regard these things as merely caused by current emergencies, and/or as a mere reflection of the temporary necessities of a compromise with the private sector?

In the letter to Sokol'nikov, quoted above, Lenin was emphatic about the need for the discipline of the market, the need to run trusts and enterprises according to 'a business-like and mercantile method'. In fact, he wished at first to reinforce this discipline with the criminal law, suggesting that managers who were unable to avoid losses might be 'brought before the courts and punished . . . by a prolonged deprivation of liberty'. This suggestion never went beyond a private letter, and looks like a temporary aberration due to prolonged immersion in the habits of thought of war communism. But, even so, the criterion proposed by Lenin for judging management was a market criterion.

It is arguable that Lenin never intended the fully-fledged Stalin model of ultra-centralisation. It is even arguable that Stalin did not consciously intend it either, but that he stumbled into it as part of the process of trying to fulfil impossible plans. Certainly, there is no sign that a model of fully centralised planning was discussed as such in the years before 1929. The arguments were concerned with the speed of economic development, with the level of investment, with policies towards the peasants, not with the techniques of planning or economic administration. Be that as it may, those who now support a major shift in the methods of Soviet planning in the direction of using market criteria are endeavouring to enlist the help of Lenin's ideas, collecting for the purpose quotations from his writings and notes of the period 1921 to 1923. The opponents of drastic reform allege that they are misquoting Lenin, and naturally emphasise his view that the retreat had ended in 1922 and that it would soon be time for an advance. To this the reformers reply: but advance for what and against whom? Against the private sector maybe, but not, surely against effective or efficient means of utilising market relations within socialism? The argument continues.

We are left with the conclusion that, as an economic theorist, Lenin contributed little after 1899. It cannot be said that his book on imperialism was particularly original, and he had no time to write about theory after October 1917. Even making full allowance for the principle of 'the unity of theory and practice', he was too totally immersed in politics to be able to contribute significantly to the theoretical assessment of either war communism or NEP. Had he not been so completely struck down by disease, had he been able to write during a period of prolonged convalescence, he might well have expressed some valuable thoughts on the economics of socialism, including the neglected micro-economics of socialism. Unfortunately this was not to be, and his successors today are left searching for fragments and odd quotations to support proposals in the realm of theory or practice – proposals whose justification ought really to be sought in the realities of Soviet life fifty years after the October revolution.

5

Some Observations on Bukharin and His Ideas

A full-length political biography of Bukharin was long needed and has at last appeared (Cohen, 1974), but this (excellent) work had not been published when this paper was written. A good bibliography exists (Heitman, 1969). I shall not try in this paper to cover all the ground. He was a prolific writer, in economics, sociology and philosophy, and he was also an active politician, with views on the nature of Russia's revolution, views that altered over time. He was also a journalist, a brilliant and witty speaker, a populariser of complex doctrines, and no mean caricaturist. All I can do is to set out some of his ideas on some matters which seem to me to be of interest. There are aspects of his thought which will not be touched on at all. For example, he argued at length with Rosa Luxemburg, in 1912–14, on the question of whether capitalism needs a non-capitalist sector for its survival, and an English translation of this controversy has appeared. He criticised Böhm-Bawerk, Tugan-Baranovsky, Struve, Trotsky, Skvortsov-Stepanov. All these things are well worth studying and analysing, but will hardly be mentioned here. I shall also have little to say about Bukharin the politician. This is a paper, not a large book.

Bukharin was born in 1888. Thus he was only twenty-nine when the revolution happened. This may help to explain a certain basic inconsistency between his youthful 'left' enthusiasm of 1918, when he was all for revolutionary wars and instant leaps into full communism, and the cautious, statesmanlike acceptance of the logic of NEP after 1921. One question we can ask ourselves is: how great was the inconsistency? Peter Knirsch, the author of a survey of Bukharin's economic ideas (Knirsch, 1959), virtually ignored those of the NEP period, and justified this by asserting (in conversation) that after 1921 Bukharin subordinated his economics to political exigencies. Rudolph Schlesinger, who had known Bukharin, told me that in his view he was a genuine enthusiast in 1918–20, but that he was so shocked ('heart-broken') by the failures of war communism that he went to the opposite extreme of moderation. Schlesinger interpreted Bukharin's political position in the 1920s as objectively pro-peasant, and he believed that

Reprinted from Essays in Honour of E. H. Carr, *London, Macmillan, 1974.*

Stalin was right to drive him out of politics (though not to shoot him), so he may have been a prejudiced witness.

Let us look at some of Bukharin's economic ideas, in and after the war communism period. It must be noted that he had had some solid training in the subject, when he was at Vienna from 1912 to 1914. He read Western languages and was familiar with the literature; thus he was quoting from Keynes's *Economic Consequences of the Peace* within a year of its publication. He had worked on problems of imperialism, and many of Lenin's ideas on this subject could well have been influenced by Bukharin, whose writings (Bukharin, 1925a, written in 1915) antedated Lenin's *Imperialism*.

What original contribution did Bukharin make to the economic ideas of the war communism period? (We must bear in mind that his enthusiasms of the period were shared by other comrades: Larin, Obolensky-Osinski and many more.)

There is, first, the concept of 'negative expanded reproduction', i.e. of the destruction of the means of production. This is a cost of revolution. What was happening was logical, *zakonomerno*. The possessing classes must resist revolution. There would then be civil war. There would be sabotage. Relations between the proletarian vanguard and the intelligentsia and also the peasantry would be strained, the one because they will fail to see or sympathise with the coercive necessities of a proletarian revolution, the other because the towns will be unable to supply the country and will try to collect food by administrative means, supplanting the market. Class war in the village, the breaking of customary links between village and urban markets, cause adverse effects on production. The proletariat, unlike the bourgeoisie, cannot learn to govern *before* the revolution. Its culture is low, it is likely to be crude and to make mistakes, all of which contributes to economic disruption. This seems to be a fair description of Russian war communism experience, extended to proletarian revolutions in general.

At this stage of his development, Bukharin thought in terms of an inevitable 'open or concealed' conflict between the dictatorship of the proletariat and a peasantry attached to anarchic commodity (market) relations. (Bukharin, 1920, p. 83.) He clearly supported requisitioning (*razverstka*) and was not one of those who pressed Lenin to introduce NEP.

Nor can he be readily identified as a supporter of the extremes of nationalisation. Let us recall that by mid-1920 even the pettiest enterprises, even windmills employing one person, were (in the main) nationalised. Yet Bukharin, co-author with Preobrazhensky of the *ABC of Communism*, had written in 1919:

'We must remember that we do not expropriate petty property. Its nationalisation is absolutely out of the question, firstly because we would be unable ourselves to organise the scattered small-scale production, and secondly because the Communist Party does not wish to, and must not, offend the many millions of petty proprietors. Their conversion to socialism must take place voluntarily, by their own decision, and not by means of compulsory expropriation. It is particularly important to remember this in areas where small-scale production is predominant.' (Bukharin and Preobrazhensky, 1919, pp. 195–6.)

Yet this popular book was certainly written in a 'left' spirit.

He also took the position that, in the 'transition period' to socialism, Marxian value categories had almost as little place as Böhm-Bawerkian Western economics. 'The basic categories of the whole system of political economy were such concepts as commodity, value, price.' But these ceased to mean what once they meant. Bukharin believed that, under socialism, economics as the study of commodity exchange relations would wither away, being replaced by *administration*, of a planned economy. In the transition period these relations, he wrote, are dying out. Value categories in capitalist as in Marxist economics are equilibrium categories. But there is no equilibrium during the transition period. Goods cease to be available.

It is evident that in the period of transition, in the process of eliminating commodity production as such, there takes place a process of the 'self-denial' (*samootritsanie*) of money. Money ceases to be a universal equivalent, becoming a nominal and highly imperfect denomination for the circulation of products.

These 'products' are no longer 'commodities'. Similarly, wages are no longer wages, both because a worker is no longer an 'employee' and because 'under a proletarian dictatorship the worker receives a ration and not wages'. (Bukharin, 1920, pp. 110–12.) 'One of the basic tendencies of the transition period is the breaking of commodity-fetishistic disguises . . . Economic theory must move towards thinking in natural units.' The process of production will be based on plans for use.

Bukharin was very open and frank in his ideas on coercion, and not only as applied to enemies of his revolution. The workers are to be the organisers of production, but 'all proletarian organisation must be under the most all-inclusive organisation, i.e. the state organs of the working class. Hence the need for state control (*ogosudarstvlenie*) over trade unions. Hence the necessity of 'universal labour service'. He boldly faces the logic of 'eliminating freedom of labour', fearing that groups of workers will counterpose their sectional interests to the general interest, 'will fail to understand all-proletarian tasks'. In the name of 'the real liberation of labour' it is necessary to introduce labour conscription and direction of labour. Then, ultimately, all coercion will end, when real socialism is achieved, through the 'concentrated coercion' of the proletarian dictatorship. (ibid., p. 147.) Meanwhile, however, one needs maximum business sense (*delovitost'*), the concentration of control in few hands, the militarisation of economic command functions, the replacement of elections by 'careful selection' (*podbor*), by the proletarian dictatorial organs of competent people.

This emphasis contrasts not only with his later criticism of selection as against election, but also his association in 1918 with those who opposed Lenin's attempts to introduce discipline and one-man management in industry. It led him briefly into Trotsky's camp on the issue of the militarisation of labour.

Of course Bukharin did look forward to the renewal of productive forces. He was vague about the organisational forms of this, though clearly he envisaged the replacement of requisitions by 'commodity exchange' in relations with the peasants. Capital assets would have to be rebuilt. It is noteworthy, in view of subsequent argument, that in 1920 Bukharin quoted approvingly the term 'primitive socialist accumulation', with acknowledgements to the inventor of the term, V. M. Smirnov. Only he interpreted it differently from Preobrazhensky's later version. He chose to stress that the capitalists accumulated capital by exploiting labour, and that therefore a socialist reconstruction would require the conscription of labour, including here the non-proletarians, the peasantry in particular. This is a kind of primitive accumulation via forced labour. Then 'the productive forces of society will be distributed between different areas according to natural conditions, such as proximity of fuel and raw material supplies. The question of industrial standards will be solved without capitalist barriers, and the development of productive forces will proceed in giant strides'. (ibid., p. 95.)

Lenin was fond of Bukharin, but made some sharp criticisms in his marginal notes on *Ekonomika perekhodnogo perioda*. These marginal notes were published in *Leninskii sbornik* in 1929, as part of the campaign to discredit Bukharin, though he was himself at that time one of the editors of that publication. It may be of interest briefly to summarise Lenin's reactions.

In many instances Lenin was pleased, even delighted ('excellent', 'absolutely right' etc.). Indeed, he was delighted with almost all the *economic* statements in the book. True, he did not agree that economics disappears under socialism, since even under full communism there will be $c + v + m$. Another 'economic' exception, perhaps, was 'primitive socialist accumulation', a term which Lenin underlined and commented: 'Ugh!' But this might have been not an objection of substance but an example of Lenin's many protests against 'excessive scholasticism of terminology'. Example of this are many. Thus Bukharin spoke of 'horizontal competition', 'vertical competition' and 'combined [monopolistic?] competition', and Lenin's comment was: 'Ugh; playing at definitions.'

But Lenin's chief objections were of a more abstract-theoretical kind. One category was philosophical. He clearly suspected Bukharin of being too influenced by Bogdanov. For example, Bukharin wrote: 'It is further clear that the dialectical-historical viewpoint . . .', and Lenin reacted as follows: 'Spoiled by the eclecticism of Bogdanov, the dialectical "point of view" becomes just one of many equally legitimate "points of view". Wrong!' And again, Bukharin wrote that 'social-productive processes' may be 'examined' from a 'point of view' and be 'theoretically interesting'. Lenin scribbled: 'Wrong words. Errors of Bogdanov terminology clearly visible: subjectivism, solipsism. It is not a matter of who "examines", or who is "interested", but of what exists independently of the human consciousness.' He seems to suspect Bukharin of not being consistently dialectical, and indeed said this also in his testament. Bukharin is also taken to task for a phrase about 'the theoretical proof of the impossibility of the reconstitution of capitalist relations'. Lenin retorted: ' "Impossibility" can only be proved by practice. The author does not probe the relationship between theory and practice *dialectically*.' Lenin may have had in mind the active and voluntaristic aspect of Marxism, which had been so strikingly demonstrated in the successful seizure of power in Russia, under (theoretically) unripe, i.e. 'impossible', conditions.

Lenin's hackles are also raised wherever the word 'sociology' appears. Phrases recur: 'Bukharin worsened Marx with sociological scholastics', or 'Marx spoke without elaborate "terms" and "systems" and "sociologies" '. When Bukharin used an unhappy phrase about 'exploding relationships' (*lopayushchikhsya otnosheniyakh*), Lenin exclaimed: 'What language, what "sociology".' When Bukharin writes a phrase about 'sociological definition of productive forces', Lenin at once underlines the word 'sociological' and comments: 'Ha, ha.' Finally, Bukharin has a footnote mocking the 'sociologist' Kautsky, and Lenin comments: 'That's great. On page 84 the "sociologist" Bukharin puts the word "sociology" into ironical quotation marks. Bravo!' Why did Lenin so hate this word?

But we shall return to Bukharin's sociology later. Let us briefly continue to discuss the 'transition period' and the evolution of Bukharin's ideas.

How did Bukharin look at his own ideas later on? Certainly, he admitted to 'illusions'. Thus in a work published as early as 1921 we find him insisting that the struggle to retain power *compelled* total control and heavy losses of productive capacity ('we did not needlessly smash crockery'). However, 'it became clear in 1921 that the Russian economy was still more obstinate [than we thought], and that the state machine had sufficient power only to keep large-scale industry socialised, and not all of that'. (Bukharin, 1921, pp. 306–7.) He came to emphasise the vital importance, for survival, of 'raising up the productive forces', and for this 'requisitions and the ban on private trade were useless'. War communism combined necessities and illusions. 'We thought that we could, at a blow and swiftly, abolish market relations. Yet it turns out that we shall reach socialism through market relations.' (Bukharin, 1925b, pp. 62, 64.) The same ideas were expressed in 1924 in *Bolshevik*:

'The adoption of NEP was a collapse of our illusions . . . This does not mean that the war-communism system was basically wrong for its time . . . War and blockade compelled us to act thus. But we thought then that our peacetime policy would be a *continuation* of the centralised planning system of that period . . . In other words war communism was seen by us not as military, i.e. as needed at a given stage of civil war, but as a universal, general, so to speak "normal" form of economic policy of a victorious proletariat. The illusions of war communism burst at the very hour when the proletarian army stormed Perekop.' (Heitman, 1970, pp. 177–8. *O likvidatorstve nashikh dnei*, 1924.)

So it was to be a long, strong haul. Short cuts were out. This Bukharin learnt by bitter experience.

Before returning to his economic ideas in the NEP period, let us pass to a completely different strand of his thought, which found expression long before he himself became a victim of party machine politics. This is the issue of possible degeneration of the so-called proletarian dictatorship.

As already noted, Bukharin stressed that proletarian cadres could not develop before the revolution. They need training. The intelligentsia and other non-proletarian elements must play a leading role. In his major work published in 1921 he referred to 'the ancient Inca state', in which 'there was a regulated and organised economy, in the hands of a gentry-priesthood class, an intelligentsia of a kind, which controlled everything, ran everything, and operated the state economy as a dominant class, sitting over the top of all the others'. (Bukharin, 1921, p. 69.)

Here Bukharin had had in mind a group of rulers of non-proletarian origin. (This was certainly Lenin's fear.) Bukharin expressed *this* fear in 1923. But in that year he made it clear that his thoughts ran deeper. He wrote the following:

'Even proletarian origin, even the most calloused hands . . . is no guarantee against turning into a new class. For if we imagine that a section of those who have risen out of the working class becomes detached from the mass of the workers, and congeals into a monopoly position in its capacity of ex-workers, they too can become a species of caste, which could also become a new class . . . After the revolution the old order collapses, the old [ruling] class is scattered and deformed, and out of it can arise a new class . . . How can we struggle against it? The answer will lie in the quantitative balance of cultural forces . . . But it is possible that the first battalions which the working class sends into higher education will become a close corporation which . . . though of worker origin, will dominate through its monopoly of education.'

This would be a new class. So it is 'vital not to let the cadres become a monopoly caste'. (Bukharin, 1923, pp. 44–7.)

In the same pamphlet, Bukharin exclaims: 'We need Marxism plus Americanism', so that 'things are done efficiently' (ibid., p. 49).

In 1922, in another article, Bukharin was again concerned with the question of administrative cadres. 'The workers cannot be other than a class culturally deeply suppressed by the whole capitalist regime.' Consequently, this

'culturally oppressed class cannot develop [its culture] so as to prepare itself for the organisation of all society. It can be ready to prepare itself for the destruction of the old world. It must "remake its nature" and ripen . . . only in the period of its dictatorship. Hence additional costs (*izderzhki*) of the proletarian revolution, . . . unknown in general to the bourgeois revolution.' (Heitman, 1970, p. 168. *Burzhuaznaya revolutsiya i revolutsiya proletarskaya*, 1922.)

But then 'how does the proletariat none the less create its cadres of political ideologues and leaders?' Inevitably, the leaders tend to come from 'the bourgeois intelligentsia', and he notes that the cultural gap between such leaders and the proletarian masses is very wide, much wider than between the bourgeoisie and *its* leaders. But he sees also the existence or emergence of a whole stratum of 'worker bureaucrats', such as exist in British trade unions or in the German unions and social democracy.

When the proletariat seizes power, it must inevitably utilise specialists who are hostile to it. The idea that this can be avoided is utopian and impracticable. However, this situation 'contains within it a major danger, inevitable in a proletarian revolution . . . *the danger of the degeneration of the proletarian state and the proletarian party*' (emphasis his). (ibid., p. 171.)

Thus far Bukharin seems to see, as Lenin did in 1921, the danger in the form of the uncultured proletariat losing out to the culturally superior alien classes, or adopting their ways ('like a barbarian victor adopting the way of life and habits, even the tongue, of the conquered people'). But he did not see further than this (the emphasis is again his):

'The cultural backwardness of the worker masses, especially in conditions of general misery, when *nolens volens* the administrative and leadership apparatus has to receive many more consumers' goods than the ordinary worker, gives rise to *the danger of a very substantial divorce from the masses even of that part of the cadres which emerged from the working masses themselves.*' (ibid., p. 172.)

He went on: 'An appeal to working-class origin and proletarian goodness is not by itself an argument against the existence of this danger . . .' Classes become deformed by the revolution. Cut off from the masses, cadres *could* (though they need not) join their more cultured colleagues and together make 'the germ of a new ruling class'. Economic backwardness and the conditions of NEP add to the danger. (Bukharin did not see that the ex-proletarian cadres could eventually turn on their 'cultured' colleagues and kill them. This happened to many a bourgeois specialist, and also to Bukharin himself.)

In 1926, when he himself was at his political apogee, he made a speech in Leningrad which was part of the campaign to destroy the Zinoviev power centre there. The speech was mostly devoted to discrediting various criticisms of the then party line. Thus we can regard the allegation about the 'sergeant-like methods' (*feldfebelskie metody*) of party rule in Leningrad as normal factional-struggle language, since very similar methods were used elsewhere by Bukharin's then allies. However, he did make a significant point of general application. He deplored 'the replacement of elected functionaries by commanders appointed from above'. This, he said, can lead to excessive "hardness" of the apparatus, which, taken to absurd lengths, would lead to fossilisation (*okamenelost*) of the apparatus'. (Heitman, 1970, p. 352. Speech at the 23rd Special Provisional Conference, Leningrad, 1926.)

And finally, on the tenth anniversary of the October revolution, Bukharin referred to 'former workers, who ceased to be members of a revolutionary class, linked by many threads with new bourgeois strata, with the new service-officialdom [*sluzhilym chinovnichestvom*: note the deliberately archaic words, to remind readers of tradition], as distant from the needs and concerns of the masses as the earth is from the sky'. (Bukharin, 1927, p. 5.)

So no one can say that Bukharin was unaware of certain dangers to the party and the revolution. Yet he could not see, until too late, the dangers to himself from the Stalin group. Or rather, he must have considered the policies and personalities of the Trotsky group to be intolerable, and fought them with all his skill and cunning, considering them a graver danger than Stalin, until the latter turned on him.

Let us now go back to Bukharin the theoretician, or rather the populariser of sociological-philosophical theories. His *Teoriya istoricheskogo materializma* must be regarded as a very fine essay in popularisation, and this is in no sense a criticism. It certainly was one of the duties of the few educated leader-intellectuals to reach the less educated party members, and Bukharin did this job with a vivid language and without simplifying the issues. This is quite unlike the catechism of Stalinist indoctrination. The readers were compelled to think. (However, he did upset such eminent theorists as Lukacs and Gramsci, both of whom criticised the book, thought it seems that they treated it as a much more finished product than it really was.)

Let us see, for instance, how he discusses regularities or social laws (*pravil'nost'*, *zakonomernost'*). He gives examples. Under capitalism the number of wage-earners shows a tendency to increase, and cyclical fluctuations occur. There are also statistical regularities, such as enable us to predict the number of births next year, or the consumption of beer in Bavaria.

Man, unlike things or spiders, has conscious aims. He seeks causes. He is also caused, part of nature, part of society. Men's aims and actions depend on something, i.e. are in some sense determined. Men are subject to necessities yet there is free will. Men choose, they are neither pawns nor marionettes, but their choices are circumscribed. To assert the total freedom of human will leads either to nonsense or to religion. Man feels free. Thus an orator is free to drink water, and also to dance the *trepak*, but he drinks and does not dance, because his throat is dry. Men make the law of supply and demand by buying and selling freely. 'Society is composed of men, each social event is made up of a multitude of individual feelings, attitudes, wills, actions.' The net result, e.g. a market price, is independent of human will, in that many would have willed a quite different result. A price so arrived at is the basis of individual valuations of the product. So men's wills cause things to happen, but what happens is different from what men have willed – until communism comes. *Then* one will have collectively organised will, with no anarchy of production and no contradiction between the individual and society. Individual will, of course, would still exist, but men will act together in pursuit of aims determined by their situation and environment.

What about accident? Bukharin quotes Spinoza: 'A thing is called accidental because of lack of knowledge.' 'If, in the intersection of two or more causal chains, we know only one of them, then the event which follows this intersection will *seem* to us to be accidental, though in fact it is *zakonomerno*.'

'Accident' should be eliminated from social science. Necessity is a concept independent of moral judgement. Necessity and inevitability are not the same. Stammler argued: 'If socialism is inevitable, why struggle to attain it? No one strives to organise an eclipse of the moon.' Bukharin replied: 'Social events are made by men, otherwise we would have square circles and fried ice. Marxism does not deny the will, it explains it.'

Of course men make history, but the will of humans is itself determined. *Ex officio*, a general's will matters more than a corporal's, and it is the same with politicians. Social interconnections give power to an individual.

Bukharin emphatically denies that Marxists treat art or ideology as mere superstructure on a material base. These, and other elements of the superstructure, do have a feedback effect on the base.

He returns elsewhere to the necessity of distinguishing causal rationality from moral judgements. He rejects '*tout comprendre, c'est tout pardonner*'.

'It is said that to understand is to forgive. Nonsense. We can only assess an event if we understand it. To understand a historical event is to present it as a consequence of a particular historical cause or causes, in other words *not* as an accidental unconditioned magnitude, but as something necessarily flowing from the totality of pre-existing conditions, i.e. causal necessity.'

This is *not* fatalism. Men act. Hegel's 'all that is real is rational' should not be misunderstood. 'For Marx the "rationality" of reality was only the causal connection between past and present, while for apologists this rationality is an argument for justifying the event.' (Bukharin, 1925a, pp. 126–7.)

In his sociology, and especially in *Teoriya istoricheskogo materializma*, the term perhaps most frequently used is *ravnovesie*, 'equilibrium'. Indeed, this word occurs frequently in many of his works. Few Bolsheviks were fond of it. Let us see what he meant by it.

In his capacity as an economist, Bukharin stressed, quite logically, that economic theories, value theories, relate to and describe equilibrium situations. And indeed this is plainly true both of Böhm-Bawerk and of Marx. In fact all economists, whatever their persuasions, assume a tendency for profits to be equal in all sectors, and, as all must surely recognise, this is not so in reality, but would be so in equilibrium. For Bukharin, however, this concept has a wider connotation, and is extended far beyond economics.

Perhaps it would be correct to define it as follows. All systems, all social relationships, are to be defined and studied in their pure form, bringing out their essence, shape, interconnections, though of course recognising that in the real world there are many complicating factors *and* that all things change. Thus Bukharin would argue that Marx studied the basic features of capitalism, abstracting for the sake of clarity from, for instance, the survival of elements of feudalism in capitalist states *Ravnovesie* could be a way of analysing capitalist market relations. It could also be a way of looking at the social structure, at governments, indeed at any social phenomena. Bukharin was well read in Western sociology, and no doubt sought to influence his colleagues, some of whom, Lenin especially, had little patience with it. Anyhow, 'equilibrium' as he used it brought Bukharin some way towards the structuralist or functionalist school. This, according to some critics, is an approach inherently conservative. Bukharin would disagree vehemently, no doubt. He would use against such critics the arguments already developed against *'tout comprendre, c'est tout pardonner'*: if we understand the inter-relationships that make up a system, then we understand. This does not mean that we approve. But his enemies later attacked him for not being dialectical, for 'mechanism', and for all sorts of sins, of which 'sociology' was one. The very word became anathema for a generation after the political defeat of Bukharin.

Bukharin's name is also associated with two highly practical applications of equilibrium-type thinking. One was his striving for the maintenance of market equilibrium during NEP. The other – in the famous *Zametki ekonomista* – concerned his plea for what would now be called input-output balance, i.e. you cannot make bricks without straw, or build factories with bricks that are not there. However, these were political-economic issues on which, it seems to me, his judgement was based on considerations of a quite non-philosophical order.

But back to NEP and to political economy. How did Bukharin understand NEP? Having decisively abandoned 'illusions', what did he see?

First, his views on world revolution. In an article he wrote at the time of the seizure of power, he saw world revolution as 'providing reinforcements' for the Russian economy. 'The victory of the Western proletariat will make it possible to heal in a planned way the economic wounds of Russia with highly developed West European techniques. The economic backwardness of Russia will be offset by the high technical level of Europe.' (Bukharin, 1917, pp. 146–7.) But the revolution had not spread. So what were they to do? In 1925 (in *Put' k sotsializmu*), and again in the following year in his address to the Leningrad party conference, he argued that it was wrong to assert that Soviet Russia in its isolation was doomed by its own internal contradictions. If imperialists attack, then the USSR could be defeated, yes. The only guarantee against this is victory of the revolution in other countries. (Heitman, 1970, pp. 313, 340.) But 'can we conclude from this that our technical and economic backwardness will destroy us?' No.

'If we do not have confidence in the sufficiency of our internal forces for building socialism, then there was no reason for us to go to the barricades in October, then the Mensheviks were right, that in such a backward country as Russia it was pointless to attempt a socialist revolution, then Comrade Trotsky was right in asserting that without the help of a victorious West European proletariat we shall necessarily face a conflict with the peasants which we must lose.' (Heitman, 1970, p. 340. Leningrad Conference, 1926.)

How did Bukharin see the peasants? He was certainly aware of the existence of strata among them, and by 1927 he was, from his point of view rather illogically, calling for 'pressure on the kulak and bourgeois elements', but even then he emphasised that 'it would be a mortal sin to break up or threaten the alliance with the middle peasant'. None the less, 'together with the middle peasant, with the support of the poor peasant, basing ourselves on the growing economic and political force of our Union and our party, we should and we must go over to a stronger offensive against the capitalist elements, first and foremost against the kulaks'. (Bukharin, 1927, p. 70.)

Earlier in the decade the emphasis was different. While certainly aware that 'the working class is an oasis in the peasant desert' (Bukharin, 1925c, p. 17), and that this argument could be used to enforce the ban on fractions, Bukharin wrote:

'Lenin taught that a conflict between the working class and the peasantry is by no means inevitable. Trotsky teaches: it is unavoidable. Lenin taught: our salvation comes from coexisting (*uzhitsa*) with the peasant. Trotsky says it will all be fatal without a world revolution. Hence Lenin's unique theory of agrarian-co-operative socialism.'

Of course Bukharin was president of the Comintern after Zinoviev, and can be credited with sincerity in rejecting 'national exclusiveness'. However, he saw powerful political reasons for asserting that, despite the peasant problem, Russia would be building socialism, and he generalised this into a strategy for backward countries. His mind was dominated by the experience of war communism, when it became abundantly clear – as already mentioned – that the peasant mass would not tolerate the ban on market relations once the civil war was over. Very well, said a maturing Bukharin, we must take this reality into account, we cannot base policy upon illusions. Thus we must generalise about reality. In doing this, Bukharin was certainly influenced not only by events but also by Lenin, the Lenin of the 11th Party Congress (1922) and of his semi-coherent article 'On co-operation', written in his last lucid days. There is much evidence to support the proposition that Bukharin thought that he was carrying out Lenin's personal line, as indeed one can see by textual comparisons. All this being so, I do not think that either Knirsch or Schlesinger was being fair to the Bukharin of the 1920s in denying to his other ideas the 'theoretical' status which they accord to the extremist thought of the 1918–20 period.

In his pamphlet *The Road to Socialism and the Worker-Peasant Alliance* (Bukharin, 1926) one sees his view of peasants and of NEP most clearly developed. For him, party rule represented, and had to represent, the dominance of the working class in the worker-peasant alliance. Thus, in a speech in the same year (1926), he rejected a naive suggestion that a peasant party be legalised; the peasant would support it against the Bolsheviks, and it is in their own interest ('hard as it is to explain to them') that the working-class dictatorship exercised by the party be maintained. (Heitman, 1970, p. 348. Leningrad Conference.)

But back to 'the road to socialism'. Naturally, he wrote, there are some differences between peasants and workers, e.g. over food prices. There are differences also between poor and rich peasants, but Bukharin could see that the problem concerned the *bulk* of the peasants taken as a whole.

Lenin spoke of a link, the *smychka*, with the peasantry. Its economic aspect was *competition*, i.e. the competition of state industry and state trade with the 'privateer'. The NEPmen try to make their *smychka*, and can succeed if the state provides goods and services badly. If 'the state economy can meet peasant needs better than the private trader, capitalist, middleman, then the *smychka* is safe'. (Bukharin, 1925b, p. 26.) Under war communism it was proper to confiscate and smash the privateers. Now times are different. Such methods are out.

He looked forward to the gradual squeezing out of the private sector by competition, using the economies of scale which represented a great and yet unused potential of socialist industry. This industry will gradually move towards overall planning (*obyedinena obshchinim planom*), but 'this sort of planning is not conceivable by itself, since our industry produces to a great extent for the peasant market'. (ibid., p. 30.) Peasant demand must be studied, the peasant economy must grow and be modernised. The peasants will gradually see the advantage of joining together. 'It is evident that we cannot persuade, or even try to persuade, the peasants to go over at once to uniting their land-holdings. Old habits have so impregnated the people that to break these habits is not possible. Yet nevertheless the peasants will inevitably travel the road towards unity' – and this will be 'through co-operation', by stages: first marketing and purchasing co-operatives, then such joint production as butter-making and other processing. These peasant co-operatives will, as a whole, 'grow into (*vrastat*') the system of economic organs of the proletarian state, and this will mean that we take large steps on the road to socialism'. (ibid., p. 37.) The parallel with the Lenin of 1922–3 is very clear. Indeed, Bukharin spoke of Lenin's 'state trade and co-operative line' and asserted: 'We shall achieve socialism here through the process of circulation, not directly through production. We shall reach it through co-operation. (Bukharin, 1925c, p. 73.) He clearly did not have producers' co-operatives in mind, but then, despite Stalin, neither did Lenin.

What would Lenin have said? Bukharin's speech on Lenin, made soon after Lenin's death in 1924, emphasised his flexibility and tactical ingenuity as far as slogans of the moment were concerned. Bukharin noted that he could advocate the Constituent Assembly, and then destroy it, because both actions were right in the circumstances. He could launch crude slogans like '*grab*' *nagrablennoe*' if this was what moved the masses. Lenin understood well that, before the seizure of power, the task is 'destructive', to identify all those contradictions which it is the task of party policy to deepen, so as to destroy. But 'now we must not destroy, we must build'. What was Marxism, a methodology or a certain number of ideas in their concrete application? If the latter, then Lenin, facing a new situation, went beyond Marxism (*za gran' marksizma*). But this, said Bukharin, is wrong. Leninism is a synthesis of Marx's methods and basic principles with revolutionary experience. 'Lenin possessed Marxism, Marxism did not possess Lenin.' (Heitman, 1970, pp. 226, 229. *Lenin kak marksist*.) He quoted Lenin (in italics): 'Many of our mistakes are due to the mechanical use of slogans which were correct in one historical situation . . . in a completely different situation.' Was Bukharin uneasily aware that his former master would have taken a more 'offensive' line had he been alive at the end of the 1920s?

It may be necessary to remind some readers just how 'gradualist' and cautious was Lenin's position in 1922–3. Lenin's co-operatives were above all to be concerned with trade. The whole population, he argued, should become so 'civilised' as to participate in co-operatives and learn to calculate. This is 'all' that is needed to move on to socialism, but Lenin put 'all' in inverted commas, because the low level of culture made it a huge task, 'immeasurably difficult', 'requiring a cultural revolution'. 'Russians now trade in the Asiatic manner, they must learn how to trade as Europeans.' Co-operatives he saw primarily as a means of ensuring the participation of the people in retail distribution, as a way of limiting private trade. State control over industry and land nationalisation would ensure that Soviet co-operatives would be unlike those existing in capitalist countries. Lenin, vol. 45, 1964, pp. 371–6.) Lenin, in his speech to the 11th Party Congress (1922), insisted that the *smychka* required the communists to learn to trade, to satisfy peasant needs better than the 'capitalist-NEPman'. He exclaimed: 'As for you, your principles are communist, your ideas are excellent, you resemble saints qualified for instant transfer to paradise, but can you run a business?' This is all quite consistent with Bukharin's mid-1920s concept of competition between the private and the state economy through the market, and the substitution of economic for administrative means of waging the class struggle. This, however, still leaves open the question of what Lenin might have thought in the circumstances of the second half of the 1920s. For him NEP was at once a necessary retreat (*reculer pour mieux sauter?*), and the right path to be followed 'seriously and for a long time'. When would he have resumed the advance? And in what direction? We can never know.

Bukharin, anyhow, followed fairly consistently the logic of NEP. Prices, the market, are the connecting link between town and country. 'Our industry will develop the more rapidly, the higher is effective demand from the peasantry. Accumulation in our industry will be the more rapid as accumulation speeds up in the peasant economy.' (Bukharin, 1925a, p. 41.) If someone says: 'Charge more for industrial goods, raise wages, down with concessions to the rural petty-bourgeoisie', then Bukharin replies: 'Nonsense, industry would then impoverish the peasantry and will itself be deprived of its market.' (ibid., p. 44.)

What of class war in the villages? Bukharin would see richer peasants striving for influence in the villages, and in co-operatives too. But, he insisted, now is not the time to rob the kulaks to give to the poor. The days of confiscation and requisitions are over. The middle peasant will become better off, will 'catch up the prosperous' by better methods and via co-operation. Even kulaks can 'grow into' (*vrastat'*) socialism via co-operation, by putting their money into state banks etc. True, they would be a species of foreign body in the system (like foreign concessions), but kulaks could only be a menace if they grow faster than state industry.

Bukharin returned again to the theme of peaceful competition, indeed coexistence, with the NEPman. Greater freedom for bourgeois elements is not dangerous now (1925) because we are stronger, he said. (Contrast this with the argument that because we are stronger we can pass to the offensive.) He denied that they were abandoning the poor, who will become less poor in a developing economy. 'Against the village money-lender and petty trader we shall use not coercion but credit co-operatives and efficient shops.' (ibid., p. 55.)

Bukharin's 'growing into' concept attracted some hostile comment at the time. He denied that his policy was based on the prosperous peasant, or that it was a form of degeneration of party policy: NEP, he asserted, strengthened the forces of socialism, 'it is not treason to the proletarian line, but the only correct proletarian policy'. (ibid., p. 66.)

Bukharin's formulations were made in the face of attack from Trotsky and his friends. Bukharin would occasionally agree that NEP was 'only a *peredyshka*' (temporary halt), and that there will be battles and offensives to come. (Bukharin, 1925c, p. 25.) But Bukharin, unlike Trotsky, was willing to be a gradualist, and accepted the logic of NEP – coexistence and competition with the private sector and a species of equilibrium relations between them – this being contrasted with Preobrazhensky's view that one must 'eat up' (*pozhirat'*) the other. The Leninist idea of a bloc or *smychka* with the peasants means a gradual and slow progress. 'We shall proceed forward slowly and bit by bit, dragging the peasant cart behind us.' (ibid., p. 64.) Elsewhere he spoke of moving towards socialism 'at the pace of a tortoise'. Some comrades would not be so patient.

One must ask oneself if Bukharin's ideas of 1927, with phrases about 'passing to the offensive against the kulaks', were consistent with his own ideas of 1925, or indeed with the growth of the peasant economy and of marketing of food at which he was aiming. Probably not. By 1927 he was already under political pressure to recant his ideas on *vrastanie*. There is an odd phrase in his Leningrad speech of 1926: 'When he shall be sufficiently strong . . . then we shall be able decisively and sharply to turn the basic masses of the peasantry onto the socialist road. But this is a matter for the future, though not a particularly distant future.' (Heitman, 1970, p. 339.) This was surely in line with Stalin's ideas of the time. Did he mean it? Probably not in Stalin's way. A few minutes earlier he had said that the kulak's economic grip was due to his value to his fellow-peasants: 'The co-operative trades badly, the kulak trades better. The co-operative has no galoshes, the kulak has. We cannot feed the peasant with good decrees and speeches about Chamberlain.' (ibid., p. 335.)

As already noted, Bukharin used the term 'equilibrium' very frequently. NEP was, of course, based on market relations, and Bukharin became a most fervent supporter of measures to achieve and maintain equilibrium in the market. A resumption of the offensive for socialism seemed, for him, consistent with market relations, for this would be an *economic* offensive, not based on coercion and police measures *vis-à-vis* the petty-bourgeois elements. So the 'goods famine' of the period after 1926 seemed to him to threaten a dangerous disequilibrium, and Stalin's coercive measures in the first months of 1928 put the final seal on a split which was to destroy Bukharin politically and, in the end, physically.

But his allegiance to NEP should not be taken as evidence that he is a kind of prophet of market socialism. This is to misunderstand his economics. It is not only the Bukharin of 1920 who saw socialism as a non-market system. Writing in 1927, Bukharin asserted: 'Despite the existence of the market and of capitalist forms of management, we are already moving from a type of economy based on profit to one based on the requirements of the masses (*pokrytiem podrebnostei mass*).' (Bukharin, 1927, p. 87.) An eminent Soviet scholar who had known both men said to me: 'Bukharin and Preobrazhensky, however much they differ on other matters, were both agreed that the law of value would have no place under socialism.' (In his opinion they were both wrong.) Bukharin accepted the 'market' logic of a mixed economy such as that of NEP. He was for building socialism *using* the market. But socialism for him would *not* be any species of market economy, and none of his writings can be cited to support a contrary view. My own belief is that experience has proved him to have been mistaken, but that is hardly the point.

Bukharin did not oppose industrialisation and was aware of the need to accumulate. 'The transfer of value into the accumulation fund at the expense of the petty producers must occur.' But this, he insisted, was *not* exploitation, was *not* any kind of internal colonialism. (Bukharin, 1925c, p. 68.) He had opposed Trotsky's demand, made in his letter of 8 October 1923, for planned industrial expansion. It was, in his view, absurd for its time, threatening the hard-won 'equilibrium' (that word again!) of political and economic forces. But he insisted even then that a plan would be needed, and industrialisation too. Either that, 'or we shall degenerate' (*pererodimsya*). (ibid.) Then again: 'We are sometimes reproached for wishing to obtain the missing capital at the cost of the people (*za schyot naroda*). But there is no other "cost"! (*scheta drugogo nyet!*).' (Bukharin, 1927, p. 66.)

Bukharin's line, therefore, should certainly not be so presented as to make him an opponent of planning and industrialisation. The essential point was that he wished to advance as fast as possible *within* NEP, and this means advancing rather slowly. His willingness to go along with anti-kulak measures (stopping, it is true, far short of expropriation and deportation) seemed, however, to be basically inconsistent with his 'NEP' premises: increased agricultural marketings were vital, and those peasants who were successful were, or would become, kulaks, to the extent to which they expanded marketings. But I have not the space here to pursue this fascinating problem of the viability of Bukharin's policies in the late 1920s, except perhaps to refer briefly to one important dimension of the discussion. Part of Bukharin's 'line' of the late 1920s was, in a sense, negative: do *not* try to build factories with bricks which are not there, do *not* make unbalanced plans, do *not* antagonise the peasantry, do *not* return to requisitions and confiscations. Yet, as any economic adviser knows, sound recommendations can well take the form of urging that the wrong things be not done. This is not really 'negative' advice either. While he was unable to say so publicly, Bukharin in the 1930s must have thought: 'If those who accepted the unbalanced and excessive First Plan, and launched the offensive against the peasants, had known the huge cost which would be incurred, which *was* incurred, would they have persisted in their policies?' After all, an agricultural surplus might have been mobilised at less cost if there had not been a decline in output, mass slaughtering of livestock, famine, sabotage etc., all these being direct consequences of the policies Bukharin had opposed. A possible answer to this would invoke Lenin's 'Port Arthur' analogy: the Japanese (in 1904) had launched an assault which failed, but learnt from this failure how to succeed; Stalin's assault led to vast mistakes and heavy losses, but in the end they broke through and built a mighty industry. Yes, but warnings which, if heeded, might have reduced the losses, must still be regarded as having been justified. It seems to be that the arguments in, for instance, *Zametki ekonomista*, about excesses in planning, were well founded and were abundantly supported by subsequent events. The man whose work we are honouring in this volume has put us all in his debt by his truly immense contribution to our knowledge of Soviet Russia, and I yield to none in my admiration. But, as he knows, in this particular area of discussion my view remains obstinately different from his.

Finally, some concluding thoughts. Bukharin was a strikingly original thinker, and it is a tragedy that he was for all practical purposes silenced at the end of the 1920s. The attacks on him, made by little men when he was forbidden to reply, make painful reading. True, he was himself a vigorous polemicist, not averse to both demagogy and 'organisational measures' in his own attacks on the Trotskyists. But argument, however fierce, is not the same as calling in the police. Bukharin himself was no administrator. He at no time headed a commissariat, nor was he a party secretary at any level. Indeed, he had grave weaknesses as a practical politician. He was a brilliant journalist and populariser, but also a man who had made important contributions to Marxian economics and was something of a pioneer in Marxian sociology. It was a great blow to this subject in particular that Bukharin's association with sociology led to the virtual banishment of the subject as well as the word from Russian academic life after his fall. It is only now slowly coming back to life. His concept of equilibrium and system, involving a kind of functionalism or institutionalism, was open to attack from those Marxists who emphasised change: he could be accused of an undialectical approach, mechanism, Bogdanovism even. Yet the study of the interaction of the parts of a system, indeed the concept of system, seems to me so obviously useful that the accusations hang in the air. The 'system' could be a market, a general staff, a planned centralised economy, a relationship between state, workers and peasants, a bureaucratic apparatus. True, it is a kind of instantaneous photograph, not a moving picture. A system changes. One may wish to overthrow it. But it has an inner logic, or essence, which are worth bringing out in analysis. (Lenin, it is true, would take exception to both 'logic' and 'essence', as evidenced by his marginal notes.)

To cite an example, Bettelheim uses a phrase, *'analyser les formations sociales en transition comme des structures complexes, dans lesquelles "tous les rapports coexistent simultanément et se supportent les uns les autres", selon l'expression de Marx . . .'* (Bettelheim, 1970a, p. 9.) Bukharin would have approved. I cannot see how one can disapprove in the name of Marxism.

However, those who silenced Bukharin the social scientist were not really interested in these philosophical distinctions, even if they really understood them. For some, philosophy or social theory was merely incidental to the real issues. (*'Kto kogo, vot nasha filosofiya'*, to cite a fictional but not untypical local functionary.) For others, what was needed was simplicity, a catechism, which provides answers which do not raise awkward questions, and which establishes unquestioned authorities and axioms. Typical of this was Stalin's well-known letter to the editor of *Proletarskaya Revolutsiya* in 1931, when an unfortunate historian, Slutsky, was castigated for daring to suggest that Lenin underestimated the extent to which the German social democrats had abandoned the revolutionary path before 1914. Stalin was not interested in the substance of the case, but he assaulted author and editors alike for daring to discuss the undiscussable. Bukharin was never this kind of populariser. He was far too much the erudite intellectual. This quality, which perhaps limited his political effectiveness, he shared with many Bolshevik intellectual victims of the Purges. (Even Dr Schlesinger had it. He once told me that he was expelled for being, in the words of the official who expelled him, 'an incurable *Privatdozent*'.) Maybe, it could be argued, dissident voices had to be silenced if Russia was to get through the crises and cataclysms of the 1930s. But we are a generation and more removed from this period. Surely the time has come for a free and open discussion of his ideas in the USSR?

N.B. All quotations are translated by the author.

6

Planners' Preferences, Priorities and Reforms

The object of this paper is to examine some concepts used in discussions of Soviet-type economies, and to relate them to some of the practical issues which are being debated in the Soviet Union in the course of the search for new and more efficient forms of managing the economy.

One such concept, widely used in discussions in the West, is 'planners' preferences'. These are often contrasted with consumers' preferences, and we are told that Soviet prices could be, or should be, rational in terms of planners' preferences. Some critics refer to the conflict between the two types of preferences said to be inherent in a Soviet-type economy. It would follow that the recent reform discussions, associated with the name of Liberman, represent an attempt to substitute consumers' and planners' preferences, and that therefore this is a change which would challenge the very foundation of the planning system. In my view, this line of thought can lead to confusion.

Let us first examine consumers' goods. What are planners' preferences? Are they represented by the product mix which state industry actually makes available to the consumer? Surely this can not be, for such an assumption is unrealistic on two counts. First, it excludes the possibility of error, of miscalculation, of faulty communication. Secondly, it treats 'the planners' as if they were one body with identical interests, though they are sometimes at odds with one another. What happens by no means always accords with what the planners wish to happen. The word 'wish' has two meanings here. The planners may wish, i.e. order, something, and what actually occurs is not what they intended. Or their 'wishes' may indeed have been carried out, but the orders themselves may have been mistaken, in the sense that they were not in accord with the objectives of the planners.

Let us illustrate these propositions with examples taken from the real Soviet world. The product mix actually available, at established prices, is in evident conflict with consumer demand. Stocks in the trading network grow rapidly, the retail trade plan is not fulfilled, there are queues of dissatisfied customers for items in short supply, money savings of the population increase and this last phenomenon is treated by Soviet analysts as a by-product of the citizens' inability to obtain the goods they need.

Reprinted from The Economic Journal, *vol. 76, no. 302, June, 1966.*

What planners did, or could, 'prefer' this situation? Their reaction to it shows that they regard it as a consequence of their errors, not of their preferences. Once one rejects the mistaken concept that the planners 'prefer' what actually is available, one starts seeking causes. The planners could have misjudged demand. Or deficiencies in the distribution network could have caused excess stocks to accumulate in one area while people were queuing for these same goods in another area. Or the price system could be clumsy and irrational. Or, quite frequently, a global plan which might be correctly related to aggregate demand is distorted in the process of disaggregation. Thus, a plan to produce a given volume of wool cloth, shoes, women's dresses is fulfilled in detail in such a way that the customers cannot obtain the design, quality or size that they happen to want. This could happen because the plan is expressed in terms of total quantity at a given average cost; or because the financial organs exert pressure to ensure the output of items which, though not in demand, carry a high rate of turnover tax; or because some intermediate authority (region or ministry) is trying to fulfil a plan in terms of gross value of output, and so on. All these various distortions are well known to students of the Soviet economy. All arise either out of ambiguities and contradictions in the plan, or (and) out of conflict and contradictions within the planning system. It is important to emphasise that the planners, or the state, cannot be treated as a single unit with uniform goals and identical interests, and I will return to this point later on.

Peter Wiles once pointed out that in the field of consumers' goods planners have no rational reason to refer a pattern of output which does not conform to consumer demand. (Wiles, 1963.) There are, of course, exceptions to this in every country. In Great Britain we tax spirits and cigarettes very heavily, do not tax books, and provide cheap milk and cod-liver oil to mothers. In the Soviet Union spirits are also taxed very heavily, children's clothes are priced low and pop records are taxed more highly than symphonies and folk-songs. These examples show that there are some cases where the state does consciously try to stimulate one kind of demand and to restrict other kinds. But Wiles's principle holds over most of the field, and planners' failures to provide the goods that are wanted are mostly unintentional.

Of course, planners prefer to be able to prefer. In other words, they have a vested interest in a decision-making structure that gives them power to take decisions. It is also a social-economic fact that, for various reasons, public authorities in charge of resource allocation often do not seem to care much for the convenience of the citizens. But this is quite another question. It does not mean that the planners prefer any particular bill of goods. They do not consciously desire that the customer be unable to obtain what she wants, though the institutional arrangements are such that she may be unable to do so.

None of the above argument would lose its force if the planners so manipulated prices that they cleared the market of the goods they had decided to produce. This is the situation envisaged by Lange (in 1938), when he wrote:

'One may well imagine a system in which production and the alloca-tion of resources are guided by a preference scale fixed by the central planning board, while the price system is used to distribute the consumers' goods produced. In such a system there is freedom of choice in consumption, but the consumers have no influence whatever on the decisions of the managers of production and of the productive resources. There would be two sets of prices of consumers' goods. One would be the market prices at which the goods are sold to the con-sumers; the other, the accounting prices derived from the preference scale fixed by the central planning board.' (Lippincott, 1964, p. 96.)

In such circumstances, too, the bill of goods actually produced could be a consequence of all the distortions already referred to, plus com-petition between different departments for investment resources, which, since capital has been provided free of charge, is really a form of empire building in which success results from political 'pull' or a well-drafted memorandum. Lange's 'preference scale fixed by the central planning board' is a myth, if by this is meant a detailed bill of goods so preferred. In Soviet reality there are very large variations in the difference between 'the market price at which goods are sold to the consumer' and the 'accounting prices', i.e. factory prices net of tax). But this, in most cases, is not the consequence of conscious design. Thus, radios, watches and cameras sell close to cost price, while wool textiles and sugar bear high turnover tax rates. This only suggests relative over-investment in radios, watches and cameras, and not anybody's preference scale.

A somewhat similar point could be made in respect of producers' goods. Here it is not disputed that planners make errors. They may choose a higher-cost variant, or issue orders at a level of aggregation which causes subordinate authorities to distort the product mix. The reasons which cause textile factories to produce cloth which is not in demand also cause rolling mills to make excessively heavy metal parts, in this instance to fulfil a plan target expressed in tons. Many prod-uction and investment choices are made in ignorance of cost considera-tions, or by blindly following a primitive and out-of-date input-output ('material balances') table, or because prices are illogical or irrational, or through regional or departmental vested interests. In the case of producer's goods, it is still the rule in the Soviet Union that allocation is by administrative order, at fixed prices, and so any imbalance between authorised demand and available supply must by definition be due to miscalculation. (The sheer scale of the planners' task makes such miscalculations all too common.) Prices, roughly based on average costs of several years ago, have hitherto played a largely passive role, and it seems unreasonable to assign to such prices any very precise economic significance. It is true, as Bergson has pointed out several times, that costs, on which these prices are based, are largely composed (directly or indirectly) of wages, and that, labour being free to move, a labour market exists. To that extent, labour cost as computed through wages has real significance. However, it has always seemed to me to be doubtful if this is a sufficient condition for regarding such prices as rational in any terms. The resource allocation decisions, which cause the demand for different kinds of labour to change, and thus affect costs, cannot be assumed to conform to planners' preferences, for reasons already abundantly explored. Wiles has argued that planners may be irrational in what they prefer, which is also a legitimate point of view. An example might be the reported preference of Stalin for the great works of Stalin to be visible from the planet Mars. But this, at least, was one despot's notion of the satisfaction of his (despotic) wants, whereas planners' allocation decisions are often due to an inability to define and observe efficiency criteria which they would like to observe, if only they knew what they were.

We must now pass on to another and related question, that of the priority of producers' goods, and of a high rate of investment over current consumption. Whatever may or may not be the planners' view of a desirable product mix of consumers' goods, they do undoubtedly assert the priority of the future as against the present. Indeed, there have been times when the pattern of consumers' goods production was largely predetermined by the productive capacity already available, or by the supply of domestic raw materials, since virtually all investments and all imports served the expansion of the producers' goods sectors. In the field of foreign trade British controls operated in a not dissimilar way: thus, in 1948 goods were divided into 'essential' and 'less essential', and we imported raw rubber, cotton and certain capital goods which could not be made at home, and severely restricted imports of clothing, luxury goods and television sets. This is undeniably an example of a substitution of 'political' choice for market forces, though it is noteworthy that, in Britain then and in Russia now, the price system was so artificial that it could not be used to express or transmit consumers' preferences.

The allocation of resources (domestic and foreign) between current consumption and accumulation to a great extent predetermines the division of actual output between what the Soviet writers call producers' goods and consumers' goods. (Peter Wiles pointed out, in his above cited work, that this is the input-output consequence of a high rate of investment and of growth.) Obviously, investment must take material forms if it is to be a reality in any economy. (Perhaps one reason for our chronic balance of payments deficits lies in the fact that when investment increases so many of the investment goods are *not* made in this country, thus greatly increasing our propensity to import. But that is another story.) Can we say that in the Soviet Union, in a way fundamentally different from the West, planners – and not the citizens as a whole – decide what proportion of the GNP should be devoted to investment or to communal as against individual consumption?

Here again, we must avoid excessively sweeping conclusions. There is the repeated assertion in the USSR of a special kind of priority for producers' goods, even though the dogmatic assumption that output of such goods *must* grow faster than that of consumers' goods is at last being abandoned. One can indeed establish a Soviet 'model' in which the volume of investment is a political decision, wholly financed by forced savings, through the prices of goods sold by the state. This can be contrasted with a Western model in which the rate of investment reflects the 'time-preference of the community' and the behaviour of individual savers. But this is a little far-fetched. Part of the investment of any Western country is state financed. Much of private investment is in fact financed out of retained profits, i.e. through the prices of goods. A citizen who buys, say, stockings in the Soviet Union is making an involuntary contribution to investment funds through the price he pays. But a British citizen does the same thing too, by contributing to the profits of the company that makes the stockings. It does not seem a tenable proposition to assert that the first is a case of forced saving and the second a manifestation of the free choice of a sovereign consumer. Admittedly, one could treat the company's decision about investment as involving choice between the distribution of the profit as dividend and its reinvestment. It is not suggested that the situation in East and West is identical. The institutional arrangements are indeed very different. Therefore, while a conflict between present consumption and future needs exists everywhere, it is resolved differently. However, it is not very realistic to contrast the two systems as if they actually conformed to imaginary models. In fact, there is involuntary saving in both. Although, especially at some periods, the *scale* of forced saving in the Soviet Union was exceptionally great, it is difficult to visualise, *conceptually*, a conflict in this respect between planners' and consumers' preferences peculiar to a Soviet-type economy.

As for the decision concerning the scale of social as against individual consumption, it is hard to discern any difference of principle between the Soviet Union and, say, Great Britain or France. Social services are financed by taxation and compulsory levies of various kinds, in East and West. If in this respect 'planners' preferences' contradict 'consumers' preferences' they do so in all these countries.

It is also desirable to make clear what is meant by 'the final bill of goods', in the context of real or imagined reforms to the Soviet planning system. Planners are criticised – by Wiles and Nemchinov, for instance – for fixing targets for intermediate goods and basic materials, and for devising a possible pattern of end-products from them, rather than vice versa. This could well be a valid criticism. However, one should be clear what sort of final bill of goods the critic has in mind. The state as such has, of course, its own claim on resources for its own purposes. These would include, for instance, missiles, submarines, the collected works of Lenin, school desks and smallpox vaccine. All these, except the works of Lenin, are required also by the British state. For the rest, it is either a question of correctly estimating or projecting consumer demand or of finding the best means (machinery, factory buildings, materials, fuel etc.) to achieve the desired ends. As already pointed out, the planners have no 'final bill of goods' in the real world. No doubt planners can and do make estimates which include a pattern of consumption. Even in the Soviet Union, there are studies of income elasticities, designed to aid planners in this task. However, we must distinguish between aggregate long-term projections and operationally valid disaggregation. In the first case we are dealing with, say, textiles or clothing in general. Planners have not, for reasons already analysed, any very clear preference *qua* planners about textiles, but they may proceed intelligently to estimate demand changes and seek to provide for the necessary capacity and inputs. (They do this also, as they must, for basic materials and fuels.) This can form an integral part of a plan for 1980. However, this level of aggregation will not ensure that blue woollen skirts of a given type are available in 1976 in Uzbekistan. Similarly, a global plan for, say, spare parts for farm machinery will not – even if globally correct – ensure the availability of carburettors for a particular type of tractor in any given area at the appropriate time. Plainly, these are quite different kinds of problems. Reformers such as Professor Liberman, and other 'decentralisers', are concerned with micro-economic adjustments, and assert that contractual relationships which convey user demand directly to the producer can help to ensure that the right things are produced. The hierarchical planning system which aggregates requirements and issues (necessarily aggregated) instructions to meet them, i.e. the 'command economy' of the traditional type, cannot ensure that requirements are rationally met, and this applies to the product mix and to the choice between and supply of inputs. The reformers are thus concerned with blue woollen skirts and carburettors this year, not with clothing and farm machinery in 1980. They are concerned with operational decisions, not with aggregate long-term projections.

The prewar Lange must be regarded as having been unrealistic when he imagined that prices could be imposed on enterprises. In his words: 'The technique of attaining this end is very simple [*sic*]; the central planning board has to fix prices and see to it that all managers of plants, industries and resources do their accounting on the basis of the prices fixed by the central planning board.' (Lippincott, 1964, p. 81.) Would it were simple! It is not surprising that every serious reform proposal, whether it be by Liberman in the Soviet Union or Šik in Czechoslovakia, envisages some price flexibility. The number of prices which would have to be individually determined by the authorities would clearly run into far too many millions to be manageable on a rational basis.

It is in the light of these considerations, too, that one must view the role of computers and of programming. This is a vast and complex subject, which can only be mentioned briefly here.

The computer's value in drafting consistent long-term plans, in speeding up and thus greatly facilitating the process of iteration, is not in dispute. Nor is it to be doubted that computers will be widely used in Soviet planning, as they are in many Western firms, to find solutions to particular problems in various sectors of the economy. However, a *system* of centrally directed computers which would permit the retention of *operational* micro-economic control at the centre is surely a fantasy. Or, to be precise, it is a fantasy for many years to come. It is already possible to conceive of a fully cybernetised system in which everything is encompassed. On a less ambitious scale, there are the 'two-level planning' experiments of Kornai and Liptak in Hungary. For the immediate future, however, Liberman-style reforms are necessary, and do not conflict with the further development of the computer as an aid to planning; the most eminent of the 'mathematicians', Kantorovich, has said this quite clearly. (VEk, no. 9, 1964, p. 81.) Similarly, Nemchinov, a leading reformer, sought to combine macro-economic 'econometric' planning with extensive micro-economic devolution to enterprises, and even competition for orders. (*Kom*, no. 5, 1964.) (This was one of his last articles, as he died later in the year. He performed great services to Soviet economics.) All this would imply the dismantlement of part of the existing system of administrative allocation of inputs and of the micro-planning of output.

Therefore proposals for micro-economic decentralisation and for the use of computers to facilitate central planning are being made simultaneously, and sometimes by the same persons. There is no necessary contradiction between them. The reform proposals now being implemented also involve a debate concerning the proper location of decision making, and this in turn raises issues such as the availability at various levels of the necessary information, the size of management units in different branches of economic activity, and so on. One must not be tempted into oversimplification, and contrast an imaginary 'command economy' in which super-planners decide everything with an equally imaginary decentralisation of all decision making to enterprise directors, guided by the profit motive. It is evident, if only from the experience of Western countries, that there is need for variety, that no single pattern of organisation or of pricing can suit the entire economy. A Soviet enterprise corresponds to a plant. A Soviet enterprise making, say, caustic soda therefore corresponds to a sub-unit of one of the divisions of Imperial Chemical Industries Ltd. Has the manager of such a plant in England any greater decision-making powers than a director of a Soviet enterprise now possesses? This is very doubtful. If it is rational to give such a director freedom to respond autonomously to price and profit stimuli in his production and investment programmes, then it would be rational to break up ICI. Examples can be multiplied. Thus, it is at the very least not self-evident, if Western experience is taken as a guide, that 'Liberman'-type reforms are universally applicable, or that management at plant level ought always to be given much greater autonomy. No one doubts that the output of, say, clothing factories could be more expeditiously adjusted to requirements by micro-economic decentralisation of management, but even there the Soviet reformers are experimenting with grouping together enterprises to form larger productive units, to which they give the name *firma*, 'firm'. Similarly, one can envisage a situation in which some prices can be left free to fluctuate under virtually free-market conditions, while others are fixed by ministries. This, for example, is an integral part of recent reforms in Czechoslovakia. This, too, corresponds to Western reality, with its mixture of free and 'administered' prices, especially if one bears in mind that the analogue to the managing director of ICI is a comrade holding the rank of minister.

Therefore the solution which is being sought will contain elements of market and of administrative planning, of centralisation and decentralisation. It is surely unrealistic to adopt an 'either/or' approach; it is simply not true that they (or we) must either adopt the whole free-market system or reassert total 'command' planning, neither of which has in fact existed in pure form anywhere. There can be viable positions in between these extremes.

But not all intermediate positions are viable. To find a balance between central macro-economic planning and micro-economic 'market' flexibility is a very difficult task, especially as the process must begin in a situation of strains, shortages, irrational prices and long established administrative 'rationing' of inputs. Perhaps the key difficulty concerns the control over investment.

The problem may be best seen by imagining that it is decided that all current production decisions be left to the free play of supply and demand, while the central planners take all the major investment decisions.

The first point to make is that a sizable part of current output consists of those goods which make a reality of the investment plan. Therefore, if the state controls the bulk of investment and does not directly control the current production programme of enterprises making investment goods there is at least the possibility of something going badly wrong. True, a simplified model can be imagined in which enterprises are neatly divided into those making investment goods and those making consumers' goods, and in which the former can only get orders from the state, as the sole 'investor'. This, however, is unrealistic on two grounds. First, the enterprises making investment goods, plus those who supply them with inputs, often make consumers' goods, or provide inputs for industries making consumers' goods. This is too obvious to need elaboration. It therefore follows that there could be unbalance and disequilibria which adversely affect the fulfilment of the investment plan.

Secondly, we must now return to the point made earlier, concerning the unreality of imagining the state and the planners to be a unified group with single interests and objectives. In practice, there are many pressure groups. Some are familiar in the West also. Thus, someone is doubtless strongly making a case for necessary expenditures on building more houses, schools, hospitals. In addition, the separate economic departments, ministries, committees, press their own claim. Regional officials (and this includes party officials) argue for 'their' projects (The report of the December 1964 session of the Supreme Soviet, to cite an example, is full of this sort of thing.) Enterprises press for grants to finance extensions or to re-equip the factory. In practice, of course, various subordinate authorities and enterprises do make their own investment plans. These sometimes depend on grants from the (central) budget, or are limited by the government's insistence on authorising every project over a certain size, and/or by global maxima of investment expenditures. However, enterprises even now have some funds of their own for financing decentralised investments, and the growing practice of allowing the banks to grant credits for this purpose provides another source of funds. All this adds up to an amount which has often been substantially in excess of the financial and material resources available, even after cuts by the central planners. The decisions taken in September 1965 will lead to a substantial increase in decentralised investments.

Soviet writers are conscious of the problem of over-investment, and have been seeking a diagnosis of its causes. Here is one such diagnosis:

'The system of evaluating the performance of productive units, of regional economic councils, of whole sectors, creates excessive demand for investments. Plan indicators of the volume of output, of reduction in costs and of increases in labour productivity can all be more easily fulfilled if more investment resources are received . . . Enterprises which achieve the same labour productivity with a smaller basic capital usually receive absolutely no reward for this . . . It will be possible to reduce the demand for investments if evaluation of economic performance, and material incentives take into account the extent to which additional capital is used.' (K. Popadyuk, *EkG*, 7 July, 1964, p. 5.)

Other writers have pointed to an underestimation of depreciation and replacement, and also of the actual cost of construction, which 'for 475 major construction sites . . . exceeded estimated cost by 25 per cent'. This lack of realism in investment planning 'leads to an unjusti-fied expansion of the building programme, which in the last analysis creates overstrain'. (Y. Kvasha and V. Krasovski, *VEk*, no. 7, 1965, pp. 3, 4.) These are only some of the more recent writings on the subject, and are cited here only to demonstrate that this tendency is known and is causing concern.

It is true that one reason for excessive investment applications is that the money is 'free' to the recipient. Under present rules there is no interest levied on basic capital, and a grant from the state budget is non-returnable. If a charge were made, some reduction in the flow of applications might occur. The reforms announced by Kosygin in September 1965 envisage a capital charge, and the bonus system has been altered to encourage enterprises to economise in the use of capital. Outright grants will gradually be replaced by long-term credits. None the less, demand may still be excessive. Yugoslav experience shows that 'socialist enterprises' can over-apply for capital, even if they must borrow from the bank, even if there is an interest charge, and indeed even if they have to submit to severe cross-examination on the expected rate of return. The snag is that, while capital for expansion is attractive for the enterprise, its possible inability to repay is not associated with any effective sanctions. The manager can, of course, be dismissed, but by the time the chickens come home to roost he may well have been transferred. The point is by no means a frivolous one. The author of these lines was told both in Prague and in Belgrade that one of the major problems of their systems is how to devise effective (non-criminal) penalties, for instance for overbidding. This mades indirect, 'monetary', control hard to operate effectively.

Below the level of the centre it pays everyone to begin as many investment projects as possible, because it strengthens their hand in bidding for another instalment of funds (or a permit to continue) in the year following. This, too, contributes to the notorious *rasplyenie sredstv* (scattering of resources over too many investments), the denunciation of which is a regular feature of the finance minister's budget speech. Shortages of materials and delays in delivery of equipment also help to prolong the period of construction and the volume of unfinished work. This is one manifestation of over-investment.

So the central planners are under heavy pressure from the lower echelons. But simultaneously they are under pressure from above, because the party leadership aims at maximising the rate of growth. This – as the Czech economist Goldmann has observed in a most original and stimulating article – leads to a recurrent tendency to over-invest, and when critical shortages develop, has sometimes caused a sharp reduction in (in Czechoslovakia even a halting of) growth, which Goldmann treats as a species of business cycle. (reprinted in Goldman, 1964, p. 99ff.)

The effect of over-investment is to create unplanned shortages, unexpected snags. This leads to repeated amendments of plans, current as well as long term. And it is precisely here that one does see planners' preferences asserting themselves, in a very real way, against consumers' preferences. When unexpected shortages develop, planning officials (and also party officials at various levels) intervene to say whose supplies should be cut off, what investment projects should be halted, who is to be allowed to use scarce rail wagons, and so forth. By long established tradition, they tend to opt for the future against the present, for investment against consumption, for factories rather than housing or schools, and steel and engineering factories rather than textile mills and agriculture. (For example, Brezhnev, in his speech to the September 1965 plenum, deplored the planners' habit of 'balancing' their accounts at the expense of the needs of agriculture, and this despite the high priority accorded it in recent party decisions.) These priorities can be, perhaps are being, modified. But so long as there are chronic shortages and bottle-necks, some priorities there must be. These affect a wide range of producers' goods.

It is the essence of the 'market' type of reform that enterprises must be free to place orders for the inputs they require. Logically, therefore, the input providers must themselves be free to plan on the basis of their customers' requirements. Thus, market forces, expressing consumer demand, would 'permeate' a large part of the economy. As already argued at length, this would not raise issues of principle over the substitution of consumers' for planners' preferences. But it could lead to chaos if the total demand for resources significantly exceeds availabilities. This undoubtedly worries the planners. It is a precondition of the effectiveness of this kind of reform that excess demand be checked, and that known or anticipated shortages become the subject of appropriate production or investment decisions, bearing in mind that there is no capital market which could permit the transfer of investment recovery from one enterprise (or section) to another. Soviet economic officials are accustomed to cope with these problems by allocating resources administratively. They have yet to learn control by what the reformers call 'economic means'. Yet they must do so if the reforms adopted in September 1965 are to make a decisive difference to planning methods and the performance of the economy.

7

'Market Socialism' and Its Critics

This paper examines the attack on 'market socialism' from the left, i.e. from those who believe that the very term 'market socialism' is a contradiction in terms, that the East European reformers are in process of retreat from socialist aims, if not actually restoring capitalism.

This view commands considerable support from the 'New Left' both in the West and in parts of the Third World. This species of criticism should be distinguished from the resistance to reform on the part of the party and planning machine, which, though it sometimes cites similar ideological arguments, is powerfully motivated by bureaucratic habits and self-interest; certainly the New Left critics think that this is so. It is perhaps less easy to distinguish the 'left' critique from one sometimes heard from another quarter: that, whether good or bad, market socialism is inconsistent with the vision of Marx and Engels. For Paul Craig Roberts, for instance, it is clear that Marx saw commodity production and markets as characteristic of capitalism, bringing alienation in their wake, and therefore the reformers are un-Marxist, indeed the prewar Lange was also un-Marxist. (Roberts, 1971.)

This type of Western critic is presumably little interested in the existence or non-existence of viable alternatives to a centralised non-market economy, or in the relative inefficiency of this or that model of a planned economy. If, indeed, it could be proved that market-type reforms were necessary and inescapable in Eastern Europe, Paul Craig Roberts would probably say: well, so be it, but it simply proves that Marx's economic vision was wrong!

This, of course, cannot be the argument of Bettelheim, Sweezy and others like them, who sympathise with Mao's position and, therefore, while opposing both the Soviet leadership (for bureaucracy and conservatism) and the 'liberal' reformers (for revisionism), must assert that they have a viable socialist economic model. The present paper will examine in detail the ideas of Bettelheim, as these are expressed in his recent work. (Bettelheim, 1970a.) His arguments are clear and succinct, and it seems to me that it is useful to consider them seriously. I am not in sympathy with their ideas, but who better than Bettelheim to compel one to develop systematic counter-arguments? In first analysing and then criticising Bettelheim's ideas, I am trying to see them from a standpoint which, for want of a better phrase, I would call 'feasible socialist economics'. That is to say, I try to see what form of organisation of production and distribution *could* work, given nationalisation or socialisation of the means of production. To put the same thing in another way: I am seeking for possible ways in which a Soviet-type economy *could* function. I realise that this approach begs an important question: feasibility is hard to define, and the impossible can, given time, become possible. Technical progress, social engineering, the impact of collectivism on human psychology, could alter many of the parameters which affect the discussion. This is doubtless so. However, such changes, if assumed, must be spelled out by the analyst, and not brought in as silent assumptions. Nor can one get round them by facile assumptions about human nature. It is sometimes said that critics of the New Left are prisoners of an outlook formed under acquisitive capitalism, that under socialism men will try to do good. Maybe they will, who knows, though a little scepticism would not be out of place: men have a remarkable capacity for equating the good of society with their own self-interest, a capacity which may have little to do with private ownership of factories and mines. But, in any case, men cannot be expected to do 'good' in economic affairs unless it is shown that what *is* good can be identified.

Let me set out Bettelheim's ideas, as I understand them. He begins by noting the 'gap which separates the theoretical propositions of Marx and Engels, concerning the socialist mode of production, and the reality of "socialist countries" '. (Bettelheim, 1970a, p. 9.) (The words 'socialist countries', when used to describe Eastern Europe or the USSR, are always placed in inverted commas.) This, he maintains, is linked with a double misunderstanding: a failure to distinguish between fully developed social systems and those in transition, and a tendency to treat as socialist those systems in transition which have in fact left the socialist road. We shall see that Bettelheim is deeply concerned with problems of transition, and indeed he realises that too rapid a move towards what he would call socialism could be counter-productive. However, he bitterly opposes the 'pseudo-decentralisation which is today attempted in the countries of Eastern Europe', which is 'none other than the restoration of the "market machanism", implying thereby the abandonment of socialist planning'. He concedes that the virtues of socialist planning have been 'obscured' by excessive centralisation, a 'hypertrophy of the state apparatus' which stands in the way of social control over production and ends up by reinforcing the role of money and market. (ibid., pp. 10–11.)

Bettelheim has no trouble in establishing that Marx and Engels defined socialism as excluding commodity and market relations. This is most vividly stated in a familiar passage in Engels's *Anti-Dühring*. 'Direct social production' will exclude commodity exchange, therefore also the transformation of products into commodities and into values. The quantity of social labour will also be measured directly, in hours. Production plans will be made in the knowledge of the *utility* of various products, compared with one another and with the quantity of labour necessary for their production. 'People will decide all this quite simply, without the use of so-called "value".'

None of this is the case in 'socialist countries' today. In practice, Eastern Europe has an uneasy combination of monetary measures (prices, value categories etc.) and socially and politically determined priorities, representing two different species of economic calculation. We shall see that Bettelheim finds good reasons to expect their coexistence in the transition period.

To make progress towards socialist economic calculation, it is necessary to begin by identifying the 'social utility' (*effet social utile*) of various products. How? 'Here is a problem which has not yet been fully solved [*sic*].' (Bettelheim, 1970a, p. 20.) All products have in common the fact that they enter into socially organised production and consumption. Bettelheim proceeds to distinguish very carefully between *economic* calculation and *monetary* calculation: the latter uses 'not measured magnitudes but *given* multitudes', in the sense that prices are given, without (in capitalism) their level being meaningfully defined or determined. 'Economic' calculation in Bettelheim's sense requires taking into account the 'substitutability' both of labour and of products, which would seem to admit, indeed require, the concept of opportunity cost. Under capitalism the object of production is the appropriation of surplus value, for which the satisfaction of needs is but a means, hence the link between socially necessary labour and the rationality of profitability as a criterion. But under socialism the theoretical context should be 'not one related to values and prices, but *social utility*', and the distribution of productive efforts should be related to *this* measure.

Why, then, has this not happened? Bettelheim advances a number of reasons, among them the inadequate development of productive forces, and also the continued existence of a capitalist world. But he devotes most space to other causes. Thus the inadequacy and contradictory nature of prices in the USSR, Poland etc. led to a search for better economic calculation, by combining plan and market. He mentions Novozhilov and Nemchinov, but remarks: 'These economists' attempts are ambiguous, since they fail to distinguish between economic calculation and monetary calculation', and while they have made an important contribution to the discussion they are none the less 'contaminated' by 'unscientific ideology' and by the growth of commodity and market relations.

Prices, he insists, conceal rather than bring out the real economic magnitudes. Computations designed to minimise costs or maximise returns are logical enough for capitalists,

'but they teach us nothing directly about the needs of development of socialist production, or the improvement of conditions of production and of the toilers' existence . . . At best they could identify those productive combinations which, within a given structure of prices, wages and techniques, would maximise the total surplus value which capital can extract from the exploitation of labour-power.' (ibid., p. 25.)

(So much for the whole Soviet discussion about optimal programming!)

According to him, socialist economic calculation has also made such slow progress because many Marxist economists have neglected use-value, and have also resisted marginal calculation, although it follows from the differential calculus. Then, he claims, Engels' reference to the 'simplicity' of socialist computation has been misunderstood. In fact, he points out,

'a product is often the result of the work of all of society, and not only of that labourer or group of labourers who have made it . . . Their work involves very large amounts of the work of others, to provide tools and objects of labour and auxiliary means, which are combined within a highly complex social organisation . . . Most are made by groupings of workers which also produce simultaneously a great variety of products, so that their contribution to each product cannot be directly measured and requires a highly complex series of analytical operations.' (ibid., p. 30.)

(It does indeed! And how does one go about it?)

So Engels' 'simplicity' seems to mean something other than simplicity, merely directness, i.e. identifying need and cost without the interposition of commodity-money relations. But neither the labour input in time nor social utility can yet be measured. So computations using commodity-money categories are in fact made in Eastern Europe. This is inevitable, argues Bettelheim, but can lead to error, and also to illusions.

Bettelheim does not agree with Bukharin's view that economics disappears under socialism. For him, unlike Bukharin, it is *not* concerned exclusively with commodity exchange. Under socialism, economic phenomena would be directly observable, instead of being hidden. Under socialism, there would be not only productive forces to be organised but also relations of production, a complex structure which can be the subject of Marxist economic analysis.

In the transition period, in which value and commodity categories persist, there must be a set of social relations which require such categories. These exist when relations between producers are 'duplicated' by relations between proprietors, and when the producers and proprietors are relatively independent and enter into purchase-and-sale relations with one another. These relations are, in Marxist terms, a form of *dissimulation*, i.e. the relations between men take on a 'phantasmagoric form of relations between things'. Bettelheim remarks, justly, that socialist planned relations can also 'dissimulate', because of the great complexity of inter-relations within a plan, which can give rise to 'plan fetichism'. This line of thought could lead, however, to stressing the *identity* of opposites, of plan and market, and thus to an identity between perfect market and perfect planning. This would mean accepting the ideas of Pareto and Barone, but he insists that this would be to confuse the different *functions* of plan and market, the confusion being similar to that between (real) economic calculation and monetary calculation.

Under socialism, insists Bettelheim, products will not be made for exchange but for use. There will be no more contradiction between private and social labour. But what about transitional society? The existence of value categories, alongside plan, must mean that 'the phantasmagoric forms of relations between things' persist, *and* that lack of information and imperfect organisation limit the action of politics (and of the state planners) upon economics.

But has not private property in means of production been eliminated? Yes, but, said Marx, 'useful objects become commodities because they are the products of private work carried on independently of one another'. Bettelheim considers, rightly in my view, that the formal ownership is a good deal less important than independence, or autonomy. That is to say, it follows from his argument that any management, whether appointed or elected by the workers, will produce 'commodities' (i.e. goods for *exchange*) if its work is organised separately from other groups with other managements. The central plan leaves many gaps, and combines administrative orders with a variety of monetary measures (profit-and-loss account, bonuses for cost reduction etc. etc.) which are only explicable in terms of an autonomous field of action for management in production and in relations with other managers. This is so even under Soviet centralisation, and is even more obviously so in Yugoslavia or Hungary.

Property is not the point. Preobrazhensky and Stalin thought that value categories survive because of the survival of non-socialist sectors. This is not good enough, writes Bettelheim. One must face up to the survival of 'commodity fetichism' within the state sector. The principal reason, he insists, is the fragmentation, the fact that relations have to be established between work which, 'though carried out independently, depends more or less on the work of others'. The process of co-ordination by plan reduces the area within which commodity relations manifest themselves, imposes constraints on exchanges. But a plan can effectively co-ordinate only on conditions, political ('effective participation of the masses') and economic ('scientific economic and social analysis') which are not yet present. (ibid., pp. 53, 54.)

But how is one to achieve what Bettelheim calls 'the effective participation of the masses in the elaboration and execution of plans', so as to achieve 'the effective domination of the producers over the means of production and the product', which for him are the essential features of socialist production relations? He is well aware that all this can be distorted by bureaucracy, privilege, indifference. In some cases the rot has gone so far as to require revolutionary changes. But he refuses to be precise on how a real socialist plan should operate. All depends on circumstances, the degree of development of production forces. There could be many combinations of central plan and the 'superposition of mutually co-ordinated plans' below the central level.

Within these conceptions, it is obvious that reforms designed to increase the influence and range of action of market forces are highly offensive to Bettelheim.

During the transition period, 'ownership' by the state could be more juridical than real. Power over property, possessions, can belong in some degree to the management. This would be analogous to the ownership by shareholders of property with a degree of *de facto* control of managers under modern capitalism. The state, if it is a workers' state, by imposing limits on enterprise autonomy, should be enforcing 'the domination of the toilers' over production, over 'the means and results of their labour'. It therefore follows that, while the existing state or planning mechanism may have many defects, in principle Bettelheim opposes the idea of enterprise autonomy, in so far as it is precisely by (correct) intervention that the interests of the whole toiling masses are given priority over the monetary computations of the enterprise. But he recognises that, even in a workers' state, there could be a 'separation of the workers from their means of production', since the state, by reason of its remoteness, may not be the best means of ensuring the domination of labour. Possibly, the Chinese communes provide a suitable model, a higher form than that of 'state property pure and simple', because they are also *political* organs, within which social-political desiderata take priority over the economic. However, it does not seem that Bettelheim is well acquainted with the Chinese model.

The word 'enterprise' requires definition, and Bettelheim finds it inapplicable to socialism, preferring 'production unit'. An 'enterprise' operates with money, pays wages, administers sub-units, possesses a profit and loss account. It is thus capitalist in its very nature, even if it is 'self-managed' in the Yugoslav manner. For, 'in the absence of socialist planning, the enterprise, whether or not "self-managed", is dominated by capitalist production relations, and must work for the return on its capital (*mise en valeur de son capital*)'. Even when the enterprises are subject to control and intervention from the planners they remain an institution within which capitalist relations reproduce themselves. 'Only a revolutionarisation of the production units can put an end to this capitalist apparatus and replace it by a new apparatus.' (ibid., pp. 70–1.) (But which?) Enterprises by their existence separate workers from their means of production and separate productive units from each other (*'double séparation'*).

In passing, Bettelheim makes the interesting point that economies of scale under capitalism could be the result of capitalist economic relations rather than of techniques as such. This is certainly a valid observation with regard to the size of firms, and perhaps also to the size of some equipment, since both could give *organisational* economies, which by no means follow if the mode of production is radically altered. However, his corollary is a more questionable one: that the Chinese have avoided the burdens of primitive socialist accumulation by not copying Western capitalist techniques, thus providing a model superior to that of the USSR.

The 'enterprise', then, is appropriate to capitalist ideology: hiring and firing, hierarchy, discipline are its features, which go naturally with production for sale. He advocates 'the ideological revolutionarisation of the workers, which causes them to affirm themselves as the real masters of production', leading to 'the elimination of money in the relations between productive units . . . the domination of the plan over productive units'. How? 'In the form of the domination of the workers over the means of production' (ibid., pp. 76, 77), a domination which the plan must express.

Bettelheim builds on the idea of state capitalism, a system of state-owned enterprises associated with the era of imperialism. He sees it as an unstable, transitional phase, which could slide into capitalism, through the growth of market relations. Surplus value under state capitalism can be used for socialist purposes by a workers' state, but it can be misappropriated by a 'ruling class' consisting of an alliance of managers and their (state) controllers.

In one of his recent articles, Bettelheim stressed the importance, from the point of view of socialism, of 'the nature of the class in power'. He notes that 'to identify "plan" with socialism and "market" with capitalism (which is true tendentially) aids the bourgeoisie (and notably the Soviet bourgeoisie), to exercise its domination under cover of a "plan" in the name of which it withdraws all rights of expression from the exploited classes'. (Bettelheim, 1970b, p. 8.) In other words, for him the plan can be 'an instrument of the domination of the direct producers over the conditions and results of their activity' only under certain political-social conditions. Only then the plan becomes 'a "concentrate" of the will and aspirations of the masses, of their correct ideas'. (ibid., p. 9. Shades of Rousseau's *volonté générale!*)

He returns several times to the need for a *calcul économique social*. 'Commodity relations link production units through their products, not through their work. The work is done in each unit separately, and *they are thus not directly related [confrontés]*. This is precisely the characteristic of commodity production . . . which renders impossible a real economic calculation, a direct measure of socially necessary labour.' (Bettelheim, 1970a, p. 81.) Yugoslav enterprises serve merely to divide the workers, who only have the illusion of self-management, since 'they cannot really dominate the use of either their means of production or of their products, since this is itself dominated by commodity (i.e. market) relations'. (ibid., p. 82.)

Bettelheim admits that, 'in the transition period', the (workers') state's exercise of power over property separates the direct producers from 'their' means of production, of which 'they are owners only through the intermediary of the state'. This would be acceptable if 'the state apparatus is genuinely dominated by the toilers'. Otherwise, the state officials become 'the effective owners'. They dispose of the surplus as they think best, and are 'compelled to grant a dominant role to the market and to profitability criteria'. (ibid., p. 87.) This can be shown from 'the history of the USSR during the past ten years' (! !). The alternative is that state property and state capitalism should be replaced 'by social appropriation' (?). Instead of this, one sees in Eastern Europe unstable combinations of commodity relations and administrative orders, the latter being sometimes obeyed by enterprise managers, and this is not a real plan. It is then a short step for revisionist critics to see the need for a strengthening of market relations in the interests of 'efficiency'.

How, then, should relations between productive units be organised? Bettelheim (rightly) stresses the need for diversity. If relations between given units are continuous and close, they could become larger 'complex units' with some species of joint management. These larger units could be inter-related 'either by the plan, or by the joint management, or by one of the units which dominates others', or finally there could be 'direct relations' between productive units.

The contradictions in the transition period between plan and market are in some respects analogous to the contrasts within a capitalist corporation between the profit of the whole corporation and that of its parts. The general social interest, embodied in the plan, must (for

Bettelheim) represent *politics* expressing the domination of 'direct producers'. Otherwise, the plan is a 'phoney' (*simulacre*).

'The means of establishing socially useful links between economic units and techniques can be increasingly concentrated at the level of the planning organs, closely connected with the various workers' collectives, corresponding to a real social appropriation.' (ibid., p. 111.) (I must admit that for me this is peroration and not economics.)

Politics dominates economics, says Bettelheim, yet the economic factor is dominant. How can this be? The answer: 'The economic is the determinant through the intermediary of politics.' But some cannot see this, and proclaim the interference of the political organs to be arbitrary. This could only be so if it is 'subjectivist and voluntarist', unscientific etc. In the USSR this is indeed often so. Ineffective forms of state intervention cause conflict and confusion. An apt phrase: the top planners 'face a screen between themselves and reality, which also acts as a mirror which transmits back to the planners an image of their own wishes'. Plans are thereby 'fulfilled' formally, but only formally.

How can one achieve the subordination of state institutions to the 'direct producers'? Only through struggle against a constant 'tendency to *separate* the functions of control and direction and those of carrying out the work. This tendency is itself inscribed in the ideological relationships produced by *institutions* . . . inherited from societies dominated by non-workers'. The fundamental law of developed socialism is the 'law of the social direction of the economy', under which one has a direct economic and social calculation, which does not proceed by the detour of the law of value, as Engels said. (ibid., pp. 124, 125.)

Since in the transition period there must be prices, these should (according to Bettelheim) be plan prices, which reflect economic policy and not 'the exigencies of the law of value'. Then the allocation of labour will be subordinated to the construction of socialism, i.e. to achieving 'the direct control of the immediate producers over production . . . therefore for the present and future needs of the producers', politically evaluated. In particular, 'the planning and investments should no longer be subordinated to the criterion of rate of return, whether financial or monetary'. Instead, we should have the criterion of '*social and political efficacy*' (his emphasis). (ibid., p. 125.) This he equates with Stalin's 1952 formulation about 'profitability from the standpoint of the whole national economy'.

In his discussion with Sweezy, Bettelheim elicited from the latter the following statement of a common position:

'When the bureaucratically administered economy runs into difficulties, as it certainly must, there are two politically opposite ways in which a solution must be sought. One is to weaken the bureaucracy, politicise the masses and ensure increasing initiative and responsibility to the workers themselves. This is the road towards socialist relations of production. The other way is to put increasing reliance on the market, not as a temporary retreat (like Lenin's NEP) but as an ostensible step towards a more efficient 'socialist' economy . . . It is, I submit, the road back to class domination and ultimately the restoration of capitalism'. (Bettelheim, 1970a, p. 21.)

Bettelheim warns against too rapid an elimination of prices and money. Their use follows from the relative autonomy of production units, from the unavoidable incompleteness of planning in the 'period of transition'. Planned prices should encourage productive units to behave in line with the plan, to minimise cost, and so on. Premature abandonment of this is likely to lead to confusion, as it has done (he maintains) in Cuba. It is too early to reconcile efficient use of means of production with purely quantitative allocation. Prices are real, sums of money are paid, and this is necessary, though this means imperfect, 'indirect' calculation and requires limitations on the role of money. (All this seems to be a case against ultra-ultra-leftism.)

Bettelheim speculates about a possible 'multi-level social unit of calculation', perhaps an international one, and promises to examine this question in a subsequent work.

He says, rightly, that rationing of scarce resources can be a consequence not of socialist planning as such, but of imbalance, of failure to co-ordinate. It is silly 'to blame money for disequilibria which it merely brings to light', and which cannot be abolished merely by eliminating money. (Bettelheim, 1970b, p. 135.)

At the end of the transition period? Well, then we would have 'ideological socialist relations', which will be constituted by the co-operation of production units with the object of the realisation of a socially optimal totality (*un ensemble*) of economic and political purposes. Such co-operation will assure the socialist interdependence of production units, achieved by 'the extension of the field of action of direct producers (*producteurs immédiats*), their domination over the conditions of production and reproduction'. (ibid., p. 134.) (Once again, to me this is eloquent rather than informative.)

So ends my summary of Bettelheim's case. What comment or critique can and should be made?

The first point that occurs to me is to be astonished at the omission of any mention of scarcity and abundance. True, Bettelheim refers to the insufficient development of productive forces as one of the factors responsible for the survival of 'commodity' relations, but he nowhere even begins to define what he regards as 'sufficient'. His repeated statements about choice leave one to infer that he means choices between alternative ends and means, that by doing or making A one is not doing (or doing less of) B. Were it otherwise, it would be his duty to say so. We must therefore assume that the needs of all the members of society are greater than the means available to satisfy them, certainly in the transition period, and presumably also when 'socialism' in his definition comes about. His definition says much about the producers' control over production and the product, and about the direct measurement of social utility without the interposition of money. The word 'abundance' does not occur. We must therefore assume that many citizens wish to obtain more of certain things that can at that time be produced, that inputs are limited, so that opportunity-cost is a reality. It is in *this* sort of situation that Bettelheim calls for his complex of socialist measures, not an imaginary utopia in which all is available in plenty to all. In any case, his critique of East European reformers can only make any sense in the context of an economy coping with relative scarcities.

Let us now tackle a fundamental Bettelheimian proposition: that the *producers* should control the instruments of production and the product. What does this mean? If the proposition affirms the right of the members of a producers' collective to decide among themselves the conditions of their work, this represents a comprehensible plea for industrial democracy and self-management. But surely Bettelheim means more than this. If he does, then he must be wrong. Suppose a group of workers are operating some physical plant which produces sulphuric acid, or bread, it does not matter which for the present purpose. It is *at least* as reasonable to assert that the product, and therefore the use to which the instruments of production are put, should be determined by the *user*, the *consumer*, as by the producer. Bettelheim criticises the Yugoslav 'self-management' model because 'the workers *cannot really dominate* the use of their means of production or of the product, because their use is itself dominated by market relations'. *But why should they do so?* If a market does not indicate what the customers (users, consumers) want, then some other person or institution must. Bettelheim might reply: 'Oh, but the collectivity of workers discuss the needs of their customers in a comradely way.' Then one must ask him: 'Yes, but under conditions of relative scarcity there will be more potential customers (at zero prices) than productive capacity. On what basis will the workers decide which need it is best – from the standpoint of society – to supply?' It is not a question of good will or bad will, but one of knowledge. This is quite unclear in Bettelheim's model. He implies that the central planners and various intermediate bodies will co-ordinate everything. But if a central planner *tells* the producers of bread and sulphuric acid what they ought to produce, then are they 'really dominating' their own equipment and products?

Choices are to be made about end-products based upon units of social utility. Presumably, these choices must be made by central planners? I cannot see how a collectivity, a group of workers, engaged in making buttons, sulphuric acid, thread, skirts, internal combustion engines or whatever, can compare alternative social utilities. At that level, this is simply not possible. How would planners carry out their vital function? Let us abstract from such possibilities as inertia, laziness, indifference. The planners, and the political leaders, are hereby assumed to be the nearest approach to angels conceivable in an irreligious world: they wish to do good by their fellow-men. How do they go about discovering men's needs, at zero price, and arranging them in order upon a scale of social utility? In what units is social utility to be measured? We are dealing here with a country, numbering millions of people, not a couple of hundred *kibbutz* members who can meet together, argue, vote (and then purchase their needs in a market economy.) We are dealing with a range of consumer goods which, fully disaggregated by type, run into millions of variants. It is true, of course, that some goods or services can be, often are, produced or supplied by political decision which is not derived from a market: water, for instance, or education. One could decide on a free ration of bread, milk, toilet paper. Museums could be free, and so could babies' diapers or medicines. The possibility or desirability of having a segment of the economy where goods or services are supplied without payment is hardly in dispute in principle. But we may be sure that Bettelheim has much more than this in mind, his vision is all-inclusive. Can he then not even hint *how*, along what lines, the measurement of social utility is to take place, and *who is to do the measuring*?

While I do not suggest that Bettelheim does or should follow the doctrines of Trotsky, it is not irrelevant at this point to quote Trotsky's ideas, because they at least grapple with the problem of scarcity, and, it seems to me, have a much more realistic view of its consequences.

Firstly, Trotsky ascribed 'the basis of bureaucratic rule' to shortages of consumer goods.

'When there are enough goods in a store, purchasers can come whenever they want to. When there are few goods, the purchasers are compelled to stand in line. When the lines are very long, it is necessary to appoint a policeman to keep order. Such is the starting-point of the power of the Soviet bureaucracy. It 'knows' who is to get something and who is to wait . . . Nobody who has wealth to distribute ever omits himself.' (Trotsky, 1964, pp. 159, 160.)

Bettelheim may object that Trotsky was writing about a poor society at a difficult moment. True. But if demand exceeds supply, at any price or at zero price, there will be queues, for bread at primitive levels, for spare parts for motor vehicles (or for motor-cycles) at higher standards of life. It is Bettelheim's duty to take this point seriously.

Trotsky again:

'Cast-iron can be measured in tons, electricity in kilowatts. But it is impossible to create a universal plan without reducing all branches to one and the same value denominator. If the denominator is itself fictitious, if it is a product of bureaucratic discretion, then it eliminates the possibility of testing and correcting the plan in the process of its implementation.' (Trotsky archives, cited in R. B. Day, 1973.)

Of course, Trotsky is talking about the transition period, and still envisages some sort of moneyless communism ahead. But quite clearly he would be unhappy about Bettelheim's notion of plan prices, because 'they open up unlimited room for bureaucratic subjectivism in the area of planning', to add another phrase from the same Trotsky source. Nor did Trotsky see the coexistence of plan and 'commodity' elements in the same spirit as Bettelheim. For the latter, conflict between plan and market forces is almost synonymous with the struggle between the workers' state and the law of value. Trotsky, it would seem, was concerned with a reconciliation or balance between them. 'Only the interaction of three elements, of state planning, of the market and of Soviet democracy can provide the country with proper leadership in the transitional epoch.' (*Byulleten' oppozitsii*, 1932, no. 5, also cited in Day, 1973.) Bettelheim may reply that he admits the survival of money-commodity categories in the transition period. But surely he does so most grudgingly, in a highly theoretical sense, and in much more abbreviated time scale, unrelated (almost) to the abundance within which full communism is alone conceivable in pure theory. (Abundance and queues cannot coexist.)

Sweezy wrote:

'It is obvious that what is needed is, in Bettelheim's words, "domination by the immediate producers over their conditions of existence, and therefore in the first instance over their means of production and their products". *The question, however, is what this mean*s and, perhaps equally important, what it does *not* mean. *There are no ready-made answers to this question* and (to the best of my knowledge) *very few studies bearing upon it.*' (Sweezy, 1972, p. 9. Emphases mine.)

One might think that such studies might antedate attacks on the East European reformers for not doing what perhaps cannot in fact be done. Furthermore, there is a basic unclarity about the meaning both of 'socialism' and of the 'transition period'. Sweezy at least distinguishes between both these terms and the more advanced stage of 'full communism' (e.g. see ibid., p. 9, 'a viable socialism . . . capable of moving forward on the second leg of the journey to communism'). Sweezy also discusses equality, and is willing to contemplate 'a high price in terms of immediate output and efficiency for achieving and maintaining it'. (Undeniably, market relations do carry with them dangers of excessive inequality, though experience suggests that a state-operated non-market economy is not free of this danger either.) He also shows a proper concern for the relationship between needs and resources. 'The absurd and ultimately disastrous bourgeois notion of insatiable wants must be decisively repudiated,' he writes. (ibid., p. 12.) One can repudiate all one pleases, but the economic and social fact of relative scarcity is not thereby eliminated.

And what about choice of means? How does one compare costs? In hours, perhaps modified to take care of unequal skills? This would be totally unsatisfactory. Firstly, as Bettelheim himself said, to measure the number of hours devoted to each product is a very complex affair indeed. Secondly, it ignores altogether the relative scarcity of different means. Novozhilov once pointed out that the latest machine is bound to be in short supply, even under full communism, unless it be assumed that technological progress ceases. How does opportunity-cost enter into cost measurement in hours? Over fifty years ago, there were many 'moneyless' schemes. In 1920 Strumilin had imagined 'the utility of products' as the criterion for output decisions, but choice of means, and indeed transactions between enterprises, were left undefined. Yurovsky's critique is worth quoting: 'Karl Marx analysed social relations in capitalist society from the standpoint of expenditure of labour on production of commodities, but this cannot of itself serve as a basis for making this capitalist principle [i.e. labour as a basic of value] a feature of socialist practice.' Strumilin and his ilk wrongly ignore gifts of nature. Has land in the centre of cities not an especially high scarcity-value? How, without money, can one compare investment alternatives? How can the organ responsible for production and investment even begin to identify economic effectiveness? At best it can achieve an input-output balance (in Yurovsky's words, *svesti kontsy s kontsami*), but is this the best way to satisfy social needs? It would make more sense if the planners could allocate resources towards those items for which people are willing to pay more, 'since the willingness to pay more is itself evidence that the given product is more wanted'. But of course this requires a market for consumer goods. The state would invest in the indicated directions, earning a surplus, 'a kind of interest rate on capital' and thereby finance accumulation. 'Only the memory of the fact that interest on capital forms a class income in capitalist society can serve as a psychological basis for a refusal to make calculations of this type. No rational basis for such a refusal exists.' (Yurovsky, 1928, pp. 115–19.)

Yurovsky's argument is the stronger because he knows (and I also know!) that the price system is imperfect, that frequently 'monetary computation and social welfare do not coincide'. (ibid., p. 94.) There are externalities, uncertainties, fluctuations, which distort in some degree every price system. This is not in dispute. Nor can anyone doubt that the *indirect* identification of wants and of means, through the medium of money and exchange, can in itself cause disequilibria: this was said long ago by Tugan-Baranovsky, and indeed underlies Keynes's analysis. It is the main reason why Say's law fails to work. But surely it behoves a critic to be aware of the function of money. It has existed for some millennia, in a variety of forms, because it fulfils a number of purposes: it facilitates choice, it is a medium of calculation, it helps to identify need, it serves in the search for the best means to satisfy needs. That it does all these things imperfectly is no reason for denouncing it unless some better method is found. Economists in Moscow's TsEMI told me that the only way in which planners could identify what people wanted was to let them 'vote with the ruble'. Otherwise, they would not know what advice to give to the political leadership concerning the needs of society. They added, rightly, that some of society's needs manifest themselves other than through the market (e.g. the need for leisure, public parks, education etc. etc.), and some that do manifest themselves ought to be discouraged (e.g. vodka).

Bettelheim repeatedly asserts the need for politics to dominate economics. What does this mean? Can he define his terms? If, with an acceptable distribution of income, *economic* forces imply an unsatisfied demand for cuddly toys, crusty white rolls, books by Dostoevsky, decorated chineware or dining tables, on what 'political' ground should such 'economic' forces be resisted? Is not all Soviet experience a warning against *not* insisting that the planners have a *duty* to respond to such economic forces as these? Indifference to people's needs is a danger to be guarded against, is it not, rather than strengthened by doctrines about the primary of politics? The same is true of choices of means. If a given machine, location, design, fulfils requirements most economically, then it releases more resources utilisable for the satisfaction of other wants. This sets up the presumption that it is the best choice to make. True, this presumption can be shown to be mistaken. Kalecki once said: 'The worst thing to do is not to calculate; the second worst thing is to follow blindly the results of your calculation.' There may be reasons, known to *all* economies, for taking a different decision: external effects, regional policies, and so on. This was known even to the tsar's ministers when they decided to build railways, and it is known to the East European reformers.

It is simply not good enough to quote approvingly Stalin's 1952 dictum about profitability from the standpoint of the whole economy. To consider *each* decision from such a standpoint is totally impracticable, because the size of resultant bureaucracy would be counterproductive and self-defeating. In all economies, decision making incurs costs. One *cannot* take all the consequences of everything into account, though ideally no doubt one should. It is necessary to identify those *kinds* of decisions which do have external effects so considerable that intervention of central authority is called for. But even granted that this happens frequently, this does not necessarily justify the emphasis on 'politics' versus 'economics'. Thus, the railway line to Odessa was of immense *economic* benefit to Russia, even though most of this benefit did not show up in the accounts of the railway itself. The Yugoslav government's successful measures to stimulate tourism on the Adriatic coast was not the triumph of politics *over* economics, but the carrying out by the state of sound economic measures. If the state is the principal investor, as must be the case if private capital does not exist, investment decisions are in a formal sense 'political', i.e. they are taken by ministers. But ministers are super-managers. The government must combine its function as board of directors of 'USSR Ltd' with its political function. Why advise it, as Bettelheim seems to do, to put political considerations first? What political considerations? What about Trotsky's 'unlimited room for bureaucratic subjectivism? Would it not have been better for him to speak of the *merging* of the political and economic, in the sort of sense in which the head of the government *is* the head of the economy, *ex officio* chief planner?

Of course, Bettelheim is for responsiveness and rationality, and he hates 'bureaucratic subjectivism' as much as anyone. But *by what criteria*, under his pattern of thinking, can a bureaucratically subjectivist decision on resources allocation or investment be identified as such, and contrasted with the 'correct' decision? One of the most astonishing of his assertions is that 'the domination of the state bourgeoisie' leads to the growth of monetary and market relations, and that this is apparent from the history of the Soviet Union in the past ten years. (Bettelheim, 1970a, p. 87.) Not only is the 'state bourgeoisie' resisting the economic reforms with fair success, but it is somehow implied that the Stalin period was in some undefined respect superior, either because the state was to a greater extent a workers' state, and/or because it was able to a greater extent to impose social-political priorities against commodity-and-market forms. Bettelheim was rather uncritical of Stalin, but surely he knows that bureaucratic indifference to the needs of ordinary people became very deeply ingrained precisely under Stalin's rule, *and* that arbitrary irrationalities in economic decision making were exceedingly common. With all its imperfections, the Soviet system under Brezhnev is surely somewhat more alive to people's needs, more conscious of the duty to study and provide for them than it was in Stalin's day. True, what Bettelheim calls the 'state bourgeoisie' feel more secure from arbitrary arrest, and their individual needs may be better catered for. This must be taken into account in any serious 'class' analysis of the present-day Soviet system. But it would be far-fetched, would it not, to ignore the reduction in wage differentials, the housing programme and a few other features of 'the past ten years', and to imply that somehow the working-class or socialist principles were in better shape in 1952 than in 1972.

Perhaps by the priority of politics Bettelheim has in mind the priority of the struggle to achieve socialism, as against a 'pure' economic rationality. But he continues to insist on this even under socialism, even under conditions where it is by no means clear who is struggling with whom for what. He should clarify.

Bettelheim himself admits an evolution in his thinking: he now realises that state ownership plus planning is not of itself enough, indeed does not prevent the emergence of a new ruling class, the 'state bourgeoisie'. (Bettelheim, 1970b, pp. 8–9.) Good. One wishes he were clearer about the connection between central planning (i.e. the systematic replacement of market relations) and the power of the political-planning-managerial machine. In the name of what Marxist-analytical principle should one expect them *not* to take advantage of their social situation? Is this not idealism? Is it sensible to compare an imaginary perfect harmony in a moneyless economy with imperfect markets? This is like a Western right-wing scholar comparing perfect competition and optimal resource allocation *à la* Chicago with the messy reality of the USSR, a procedure I once defined as 'comparing model with muddle'.

Finally, let us get down to a key point of the entire argument. Bettelheim *rightly* relates 'commodity production' not to property but to fragmentation, division. It follows that he must face a contradiction. If *'les producteurs immédiats'* are to feel that their means of production are under their control, then clearly they must be in a position to decide what is done with them. In Yugoslavia, the elected management committee decides by reference to the market. In his scheme, the decisions *must* logically be subordinate to the planning apparatus. A factory making sulphuric acid or machine tools is a segment of a closely inter-related whole, as Bettelheim knows, indeed insists. In the absence of market-type links with the rest of the economy, the workers can no more be allowed to decide on their own what they should do than the railwaymen at Crewe can decide what trains should run through Crewe. When, in a market economy, systematic links are very tight-knit, they are often of a non-market type. The use of Crewe station is such an example. Not the invisible but the visible hand governs its operations. Of course, a 'socialist' Crewe would also be in this position, taking *instructions* about its operations. Bettelheim's marketless world of collectivities must also be subject to the visible hand. How can they decide for themselves? Every decision about what to produce, whom to supply, whence to draw inputs, has external effects, in the sense that it calls for economic decisions and has consequences in places for which the given collectivity is not responsible; it has consequences which it cannot even estimate. It is *not* a question of pessimistic assumptions about the goodness of Man. We are discussing the identification of what is the right thing for Men (or a given group of men) to do, what Man *must* know to be able to take decisions.

To operate such a system requires a large body of officials. At the very least it must lead to the danger of bureaucratic deformation. Appeals to democracy are of little relevance, not because democracy is unimportant, but because it is hard indeed to apply it to the complex task of managing and planning a moneyless economy. A simple example will suffice. The phrase 'voting with the ruble' has some operational meaning as a guide to what people might prefer, though the mechanism does work imperfectly in the real world and cannot be expected to be perfect. But 'voting through the ballot-box' *cannot* be an operational means for ascertaining people's wants, save in the form of very broad priorities which are at best general indications to planners (e.g. more housing and schools). The ballot-box is even less relevant to decisions about the use of plastics, alternative ways of power generation or other questions to do with means.

Of course, one could envisage upward and downward communications, involving citizens as consumers, production units, local authorities, industrial associations, planners, political leaders. But the existence of information flows cannot, with the best will in the world, be more than the first precondition for correct choice between alternatives. It can quite easily multiply the number of possible courses of action between which choices must be made.

Bettelheim seems silently to ignore the question of conflicts of interest, apparently believing that in a socialist society everyone is in some sort of mystic communion with everyone else. This seems to me to be either Rousseau's '*volonté générale*', or idealism, or both. Of course, class differences can lead to conflict. But are there not other contradictions too? Call them non-antagonistic if you must, but they must go on existing, if only because, to a Marxist, a world without contradictions is a world without movement.

Let us look at a few contradictions relevant to our theme. They all arise from the fact of scarcity in relation to possible or potential desires of people – for beautiful houses, bridges, roads, television sets, clothes, holiday trips, pictures etc. etc. In a world context, even simpler desires are unlikely to be fulfilled for the bulk of the people for many generations, and we must meanwhile organise an economy which is capable of meeting as many needs as possible (subject to constraints imposed by ecology as well as productive capacity). The word 'equality' figures in this book of Bettelheim's as little as does scarcity, but let us assume that he desires a considerable degree of equality. It remains the case that differences of opinion will arise even on what constitutes equality. (Per family or per capita? What compensations for unpleasant nature of job, heavy responsibility etc.; how much interchangeability of occupations? How much higher education should be provided and for whom?) Inhabitants in a given area will strive for improvements which inhabitants elsewhere might prefer to have in *their* area. Producers of a given product might prefer not to make the effort needed to give greater pleasure to the users of the product, claiming (and how will it be disproved?) that the effort is greater than the extra satisfaction which it yields. Professor Bettelheim's wish to extend library holdings in Paris on his subject may come into conflict with the wishes of his confrères in the University of Rennes (or of Calcutta). My desire for a new theatre in Glasgow is not necessarily shared by those who wish to build more houses or schools instead.

All these examples are unrelated to class conflict. They must occur if resources are insufficient to meet needs. Some of these conflicts have to be reconciled by a political process in all systems. My point is that Bettelheim *puts into this process the whole economy*, even while he withdraws such objective guidelines (via the hated 'law of value' and price mechanism) as can be available to the decision makers.

The whole complex issue of centralisation-decentralisation is complex precisely because people see things differently at different levels. This is so partly because of their situation (i.e. what they know, what they are responsible for), partly because of interest. ('Nobody who has wealth to distribute ever omits himself,' wrote Trotsky. Please note the word *'ever'*.) One cannot assert that the right action will always be discerned either at the centre, or the periphery, or at some intermediate level. Bettelheim does agree that a variety of organisational forms would be necessary. What he seems unable to grasp is that, in a modern integrated economy, the lower levels will have nothing to guide them except instruction from the higher levels, *unless* they base their activities on some objective criterion such as might be provided (though imperfectly) by price-and-market signals. The invisible hand *might* be consistent with workers' self-management. The visible hand *must* imply a vastly complicated system of instructions and administrative allocation, operated by a large and complex group of people whose role and functions incline them to bureaucratism. The 'struggle' against bureaucratism could not be carried on by fine phraseology (to which the French language well lends itself) about the toiling masses, or even by denouncing bureaucracy. One must devise ways in which *objective* measurement becomes both a check on bureaucratic distortion and a guideline to the conscientious official anxious to do his job well. Alternatively, one must find means to remove from the 'bureaucrats' responsibility for various decisions, which compels one to seek alternative *criteria*, which enables one to dispense with overcentralisation. How is all this to be done? In Bettelheim's transition period it cannot be done at all if economists advise the government that they should alter prices so as to facilitate the achievement of the plan. If they do this, they cannot discover a basis of determining what the plan should be. It is by no means clear to me how they determine it when 'socialism' in Bettelheim's sense is reached.

I wish that Bettelheim, or those who think like him, would criticise the Hungarian or Soviet reformers from a standpoint which bears some relation to what in fact could be *done*, within a reasonable time-span, in the countries concerned. Might he not at least contemplate the possibility that the attempt to replace 'the law of value' with central resource allocation is itself partly responsible for the bureaucratic deformation that he denounces? How can a 'worker' state' be one, or remain one for long, if a multitude of officials control the productive apparatus of the economy? They *are* the substitute for the market, a substitute also, surely, for meaningful 'self-management'. To fulminate about the bureaucratic behaviour of bureaucrats is satisfying to the psyche, but is not very useful. The *zamglavmetalsnab* in Moscow acts as he does because of the whole logic of his functions, not through ideological backsliding or hostility to 'the working class' from which he has himself probably sprung. In Mao's China he might have to spend a period hoeing cabbages in a village, but I doubt if this will affect his behaviour as a *zam*.

This is not an attack on socialism, or a disguised glorification of the market mechanism in any form: only a plea for some hard thinking and for avoiding question-begging generalities. It is unreasonable to ask Bettelheim for any *precise* blueprint of his future world, but it is not unreasonable to request him to indicate in the most general form how his economy *might* function. Quotations from Marx and Engels are not enough. In his speech following the death of Lenin, Bukharin listed a number of phenomena which had arisen since the death of Marx and could not have been known to him. He asked: 'What do we mean by Marxism? It is a methodology – a system of investigating social phenomena . . . is it a certain set of ideas . . . and in addition a set of concrete guidelines (*polozhenii*)? He then went on to assert, rightly, that Leninism, while consistent with Marxist methodology, went beyond 'the sum of ideas that Marx actually had' about the reality which he knew. (Heitman, 1970, pp. 223–4. *Lenin kak marksist*, 1924.) Marx and Engels, especially the Engels of *Anti-Dühring*, could simply have been mistaken about how a modern industrial socialist economy could be run, just as they might well have been astonished had they seen Russia as the first country with a 'Marxist' regime. Other things which they could not have foreseen could have modified their views. They did several times insist, did they not, that the shape of a future socialism was not known to them?

Counter-attack invited. *Messieurs, c'est à vous de tirer.*

8

Some Developments in East European Economic Thought

The state of Soviet economics at Stalin's death was well described by the late Professor V. Dyachenko:

'Until recently, dogmatism and scholasticism (*nachyotnichestvo*) showed themselves quite openly in quotationism. Instead of independent and deep economic research, the authors of many works busied themselves with a selection of, and commentary on, quotations. Facts were selected and presented merely to illustrate and to confirm the assertions contained in the quotations. Matters went so far that the number of quotations was regarded as an indication of the author's erudition. An economist who found a quotation which had not been used many times in the works of other economists considered himself a creative researcher. After serious criticism of dogmatism and scholasticism in the party press, quotationism diminished, but only on the surface. In many instances matters went no further than the omission of quotation marks, editorial redrafting of the quotations, but in essence things remained unchanged.'

He went on: 'The elaboration of key problems of political economy is most backward. For many years not a single solid theoretical work has been published in this field.' (*VEk*, no. 10, 1955, pp. 3–4.) Great indeed has been the progress in recent years. In the words of Alfred Zauberman, a leap from the abacus to the computer. From dreary apologetics, and works with titles such as 'Raise still higher the productivity of the pulp and paper industry', the best economists of the Soviet 'sphere' have moved to levels of sophistication and subtlety which can stand comparison with any, as I shall endeavour to show.

However, Soviet economics did not begin in the 1950s. What had happened was once described by Wassili Leontief as 'the fall and rise of Soviet economics'. The Stalin regime destroyed a flourishing and original science, and did it so thoroughly that very few survived the prisons and camps to which they were dispatched. I met one such survivor in Moscow in 1969: Albert Lvovich Vainshtein, one-time deputy head of the research institute of the People's Commissariat of

Paper presented at symposium to mark the 500th anniversary of the University of Uppsala, to be published by Croom, Helm, London.

Finance, whose director in the twenties was the world-famous Kondratiev, of the 'long-wave' trade cycle theory. Both men were arrested in 1930. Vainshtein told me of his own fifteen years in prison and exile, and that Kondratiev had been sentenced to twenty-five years when he was re-tried in 1938, and had died in prison in 1940, in a state of mental collapse. Yet his name was still appearing, twenty years later, as an honorary vice-president of the Econometric Society! May I add that Vainshtein himself, after his rehabilitation, had time to write some valuable books and articles, including one on 'The national income of Russia and the Soviet Union', before his death in 1970. He was able to publish a (delayed) obituary on another notable economist of the twenties, Fel'dman, about whom Domar wrote a well-known essay. Also arrested and imprisoned, Fel'dman was able to resume in exile his previous profession of engineer, and in due course returned to Moscow and died there, without writing another word of economics. Less drastic was the fate of Slutsky, whose famous 1915 article on demand functions is known to many. He was never arrested, but simply fell silent.

One day many other distinguished Russian economists of the period will receive belated recognition. They are virtually unknown in their own country. Western writing on this period, with very few exceptions, has been confined to one controversy: the so-called industrialisation debate, primarily a dispute within the party, whose principal protagonists were Bukharin and Preobrazhensky. Both are worthy of a mention in any history of economic thought, particularly Preobrazhensky, who developed with skill and ingenuity the Marxian two-sector growth model, extending it to the relationship between large-scale industry and the petty commodity (mainly peasant) sector, in the context of 'primitive socialist accumulation'. But alongside the *political* economists were eminent professionals, mainly non-party or former Mensheviks, who worked mainly in the various planning and financial institutions, and who responded positively and constructively to the challenge of the time: that of devising a development strategy with appropriate investment criteria. In the one Western work devoted to these men, J.-M. Collette drew our attention to the fact that they were far ahead of their time, raising many basic issues of development economics thirty years before these matters were taken seriously in the West (Collette, 1968). Bazarov, Maslov, Yurovsky, Bernshtein-Kogan, Yushkov, Barengol'ts, these are some of the names, which probably mean nothing to you; but they discussed, fifty years ago, such matters as choice between labour-saving and capital-saving investments under conditions of labour surplus, the theory of comparative costs in the context of an industrialisation programme, the choice of priorities in a development strategy. Such concepts as backward and forward linkages, or the debate about balanced and unbalanced growth, or the extent to which plans should reflect current requirements ('genetic') or aim at fundamental structural change ('teleological') were tackled. Other men, among whom Popov and Groman should be mentioned, struggled to draft a 'balance of the national economy', a first crude ancester of input-output tables. At this period, with hardly any exception, Western 'mainstream' economics was totally unconcerned with growth, or development, or investment criteria. These men were pioneers.

This was the consequence of the situation of their country in the period of 'NEP': a mixed economy, but with the 'commanding heights' in the hands of the state. The Soviet Union's economic potential was vast, and the government was bound to desire the resumption of industrialisation begun under the tsars: for national security, and also to enlarge the proletariat and the material basis of a future socialism, in a largely peasant country. How was this to be accomplished? Given that the bulk of industrial and 'infrastructure' investments would be made by the state, by what criteria should the resources be allocated? Circumstances placed all these questions on the agenda, and the economists of the period tried to consider the answers. At the same time the first attempts at deliberate planning of the 'proportions' of the economy compelled the study of the existing interconnections of the various sectors of which it was composed. Leontief developed input-output *techniques* long after he left Russia, but I am sure he would not deny that the situation in the Russia of his youth started him thinking about the 'balance of the national economy'. (In *PKh*, no. 12, 1925, Leontief commented on the first efforts of Soviet statisticians to construct a balance of the national economy, which he described as a species of *tableau économique*.) Did the Russian discussions of the twenties have any influence on Western postwar development economies? Apart from Leontief, I can trace two possible lines of influence. One relates to Kurt Martin (Mandelbaum), author of one of the pioneering Western works, who told me that, in Germany, he had closely followed the Russian controversies. The other line stretches from Fel'dman through Domar. But of course circumstances played a decisive role, and the bulk of Western development economists were quite unaware that they had Russian predecessors.

How far all this was from the interests of even the most distinguished and imaginative Western economists of the twenties.

Yet within a very few years almost every one of the participants of the debates – whether Bolsheviks or no – were in prison. Bukharin and Preobrazhensky were both shot. They at least could be said to have been punished for their politics by a vengeful Stalin. But why imprison economists, why snuff out a debate which was surely of value to the regime itself? Was it not important to devise criteria for the best use of scarce capital, for instance? It may be objected that static, conventional profitability criteria are of no use at a time of drastic, politically directed structural change. True. But the best of the economists of the twenties were not advocating such criteria, accepting (as did Bazarov, for instance) the need for developmental priorities. And what objection could be made to the 'balances' method, which could help to ensure the necessary material underpinning of investment plans?

I think that the answer is as follows. An essential part of the Stalinist despotism was the enthronement of the arbitrary, and therefore the rejection of objective criteria, by which the actions of party and government could be judged. One does not judge the infallible; it is *lèse-majesté* to try. With this went the 'campaign' or military approach to planning: one spoke of 'fronts', 'bridgeheads', 'shock-brigades'; 'there are no fortresses the Bolsheviks cannot take'. If a bottleneck developed, one launched a 'battle' to enlarge it. A claim that objective difficulties existed was, for a time, treated almost as evidence of 'right-wing deviation'. To demand the apparently impossible was all the more necessary because in all probability reserves were being concealed. This was 'unbalanced growth' with a vengeance. Mass mobilisation, forced labour, suppression of data, exaggerated claims to success, the disaster of forcible collectivisation, the virtual elimination of market forces, artificial and 'passive' prices, left little room indeed for economists and economics.

In this atmosphere, as is evident, not only non-Marxist but orthodox-Marxist theories withered. No textbook on economics was in fact published between 1930 and 1954 (and the 1954 textbook was appallingly bad). Subtle variations on Marxian value theory devised by the distinguished scholar I. Rubin were denounced, their author abused and killed. Even generalisations on planning methods were suspect. A textbook was being written by the chairman of Gosplan, Voznesensky, when he was arrested in 1949. The manuscript was confiscated and has never been found, its author shot. In his very last work, Stalin warned economists off the whole field of planning and economic policy: this was the job of the political organs. It is scarcely surprising that surviving economists dared not advance any original ideas.

None the less, 'oases' appeared in this intellectual desert. The first related to investment criteria of the most practical kind. A given result could be achieved by several means; which was the best? Despite the negative attitude of the more boneheaded ideologists, practical planners did start asking important questions. Khachaturov is an example. The second was Kantorovich's 1939 discovery of 'determining multipliers', linear programming techniques. Here he was helped by the fact that the boneheaded ideologists did not understand the implications of the techniques. But, while he avoided trouble, he had to withdraw into pure mathematics until after Stalin's death, and his ideas were left unused.

There were, needless to say, intelligent individuals who bided their time. Novozhilov, for instance, or Konyus, or in his own way Varga. But, except for a brief false spring in 1946, they were allowed very little scope.

What of Eastern Europe? These countries had different traditions. Czechoslovakia and Hungary had been greatly influenced by the Austrian school, but Poland possessed three eminent economists who were of the socialist persuasion: Lange, Kalecki and Lipinski. (We should in passing pay tribute to Edward Lipinski, who, soon to be 90, is even now publicly demanding reform and intellectual freedom in his country.) However, Stalinist order was imposed after the first postwar years, in Poland as in other parts of Soviet-controlled Europe. Here as well as in Russia, original ideas could develop only after the death of the despot. Lange, in a lecture in Belgrade in 1957, spoke of the Stalinist phase as 'a war economy *sui generis*', and this, as well as the specifically political factors, helps to explain the down-grading of economic theory. The quartermaster-general of any army allocates scarce resources, but he is not, as a rule, an economist.

Economics revived rapidly once it was understood that Stalin really was dead, but at a very uneven rate in different countries, and indeed in different segments of the discipline. Some official apologists ascribe the rapidly growing interest in allocational efficiency to the shift from extensive to intensive growth, but this is to oversimplify. True enough, by the mid-fifties the shift of peasants to the cities had slowed down in the USSR, and more attention came to be paid to raising capital and labour productivity. But the more advanced countries – Czechoslovakia and East Germany, for instance – were already well into the 'intensive' stage. While not as highly developed, it was not because it was appropriate to their needs that Hungary or Poland had adopted Soviet practice (and theory, such as it was). The political requirement to copy the Soviet Union was the primary cause. As for the Soviet Union itself, an important factor was the shift in priorities, or rather their dilution: it became necessary to stress the needs of agriculture, housing, consumers' goods, retail trade, and this caused much greater consideration of scarcity in relation to competing needs. In addition, the growth of the economy placed very great strain on the 'traditional' techniques of centralised planning.

The revival of the subject was thus due partly to the autonomous actions of the brighter economists, no longer terror-stricken, partly to the much greater interest in efficiency of the party-state leadership (an interest itself caused by new challenges and new problems), and the promise that new methods could enable them to satisfy more of the urgent needs of their society, and thus enhance the political security of the regime. In some countries, however, the dogmatists were powerfully entrenched and took longer to shift, and they were particularly strong in their defence of Marxian value-theory (as they understood it) against any 'mathematical' marginalist innovations. The need to improve planning methods, and the evident relevance to this of computers and programming, forced the dogmatists to retreat, in this sector at least, though they still counter-attack. Oddly enough, some of the strongest opposition is within Gosplan. Or maybe it is not so odd: one of the opponents of new methods claimed that if there were indeed an effective objective criterion for an optimal plan, 'active planning would from that moment be liquidated'. (Boyarsky, 1962, p. 347.) In other words, planners beware! You have nothing to lose but your jobs! (Surely there is no such danger!)

A full survey of ideas and personalities in Eastern Europe would require a long book. It therefore follows that I will have to concentrate on a few selected issues and individuals. The choice will inevitably be a subjective one.

What role can be ascribed to Marxist political economy in the development of East European theory? This is a highly complex question. One must disentangle Marx's methodology from the use to which it is put by dogmatic conservatives, and indeed also by those who are not Marxists at all, but who must quote Marx or Lenin in order to get a hearing for their views. A vital question concerns the relevance and applicability of Marxian value theory in the Soviet context. For this theory was primarily concerned with capitalism, it analysed a market economy in which economic laws manifested themselves spontaneously. Marxian value theory dwells on a high level of abstraction, and was much more concerned with surplus value, exploitation, 'the relations of production', than either with microeconomics or with the problems of a planned socialist economy. Indeed, an important element of the Marxist tradition (represented, for instance, by Plekhanov and Bukharin) denied the very existence of an *economics* of socialism, in so far as economics was concerned with unplanned exchange, purchase-and-sale, 'commodity production'. Others do not deny that some form of economics would exist under socialism, but it would not be concerned with commodity production. In a real socialism, under conditions of abundance, production would be directly for use, not for exchange, there would be no market, no prices, no inequality of income or of function.

However, I must add, unlike most Western neo-classical theorists, Soviet and East European economists have to take into account the problems of planning and of efficiency in the world in which they live. In order to grapple with the theoretical, as well as practical, issues involved, they had to clear away what could be called vulgar-Marxist or dogmatic obstacles. Thus one can scarcely ignore opportunity-cost merely because Marx did not refer to it directly in expounding his value theory. (Novozhilov devoted many pages to 'legitimising' this concept, which is taken for granted by first-year students in the West, in his contribution to *The Use of Mathematics in Economics*.) (Nemchinov, 1964.) The factor Time is of evident importance. So is demand elasticity. Even if rent was a source of exploitation income under capitalism, land cannot be treated by planners as a free good. Marxists dislike marginal utility, but decisions of a marginal character are none the less taken, and marginal valuations ('objectively determined valuations', to use Kantorovich's phrase) emerge from computerised programming.

The problem of utility, or use-value, gave the reforming economists a lot of trouble. The issue was presented in its most vivid form in three articles in the house organ of the Mathematical Economic Institute (TsEMI) in Moscow. (*EkMM*, no. 6, 1974, nos. 1 and 2, 1975.) Planners choose. In choosing they make valuations, aiming at maximising social utility. Of course, there are problems in defining what one is maximising (more of this in a moment), but quite plainly it cannot be *labour* values. Only in and through a market can labour values be brought into conformity with use-values. This is indeed so: the mere fact that the same effort (howsoever measured) has been expended on two baskets of goods cannot, of itself, lead to the conclusion that the two baskets have the same value (value-in-use) for society, or indeed for anyone.

This attracted a vigorous counter-attack from an intelligent dogmatist, Yakov Kronrod. (*PKh*, no. 8, 1975.) He takes the authors to task for heresy: Marx said in *Das Kapital* that commodities have in common *only* the fact that labour is expended in their production. Utility, marginal utility especially, is subjective-value-theory and hence doctrinally invalid. Utility is indeed a precondition for any product to have any value, but utilities of different products are incommensurate. He also refuses to accept that the 'law of value' does not operate in socialist planning.

Some of the 'mathematicians' argued that at least *ordinal* utility comparisons are possible, indeed necessary, and also that one must distinguish between deliberately chosen objectives – which in a socialist society should be related to social utility and not to Marxian 'values' – and micro-economic operational choices, *within* the broad objectives of the central plan. The central plan *cannot* encompass micro-economic detail. This has therefore to be settled by negotiation between autonomous productive units, whose actions will be influenced by their material interests. In *this* area the 'law of value' (i.e. commodity exchange) should and would operate. The implication of this view is that there should be two quite distinct principles of pricing (or valuations): those derived from the attempt to write an optimal programme in pursuit of (necessarily aggregated) social objectives, which can be seen as planners' shadow prices, and the current prices used in current micro-economic transactions. *Neither* would in practice conform to Marxian labour-values, because both would have to be influenced by considerations of relative scarcity and utility. (I doubt if this would unduly worry Marx, as distinct from his dogmatic followers; as another mathematical economist, Petrakov, pointed out, it is improper to have equilibrium prices in non-equilibrium situations. Nor would Marx expect fillet steak and oxtail to have the same 'value' because the same amount of labour is expended on their production!)

So one can discern two very different approaches to Marxian 'values': one, probably the majority view, asserts that the law of value does operate, but that the vulgar-dogmatists have misunderstood the relationship between this 'law' and *any* price system. Nowhere do actual prices conform to the law of value (or to its 'transformed form') because the real world abounds in disequilibria, joint products etc. Quotations can be assembled from the Marxian classics to show that it is 'an illusion that the prices of an optimal plan [i.e. the duals] do not have a value content', to cite Novozhilov. (Fedorenko, 1964, p. 321.) The other school, as we have seen, separates the programming procedures and the derived duals from the 'law of value' altogether, but (unlike Bettelheim) sees the necessity for its survival in the micro-economic area, where some species of market relations are irreplaceable.

This leads one to the fundamental issue debated by economists in many 'Eastern' countries: what sort of controlled market models are feasible, what sort of mix between central planning and managerial autonomy? Can the two principles coexist? Is there in fact any alternative in real life, given that a fully disaggregated central plan is quite obviously impossible, even with more and better computers?

Impossible it certainly is. Novozhilov (in 1964!) quoted Glushkov's quip that, with existing methods, the entire population of the Soviet Union would have to be engaged in planning by 1980. Antonov, the aircraft designer, remarked that 'Kiev mathematicians have calculated that, in order to draft an accurate and fully integrated plan of material-technical supply just for the Ukraine for one year, one requires the labour of the entire world's population for ten million years. (Antonov, 1965, p. 23.) (Well, maybe not *ten* million years.)

There is a rich field here. To cite Novozhilov again, 'the degree of conformity of "local" criteria with general criteria can serve as the criterion of the optimality of the organisation of economic management' (op. cit., p. 315). Soviet, Hungarian, Polish and Czech economists pointed out, with a wealth of detail, how the attempt at an impossible centralisation, with the fulfilment of central plans as the duty of subordinates, failed to stimulate management to act in accordance even with the preferences of the planners, and the adverse effect of all this on quality, innovation, conformity to the needs of users, initiative. The events of 1956 in Poland and Hungary gave a particularly strong impetus to discussions there. Alternative models were proposed. In Poland the discussions, though of great interest as such, led to few changes. Of particular interest has been the work of W. Brus on socialist models containing elements of market and plan, and workers' participation, and the relationship of these things to changes in the political system. A number of distinguished Polish economists, including Brus, have had to leave that country, and the centralised system has only cautiously been modified by giving greater autonomy to industrial associations. In Hungary, however, important reforms in 1968 introduced much stronger elements of market into the system. This has given rise to a fascinating literature on the costs and benefits of this type of reform, the expected and unexpected snags that arise in an endeavour to combine macro-economic (and 'mezzo-economic') planning with a controlled micro-economic market. Important indeed is the role of prices in such an economy. One learns of the need for competition and the obstacles to it, the dangers of inflation, the method and problems of control over incomes, the function of banking and credit, the criteria appropriate to foreign trade, and so on. The writings in Hungary of B. Csikos-Nagy on prices, the late I. Vajda and S. Ausch on foreign trade, and the Polish studies on foreign trade criteria by W. Trzeciakowski, are just a few noteworthy contributions from the smaller countries of Eastern Europe. One should also mention the recent work of Rybakov in the USSR on foreign trade criteria. More should probably be said here about Kalecki's postwar output. Those interested may be referred to a recent book wholly devoted to Kalecki by G. R. Feiwel, of the University of Tennessee. Kalecki developed an interesting growth model. My excuse for not analysing it is that I am allergic to growth models in general. (This 'allergy' found unexpected support from a highly sceptical seminar paper on the subject delivered in Glasgow by Evsei Domar.)

But we must return to the issue of the 'join' between central plans and micro-economic decision making, between centre and periphery. 'The central planning bodies,' wrote Maurice Dobb, 'should concentrate their attention and their refined techniques upon the macro-economic-relations and magnitude of the system, defining and establishing the structural framework within which the (limited) autonomy of enterprises should operate. Here it is not easy at first sight to see where the line between the macro and the micro should be drawn.' (Abramsky and Williams, 1974, p. 335.) It cannot be drawn, as Dobb suggests, between investment and current output, if only because investment goods *are* current output. We have seen that some of the 'mathematicians' wish to draw the line between aggregated objectives and disaggregated detailed operations. But the problem of the 'join' remains. How can the small magnitudes be made to add up to the desired large ones? If the latter are built up out of the former, then the plan is but the summation of the micro-market, and the purpose and advantage of planning disappear. True, information derived from the market is important for the central plan itself: how can one know what people want unless they have the opportunity to 'vote with the ruble', thereby revealing their preferences? The same argument applies to choice of means: working managers often know best what kinds of equipment or materials they require. So in practice there has to be an interpenetration of micro-demand and the aggregated plans, each influencing the other. Easy to write such a sentence. Less easy to achieve in practice. But the attempt has to be made. There must be a search for optimal decision-making structures.

In this connection, it is useful again to quote Novozhilov: he stressed how often lower-level management and its subordinates are motivated to conceal potential and to distort information flows. If this can be altered, 'this would give greater potential for growth of the socialist economy than would mathematical programming if the existing relations between higher and lower echelons are retained'. (Fedorenko, 1969, p. 32.) One must find ways of encouraging initiative and the flow of correct information, while providing criteria for autonomous decision making below the level of the centre, and make it conform to the (aggregated) plan.

This brings one to the role of prices and profitability as 'the' local criterion. In naive formal models their role seems clear enough. The optimal plan prices, which emerge from the programme, which indeed are an integral part of the programming process, can be used as the basis for local optimisation, so that 'what is profitable for the enterprise is also profitable for the economy as a whole'. Alas, this is all much too simple.

East European experience should also help us all to rethink the theoretical treatment of monopoly. One-dimensional marginalism is usually accompanied by two-dimensional monopoly theory: the two variables are volume and price. From this it might follow that it is sufficient to set an upper limit to price, or else set some financial target (e.g. a given rate of return) to give a nationalised industry the necessary operational or investment guidelines. This is plainly not so. Thus, to take an example 'borrowed' from Poland, the retail trade organisation will show the economically 'best' results if customers are standing in line all day and every day: one gets the highest product-

ivity per employee, the most effective use of buildings, the lowest costs
in relation to the volume of sales. To improve service would worsen
these indicators, and lower profits, too. Conversely, the worsening of
quality and of after-sales service, and also of such indicators as
reliability, punctuality etc., will usually 'pay' *unless* there is fear of
competition (i.e. there is a financial penalty for loss of goodwill), *or*
unless there is a *duty* (imposed if necessary) to provide goods and
services of some defined quality or standard. Western textbooks on
micro-economics will, practically without exception, have no entry in
the index for goodwill, duty, standards or even quality (or, for that
matter, sub-contractors), despite their evident significance in real life.
Hence some remarkably naive criteria proposed for nationalised
industries, for instance in Britain. Hence also some rather naive advice
to East European reformers: the 'advisers' forget that the profit motive
under monopoly can produce some perverse results.

Many economists have pointed to the reason why the role of prices,
though of great importance, 'should in no circumstances be overstated',
to quote the words of the Soviet mathematical economist, Pugachev.
(Pugachev, 1968.) Malinvaud made the same point in his contribution
to an international symposium in Moscow: 'The price system that a
statistician can construct by observing actual price schedules and
transactions is a very poor thing in comparison with these theoretical
requirements' (for plan optimisation). (Khachaturov, p. 26.)

Kornai, the able and original Hungarian, devoted to this same point
many pages of his book *Anti-equilibrium*, stressing the vital importance
of non-price information, especially with regard to the future.
Pugachev pointed out the limitations of conventional criteria whenever
major structural changes are involved. Thus if one is seeking to decide
upon 'the growth over five years in the production of mineral
fertiliser', the decision is essentially non-incremental and will itself
affect prices and profitability in the future, and not only in the
fertiliser industry. (Pugachev, 1968.) This is partly a short-run versus
long-run problem; in the short run we can assume that production
decisions will not greatly influence demand. However, to cite the
director of the Siberian Institute of Economics, Aganbegyan, in the
longer run 'success in developing production generates new demands
and modifies the objective. In normal optimisation problems . . . there
is ordinarily no inter-relation of objectives and means'. (Khachaturov,
1976, p. 76.)

It is worth mentioning that the work on investment criteria in the
context of structural change, by V. Krasovsky and Y. Kvasha, with
its stress on complementarities, interdependencies and sequences, is
far more realistic than the conventional presentation of investment
criteria in Western textbooks. (Who has not read dreary essays, by
students whom we teach, on the difference between internal rate of

return and discounted cash flow in the comparison of investment variants, as if this were the key issue!)

Corresponding to the problem of decentralised decision making is that of disaggregated prices. The prewar Lange model envisaged the central planning board 'managing' the economy through setting the prices to which socialist managers reacted as would textbook entre-preneurs under competitive capitalism. The model was unreal for a number of reasons: it abstracted from growth, technical progress, structural change, externalities and indeed motivation of all con-cerned. It abstracted, too, from the unmanageably large number of prices to be administered.

Lange wrote in 1938, before the computer era. In postwar years he wrote on economic cybernetics, but the number of prices remains unmanageable. In the words of Novozhilov, 'in view of the enormous magnitude of the national-economic plan, the prices corresponding to [the optimal plan], the duals, can relate only to a relatively small number of aggregated groups of commodities'. (Fedorenko, 1969, p. 30.) An optimising programme might conceivably contain a thousand commodity groups. One of them would be 'agricultural machinery'. But there is no price for agricultural machinery. There are prices for at least a thousand different agricultural machines. How, then, does one disaggregate?

Two approaches may be identified. One, typified by Pugachev, lays stress on consecutive aggregation, with plans and prices at various levels linked with the help of 'algorithms based on the principal of iterative aggregation'. Since he also speaks of 'horizontal' micro-economic links, his implied model must resemble that put forward by the TsEMI 'mathematicians' referred to earlier, i.e. a micro-economic market, which (to re-use my previous example) would actually deter-mine the prices of manure-spreaders, harrows, ploughs etc. etc. A somewhat different approach was developed by V. Nemchinov: he envisaged the central planning agencies acting as principal and bargaining with enterprises about prices and conditions under which the enterprises would carry out the tasks of the plan. This certainly implies prices which are determined by negotiation, but the practical implications of the proposal are obscure. (Those interested in the practical limitations and possibilities of price control may be referred to the works of B. Csikos-Nagy.)

Inevitably one is very far here from prices conforming to 'values', since relative scarcities are of key importance. So, needless to say, is opportunity-cost, or 'feedback costs', as Novozhilov called them. Terekhov, another of the 'mathematicians', pointed out that since Marxian values depend on, indeed are defined as, the quantity of labour used, '*any* production plan in which resources are fully used would be optimal' in terms of labour-values (provided, let it be added, that the products are of *some* use), and therefore one cannot usefully try to optimise the 'value' of output in this sense. (Terekhov, 1968, p. 185.)

Structures, hierarchies, centre-periphery relationships, the valuations appropriate to the problem of connecting local (or partial) with national-economic optimising, bring to the fore two questions to which 'Eastern' economists have been devoting much attention: one is the problem of defining meaningfully an *economic optimum on the scale of the economy as a whole*, the other is the analysis of the economy as a *hierarchical system*. Both appear to me to be areas of great importance for economics, to which our 'Eastern' colleagues are contributing much and will contribute a lot more.

Let us begin with the first of these questions. The view used to be expressed that programming techniques are peculiarly applicable to a Soviet-type system because, unlike the West, the institutional means exist to determine (and enforce) objectives. In this interpretation, the party leadership decides what society needs, and the techniques of programming and optimisation will enable these objectives to be realised most expeditiously, the vast number of simultaneous equations being solved by computers. This view is certainly wrong. Not only because the sheer volume of micro-decision-making would overwhelm the planning apparatus, but also because 'the party' or 'the central planners' are in practice a coalition of interest groups, with quite different ideas as to how resources should be utilised and for what purposes. I call this 'centralised pluralism'. In his excellent paper, Malinvaud pointed out that 'to regard the decision process as the solution of a mathematical programme assumes a single decision-maker. But this is never the case. Actual processes involve many participants whose interests inevitably conflict.' (Khachaturov, 1976, p. 34.) Radmila Stojanovic, of Yugoslavia, put the same points as follows: 'The problem of finding an answer arises when there are many conflicting objectives, such as is the case in all social systems'. (ibid., p. 152.) She spoke of the plan 'as the broadest social coalition'. In any case, planners' preferences have to be based on something other than the preferences of the planners. As one Soviet mathematical economist puts it in private conversation: 'We cannot use the desires of the party leadership as the objective criterion, because the party leadership turns to us for advice as to what its objectives should be. If we reply that our criterion for correct action is what the leadership decides, we would be quite useless.' The maximisation of some aggregate measure, such as national income or growth rates, plainly will not do. One has only to recall the title of that old article of Peter Wiles, 'Growth versus choice'. No single general formulation can possibly be satisfactory. The debate continues, as it must.

Probably most 'Eastern' economists would agree with I. Birman that 'there are no reasons why it is impossible to determine a national-economic criterion, if it really exists. However, one must sorrowfully admit that so far the attempts to determine it have not been successful'. (Birman, 1971, p. 39. I. Birman has emigrated to the United States.)

Pugachev, while confidently asserting the existence of a 'national-economic criterion of optimality', insists on the many important elements of 'qualitative analysis and choice', which 'immensely complicate' the problem. He and many others have debated at a high level the problem of defining what it is that one is optimising. Conceptually, and to some extent in practice, he considers that the consumers' desires can be identified, so that one could seek either to maximise the quantity of a given assortment (taking demand elasticities into account) or minimise the costs of a given quantity. (He envisages basic limiting variants of a plan, one realistically optimistic, the other realistically pessimistic. Studies of demand elasticities would affect the commodity composition.) By basing much of the analysis on 'statistical studies', he shows that he assumes the existence of a micro-market in which preferences can be revealed. They would be reinforced by other studies of utility and preferences, and he does not exclude the state influencing the pattern of consumption. There is, however, a problem of 'weighting' present as against future needs, since 'any criterion without (time) weighting or with incorrect weighting inevitably leads one to absurd results'. He devotes an interesting chapter to discussing how time-weights should be chosen. One must, of course, add social needs (defence, health, education etc.), and Pugachev here formulates familiar difficulties without being able to resolve them, as is hardly surprising.

Pugachev and other 'realistic mathematicians' insist on the importance of uncertainty, not least in the vitally important area of technical progress. Chernyak, whom we will quote later, in his presentation of systems analysis insists on the necessity of bringing into the decision-making process considerations of 'social, political, moral, ethical and other factors . . . which sometimes have a decisive effect on the formulation of aims and the selection of means and on the valuation of resources', and which 'in principle are not quantifiable'. (Chernyak, 1975, p. 50.) There is no alternative here to seeking expert advice, on the basis of which human (and fallible) decisions have to be taken, and corrected in the light of new information. We are very far here from abstract elegance. Admittedly, we are far also from formally optimal solutions, but in the process of grappling with the real difficulties the East European economists have, I believe, much to teach us about the potential and limitations of programming and optimisation.

Too little has been said here about the pioneering work of Kantorovich, who so deservedly received the Nobel prize last year.

This is partly because this great man's mathematics far surpasses this author's understanding, and partly because the concentration of attention here is on the development of theories which *apply* the techniques of programming and optimisation in the complex circumstances of the real world. To this too Kantorovich has made a notable contribution (in English we have *The Best Use of Economic Resources*, 1965, and also his contributions to *The Use of Mathematics in Economics*) (Nemchinov, 1964), not least in the work he wrote jointly with Makarov (Kantorovich and Makarov, 1965). He fought the first battle against the dogmatists to legitimise his system of shadow prices or duals ('objectively determined valuations'). No words of mine are needed to draw the Western reader's attention to his work and stature.

Less well known, but deserving of close attention, are Novozhilov and Pugachev, whom we have already cited, and also men of a wide range of ages and views: Nemchinov, who did so much to further the new methodologies, Fedorenko, under whose management TsEMI developed so fast and so well, Konyus, Vainshtein, Lurie, and younger men such as Shatalin, Belkin, Dadayan, Volkonsky, Maiminas, Aganbegyan, and also Katsenellenboigen (now in the United States). Valuable work in this field is pursued also in Poland (by Porwit, for instance) and in Hungary (Kornai and Liptak, especially on two-level optimising). No major contribution to these problems has come to notice from East Germany. East Germany has the most efficient economy in the communist world, thereby yet again illustrating the proposition that there is an inverse correlation between the quality of economists and the performance of the economy.

My own view is that a social preference function is inherently undefinable. I agree with Spulber and Horowitz about 'the pitfalls and difficulties that any entire population, a small group of policy makers or a single individual would encounter in attempting to define a preference function to guide social policy'. (Spulber and Horowitz, 1976, p. 87.) It is not surprising that 'Eastern' economists have not resolved the unresolvable. But we can learn a lot from their efforts. The nature of central planning, and the techniques which Kantorovich and his colleagues did so much to develop, virtually compelled them to try. While no model can be satisfactory, the attempt to specify the elements which enter into an objective function at least have the merit of reducing somewhat the area of arbitrariness, by systematically listing the relevant factors. As Kantorovich himself pointed out: 'Sometimes one has to reject models which were the most complete and precise in their design in favour of one which promises practical results even with some loss of perfection.' (Khachaturov, 1976, p. 71.) (When he visited Glasgow in 1966, when we awarded him an honorary doctorate, Kantorovich showed himself quite ready to be realistic, stressing 'the importance of knowing what we do not know' and adjusting to such knowledge. The example he gave in a lecture was women's fashions. Since we do not know what they will be in three years' time, it is rational to choose multiple-purpose rather than narrowly specialised machinery.) Novozhilov too (in conversations with me in Leningrad) was always ready to aim for realistic targets: what he called 'cosmic mathematics' cannot achieve an unrealisable perfection; *better* plan objectives, internally balanced, plus a planning-and-pricing system which motivates subordinates to act consistently with the chosen objectives, would satisfy him. Mathematical methods would help in achieving this.

Now on to systems theory. Here it appears to me the advances have been considerable, and along several lines which may well prove relevant also for the development of Western economics.

A major role must be assigned to Janos Kornai, whom we have already noted as co-author of a work on two-level planning, and indeed also of a book on *Mathematical Planning of Structural Decisions*. The basic ideas in the present context, however, are contained in *Anti-equilibrium*. (Kornai, 1971.) Primarily an attack on neo-classical general equilibrium theories derived from Walrus, this book was motivated by the evident irrelevance of mainstream theory, in East and West alike, to the problems raised by Hungarian economic reform: 'Theory has proven unsuited to practical application. It was my exasperation with its inadequate and unworkable character that inspired this book' (p. xvi). Kornai attacked the obsession with equilibrium, the unreality of the behavioural and institutional assumptions of typical neo-classicism, the deplorable fact that 'macro-economics and micro-economics have developed almost hermetically separated from one another' (p. 373), leaving, be it added, many of the most important problems in the gaping space between them. Kornai emphasised the vital importance of information, uncertainty, organisation, structure, systemic inter-relationships, complementarities. As already mentioned, he showed that rational action is scarcely possible based upon price information alone, particularly over time:

'The nature of the decisions is different in the case of a textile mill deciding to produce 100,000 or 105,000 metres of fabrics next week and an electricity company deciding whether to create a new hydro-electric plant . . . In making the latter decision it is not customary to say: "The price of electricity has risen, so let us build a new power plant", or "The price of electricity has fallen, so there is no need for a new investment in power plants".' (p. 339.)

Kornai and several other 'Eastern' economists have also investigated the causes and consequences of the sellers' market and taut planning, pointing to the *undesirability* of an equilibrium based upon full resource utilisation (and indeed the inconsistency of equilibrium with any dynamics). Thus, even if demand is matched by supply, in aggregate total, it *must* lead to shortages of some items, over-supply of others, because of unpredictability of demand, for particular materials, machines, consumers' goods and services. If I may take an example of my own, if our concept of equilibrium implies that there are no unoccupied seats for lunch (otherwise resources are unemployed, and Pareto conditions are not satisfied), it also requires that consumer preferences on each day for each restaurant – and, presumably, for each item on the menu of each restaurant – are known in advance. But this is nonsense, in any economy that exists or could exist. Consequently many restaurants should have spare capacity. The attempt at precise balance between supply and demand under full employment *must* lead to imbalance, shortage, sellers' markets and all the phenomena associated with these. Kornai calls his book a 'semi-finished product', and it does have loose ends. But its subtitle points the way: '*On economic systems theory*'.

Kornai, and also every thoughtful reformer in Eastern Europe, has to consider the problem of optimal decision-making structures. So, of course, must a realistically inclined Western economist – well, 'any economist who has encountered a real firm (which must, I suppose, exclude the vast majority of the profession)'. (D. P. O'Brien, 1976, p. 621.) Within corporations, as well as in the 'centralist-pluralist' economies of the East, decisions often represent compromises, are the product of coalitions within the management structure. What seems most advantageous must depend in some degree on the area of responsibility of the decision-maker, on the incentives affecting him (or her). Western corporations as well as 'Eastern' economies are complex hierarchies. Since the centre cannot encompass all, there must be division, devolution, some sort of decentralisation, which means boundary lines. Wherever there are boundary lines, there must be problems of sub-optimisation, externalities, conflicts between the partial and the general interest.

Micro-economics is too often taught as if firms behave as maximising automata, 'equating marginal everything with marginal everything else', to cite Shubik's phrase. Of course, the Walrasian system recognises, indeed stresses, the interdependence of everything, but only in the context of infinitely divisible micro-decisions in the market. Contrast the implications of a Soviet (or American) decision to develop oil in West Siberia (or Alaska). Like all major investment decisions, this one requires the best estimate of future supply and demand (alternative sources, costs of other fuels, development plans of oil-using industries, the impact of technical change on costs in the oil industry, and so on). Current prices would be of very little relevance. 'Shadow' prices cannot be calculated without the information about the future. Where is this information most likely to be found and assessed, so that error is minimised? Clearly at the centre. Then, if it is decided to go ahead, there will arise a multitude of choices, of marginal decisions: pipeline or tanker, what sort of pipeline taking what route, where to locate what kind of refining and petro-chemical plants, where to place new settlements in what was a wilderness, what kind of drilling equipment to use etc. etc. But these are not the marginal decisions of the textbook, since they make sense only *within the complex*, being means to a given end, and in this sense the margins are multi-dimensional, best seen as an integral part of a *hierarchical system*.

Soviet theory and practice has had to grapple with this problem. Thus the West Siberian oil complex was the responsibility of several ministries, each of which had its own plan objectives and success criteria. Paradoxically, Western oil firms found it easier to organise the complementary activities in the right sequence, *administered* directly or through a principal-and-sub-contractor relationship.

Independently of Kornai, Soviet mathematical economists developed the concept of optimally functioning hierarchical systems. One sees this in many books and articles, and I will cite only two, with nine years between them: one by Katsenellenboigen, Ovsienko and Fayerman (1966) the other by Chernyak (1975). There is a most interesting parallel between this work and some developments in the West, and it is significant that Chernyak cites Western work on systems theory, which first developed in defence planning (e.g. C. Hitch, S. Young, B. Radwick), but must surely soon 'invade' main-stream economic theory. (My own attempt to combat conventional micro-economics with the aid of systems theory suffered from many shortcomings.) (Nove, 1973.) Recently we have O. Williamson writing significantly of *Markets and Hierarchies*, treating '*transactions*' as the basic units of micro-economics. (Williamson, 1975.) This has its analogy in Soviet formulations, one of which defines the basic unit of decision making as 'an operation' (*operatsiya*), the other as '*a problem*' requiring solutions. Another Western work, significantly by scholars who have studied Soviet planning, has sought to apply the concept of 'multi-level, multi-goal hierarchical systems' to a general analysis of *Quantitative Economic Policy and Planning*, to cite the title of the book. (Spulber and Horowitz, 1976.) Contrasting the neo-classical model of the firm with the real world of real firms, the authors point out (p. 6) that

'management does not make a single output decision for a given production period in isolation from all other problems and aspects of the firm's operations, and its past and future history. Rather the decision-making process in a modern corporation entails a planned *sequence* of decisions – that is a *strategy* – that establishes a prod-uction, pricing and inventory *policy*. This strategy will be followed over a *series* of time-periods, and will evolve *tactics* for dealing with individual *contingencies* that might arise in the future. Modern management must also live with imperfect information.' The emphasis is in the original.

The chapter from which this quotation is taken is entitled 'Policy analysis in a systems control context'. Another vigorous attack on orthodoxy is *Choice, Complexity and Ignorance*. (Loasby, 1976.)

Is this not the road to analytical relevance and realism, not only in micro-economics but also the no-man's-land between micro and macro in which many of the key problems are located?

It is perhaps remarkable that the Russians have been so slow in integrating systems theory and economics, because, given the nature of their planning system and of its hierarchical structure, its problems should have found theoretical expression long ago. (Indeed in the early twenties the highly original maverick Marxist Bogdanov developed a kind of organisation-and-system theory which he called *Tektologiya*.) But even more remarkable is the fact that input-output techniques, so obviously useful to the Soviet planners, should have had to be 'imported' from the West after long delay, or that Kantorovich's brilliant ideas on programming should have lain unused for twenty years and more. This is just part of the cost of Stalinism. Now, however, the brightest economists of the 'East' are able to develop their own ideas, drawing upon their traditional distinction in mathematics, and utilising Western ideas too, though this still meets with resistance in some quarters. It was a major service of the late Academician Nemchinov to Soviet economics to have persuaded the ideological watchdogs to admit input-output and linear programming techniques, and he used as strong supporting arguments the (scientific-ally not very relevant) fact that Leontief graduated in Leningrad and Kantorovich in Moscow. (Internationalism in ideology does not exclude nationalism in practice!) But this was still 1959. The mathematical school today can cite Western authors without apology (though in the USSR at least they must still repel critics who accuse them of replacing Marxism by subjective marginalism).

Whoever has had the patience to read this far will have gathered that this author feels deeply the irrelevance (or triviality) of much of the economics that we teach, and nowhere more than in courses on micro-economics and the theory of the firm. *Of course* one needs formalised theory and quantification, and of course all theories must in some degree abstract from reality. No one, certainly not Kornai, would deny that 'traditional' marginalist micro-economics provides useful insights in respect of certain situations frequently encountered in East and in West. But we all live in a world in which large structure-altering investments, stimulated by the scientific-technical revolution, are made by large and complex organisations. Complementarities, externalities (or 'internalities') (see Nove, 1969, p. 847), interdependencies, hierarchical relationships, margins within margins (exemplified by decisions of the 'not whether but how' type) are far too common to be excluded from the main body of theory, far too important to be relegated to footnotes or 'exceptions'. The inadequate treatment of investment criteria in most textbooks cries out for remedy. (See, for instance, the treatment given this topic by R. Lipsey, in his otherwise very useful textbook.) (Lipsey, 1973.) The systems approach is a very promising one.

In a situation in which Stalinist centralism is patently inadequate, and the authorities require advice about remedies to real ills, the economists' minds in Eastern Europe are increasingly concentrated on devising models which can be judged by the criterion of present or future applicability. The ideological function of Marxism being what it is, orthodox political economy cannot change, but the road does now seem clear for major advances in the direction of integrating systems theory with a realistic economics.

Even in this very abbreviated presentation, it is (I hope) apparent that serious and relevant work is being done. The best of it is rigorous in the proper sense of that much misused word: systematically and rigorously taking into account all the relevant factors, as distinct from producing internally consistent and elegant abstractions. The combination of a problem-oriented systems approach with mathematical techniques, in the skilled hands of people aware of the limitations of purely quantitative analysis, may well lead to important advances in theory, in understanding, and in practice too, though it must be stressed that the existing institutional structures in Eastern Europe are not conducive to the methods of optimal planning, or to the flow of reliable information without which the best techniques become useless. The best work is brave not only because it tackles formidable conceptual obstacles, but also because the implications of the institutional changes proposed or implied represent a challenge to the strongly entrenched interests of the party-state machine.

NOTE

1 See, for instance, Porwit's contribution to Khachaturov, 1976. For a survey of Soviet advance in mathematical economics and programming, see especially Zauberman, 1975, and Ellman, 1971.

Part Three

Contemporary Economic Problems

9

The Politics of Economic Reform

What Reform?
What is it that is being reformed? Essentially, the centralised 'traditional' system inherited from the Stalin era. The basic features of this system are familiar: the model is based upon the following propositions:

(1) The centre knows, or can discover, what needs doing, for the real or supposed benefit of society.
(2) The centre knows, or can discover, how it should be done.
(3) Subordinate units (managers, enterprises) have the primary duty of fulfilling plan *orders*, and are judged primarily by the criterion of plan fulfilment.
(4) Consequently, *commercial* criteria, prices, profits, play a subordinate role.
(5) Obligatory plan targets, including production, delivery, material-technical supply and utilisation norms, wages fund etc., are determined by superior planning bodies.
(6) These bodies include production ministries and co-ordinatory-functional units (Gosplan, Gossnab etc.).
(7) The role of workers and employees in managerial decision making is, in practice, negligibly small.

Again very briefly, the problems to which this system gives rise are:

(1) Informational indigestion. It is simply impossible for the centre to collect, process and act upon micro-economic information. (This is exacerbated by the fact, inevitable in all large organisations, that information is seldom 'pure' when those who provide it are interested in the actions which will be based upon it.)
(2) The unavoidable division of responsibility (e.g. between ministries, and between them and management) makes co-ordination very difficult. The system becomes *de facto* decentralised. (See the excellent account of the system's logic by Maria Augustinovics in Bornstein, 1975.) Much criticism of *mezhduvedomstvennye*

Paper delivered at NASEES Conference, March 1977.

baryery (interdepartmental barriers) shows that, paradoxically, by centralising everything one frustrates the very objects of centralised co-ordination.

(3) Inconsistencies and other species of malfunctioning become unavoidable (e.g. supply does not match production, production targets do not 'fit' in with demand, financial plans do not 'fit' with amended output and investment plans etc. etc.).

(4) Thus the centre often does not know just what needs doing, and/or is not capable of issuing unambiguous instructions that it be done, not because of bad will or bureaucratic stupidity, but because of the nature of the system itself. (Note: it is sometimes thought that the boundary between what can and what cannot be planned runs along the line between investment and current decision making. This view is misleading. Many investment decisions – e.g. on re-equipment or machinery production and design, or completions of buildings already started, are operationally analogous to current 'micro' decisions, whereas oil, natural gas and electricity production and distribution can be and are fairly successfully centralised.)

(5) Computers cannot save this kind of system from intolerable inefficiencies. (In her already cited article, Maria Augustinovics points out that even the most rigid 'traditional' bureaucracy is infinitely more flexible, in its adjustments to the unexpected, than the best computerised programme.)

The net effect is that the desires of the centre are far too often frustrated by the system. This applies as much to technological innovation as to the failure to provide shoes that fit. *Hence the centre's interest in some sort of reform*: it desires greater efficiency, less waste, better quality (see Brezhnev's slogans: 'A quinquennium of effectiveness and quality', 'A more effective struggle for effectiveness' etc. etc.).

But in what direction to go? There are two serious alternatives and one irrelevancy. The two serious alternatives are:

(1) *A greater role for the market mechanism*, contract, commercial calculation: demand is transmitted from the user (directly, or through trade intermediaries) to the producer. An active role for prices, the use of profits as a major managerial incentive. Note that such a reform could be combined with some degree of workers' participation in enterprise management. The *level* of management to which the reform applies can vary: thus there could be mergers, 'socialist corporations' or, at the other extreme, small producers' co-operatives, depending on whether the product is (say) giant turbines or safety-pins. There are also different possible roles within the model for central intervention (see

Hungarian discussions on a 'controlled' or 'limited' market model; see also the works of W. Brus). All the versions involve the complete or partial dismantling of administered material-technical supply. All imply (more or less) supply-and-demand-balancing prices (with subsidies where socially or economically necessary). In the smaller countries, the link with foreign markets is, understandably enough, considered vital too.

(2) *A streamlined centralised system* based upon the East German 'cartel' (VVB) or *obyedineniye*, in which the centre's task is to be rendered less onerous by reducing the number of units which are the subject of planning, by merger. The 'cartels' subdivide tasks among their subordinate management. Attachment to them of research institutes is supposed to facilitate innovation. (Opinions vary whether the relative success of the East Germans is due to their model, or to the fact – according to Granick's very valuable book (1975) – that the planners allow more 'slack' and reserve capacity within the plan, or, finally, to the fact that they are Germans.) There is no place in this version for meaningful workers' participation.

The unreal 'alternative' is best seen in the works of Charles Bettelheim and Paul Sweezy. I will confine myself to one quotation: 'Centralised bureaucratic control versus the mass line.' This is to contrast a *functional method* (though a deficient one) with a *slogan*. There exists quite widely a set of ideas aiming at reconciling the irreconcilable: centralisation with the abolition of bureaucracy and with 'control by the direct producers', price control (below the prices at which supply and demand balances) with availability of goods in the shops without queueing or a black market etc. etc. It would be nice to imagine that the waste inherent in a competitive market *and* the waste caused by centralised 'Stalinist' planning could both be eliminated. No one has yet discovered such an optimum. But the fact that people *think* that it exists produces, as we shall see, pressures of which politicians must take cognisance, in Britain as in the USSR or Poland, even if they seem to be of the 'have-your-cake-and-eat-it' species.

Who, then, is for Reform?
First of all, one must consider the evidence, or, rather, the lack of good solid evidence. Beware of baseless generalisations! Examples: 'The managers are for'; 'The party (or the party professionals) are against'; 'The working class is opposed.' Opinion polls are few and can be misleading. Press reports, articles, speeches at symposia, may be unrepresentative of managers and officialdom, and as for the workers, their views usually remain unreported anyhow. This warning must be

given, in view of the fact that in the pages that follow I do try to put forward some generalisations about attitudes to reform on the part of certain strata. These are deduced more from what may be the objective situation of various groups in Soviet society than from adequate evidence about who wants what.

There is also what the economists call 'revealed preference': thus if certain reforms are not adopted, this suggests a predisposition on the part of those in power not to adopt them.

After these necessary warnings, let us try to set out a possible political balance of forces.

Let us start with *party officials*. By this I mean party *apparatchiki*, not officials of state agencies who are party members. Objectively, their interests can depend very much on their position in the hierarchy. Thus at the very top (the politbureau level) there is no time to go into micro-economic detail, and, with major investment decisions necessarily centralised, the adoption of economic reform of the market type would probably affect the powers of the leadership relatively little. It is true that the centralised system does seem to maximise the power concentrated at the apex of the pyramid, and no doubt Brezhnev and his colleagues prefer things that way. However, granted that the present system frustrates the desires of the leadership for more efficiency, better quality, the reduction of potentially dangerous consumer dissatisfaction etc. etc., they can hardly just stand still and confine themselves to exhortation. They do seem to have some general notion as to what needs doing. Thus Brezhnev urged much more attention to 'effectiveness and quality', deplored 'the chase after intermediate results' (e.g. plan fulfilment in tons), wants greater influence of the customer over production, more use of 'economic stimuli'. He said: 'The scientific-technical revolution requires *radical changes*' in methods of management and planning (see Twenty-fifth Party Congress reports). So there appears to be pressure for reform from above, motivated by the desire for results.

But the septuagenarian leadership is intensely conservative and dislikes risk – and one must admit that any major reforms in economic planning do carry with them a risk of things going wrong. Furthermore there are the views of those particularly concerned with military and other top priority sectors, who feel, with justice, that the present kind of centralised control gives the greatest advantage to the sectors for which they are responsible: thus it would be surprising indeed if a man like Ustinov favoured any drastic change. Or rather, since change there must be, the predisposition would seem to be towards the *obyedineniye*-cartel kind of reform: fewer units to plan, more devolution to the most senior levels of management, yet at the same time the maintenance of centralisation not only in determining priorities but also in execution of key projects, in which the central committee's economic apparatus can continue to play a vital role. The basic question, of course, is whether such a policy will bring the desired improvements in performance. If it does not – and my own view is that it will not – then among the next generation of leaders there may arise some who will pin their own hopes of political advancement to the advocacy and adoption of more drastic changes than these.

What of the *regional* and *republican* party officials? They were supposed to have benefited from the *sovnarkhoz* reform, since powers exercised locally (nominally by state officials) give them more scope. It is evident that the more decisions affecting resource allocations are taken in Kiev, Tashkent or Tallin, or at *oblast'* level, the more scope there is for the party secretaries at that level. The *sovnarkhozy* were plainly not a success, for reasons abundantly discussed in the literature. There is, however, an aspect of the *obyedineniye* type of reform which should appeal to regional secretaries: some *obyedineniya* are regional or republican. While it is probably nonsensical to sub-ordinate *all* industrial enterprises to a regional body, it is more practicable to have region- or republic-based mergers within a given industry. The trend in the period 1965–73 was all the other way, towards the creation of more *all-union* economic ministries, the down-grading *de facto* of republican planning and administrative bodies (such a key institution as Gossnab has republican offices, but there is no republican *snab* organ as such). True, the present pattern of *obyedineniya* cannot satisfy them. Some are all-union. Others, though regional, cross the geographical boundaries of republican or regional officials. Thus, to cite two examples, the Leningrad-based *Skorokhod* footwear corporation has several factories outside the Leningrad *oblast'*, and a recent article in *Voprosy ekonomiki* (no. 1, 1977, p. 22) advocated the creation of a *Donugol'* trust which would control mines both in the Ukrainian and the RSFSR portions of the Donets coalfield. This would surely be opposed by local party officials, and supported by those *obyedineniye* managers who desire to be free of local party interference.

As for market-type reforms, local officials would surely dislike them, as strengthening inter-managerial ties which of their nature cross all kinds of regional boundaries. Besides, the lower down one goes, the greater the party officials' role in interfering and controlling: they cope with supply bottlenecks, they issue *ad hoc* orders on a variety of topics, they reallocate resources. This is particularly obvious in agriculture. What would rural *raikomy* do without campaigns to sow, to harvest, to deliver, to mobilise, and so on? We are surely not wrong to regard the party *apparat* below the central level as very much opposed to any kind of change that might do them out of a job.

The same is emphatically true of *the planning and financial bureau-cracy*. It is worth quoting at this point the words of Boyarsky: if, he warned, there were devised some 'automatic' criteria for an optimal plan, 'active planning would from that moment be liquidated' (1962, p. 347). The planners must feel that their status and employment are threatened. They earn their living replacing the invisible hand. Automatism of any kind threatens them. No wonder it is possible to assemble many quotations from officials opposed to the entire logic of market-type reform: see, for example, Sitnin, Bunich, Drogichinsky, Bachurin and others. They are bound, by virtue of their position, to defend administrative allocation of materials, obligatory production targets, the right to alter plans in the course of their execution, and so on. They deliberately 'dilute' such reform proposals as would give an active role to either prices or profits: thus the profit-related bonus of management becomes payable only on condition that the obligatory plan-goals are fulfilled.

Less obviously, they are also opposed to some aspects of the *obyedineniye* type of reform, or so it is asserted by Aron Katsenelenboigen in an unpublished paper. He argues (also in correspondence with me) that the logic of region-based *obyedineniya* is the transfer of many Moscow-based officials, now engaged in ministerial *glavki* (and possibly also in detailed supply-and-production links) to the provinces, and this they hate as much as they hated any transfer to *sovnarkhozy* under Khrushchev. If this analysis is correct, it follows that they will obstruct the creation of *obyedineniya*, or else so influence their formation as to make minimal changes in their own position. Two variants would seem to suit them:

(1) All-union *obyedineniya* which simply perform the tasks of the *glavk* with the same officials; and/or
(2) Small local *obyedineniya*, with limited powers and functions, which will leave the centre in its customary dominant role.

In fact this analysis fits the facts rather well. The creation of *obyedineniya* is well behind schedule, and many are indeed quite small. (See *PKh*, no. 1, 1977.) Furthermore, a whole series of complaints have been published to the effect that *obyedineniya* have no greater powers than did the ordinary enterprises, and even that their 'general directors' have no higher salary to compensate for the greater responsibility they are supposed to carry.

Which brings me to the *managers*. Many years ago, when I claimed that, judging from their published articles, the managers were in favour of a market-type reform, my Soviet colleague replied: 'Those who are capable of writing articles which are publishable may well be in favour, but what about the others?' Indeed one must bear in mind that:

(1) Some people do not care for responsibility and risk, and prefer the 'shelter' afforded by the centralised system, within which they can play familiar 'games', along with their network of official and unofficial contacts. The fear of the unknown may repel such persons.

(2) No one actually likes competition, except in theory, if one is subject to it oneself. It is not disagreeable to be within an administratively created monopoly, in which customers are tied to you and cannot go elsewhere. (True, the penalty is that one is also tied to one's own supplier, but one cannot have everything!)

(3) As against this, there are certainly some frustrated would-be entrepreneurs, and many who write to complain about *melochnaya opeka,* and indeed loudly claiming that many matters which the 1965 reform left for *their* decision are the subject of detailed orders from above. Many must also be fed up with the quality of their products, quality cannot be improved within existing plan targets, supply arrangements etc.

A document of importance in this connection is the result of a survey of managers in Siberia, reported by Aganbegyan (*Pravda,* 12 November 1973). Of 1,064 managers, 80 per cent complained that they are given orders on matters which should be within their own powers to decide, that 'breaches of *khozraschyot* rights [of management] are of a mass character'. A partial survey of affected enterprises showed 1,554 'corrections' of the annual plans during the year, and this without any consequential amendment of financial indicators. 90 per cent of directors expressed the desire for a 'substantial' increase in the economic powers of decision making at enterprise level: 66 per cent of them wanted more powers in the realm of labour and wages, 36 per cent in financial questions, 35 per cent in capital investment, 31 per cent in choice of product mix. 44 per cent of these managers gave their biggest problem as being that of material supplies, 27 per cent as unstable plans and arbitrary planning, 26 per cent as lack of directorial powers, 14 per cent as deficiencies in payments to labour. One would like more information about this questionnaire, but the results are plainly of interest even as they stand.

More freedom to decide, to make contracts, to employ labour, obtain needed inputs, to have a stable plan over the formulation of which they have more influence, these seem to be management desiderata.

The attitude of management to the *obyedineniye* type of reform must be expected to differ according to the level and ambitions of the manager. Clearly an enterprise boss in (say) Baku or Krasnoyarsk whose ministerial controllers are in Moscow has greater scope than if he were made a part of some *obyedineniye*'s general director's 'empire';

in many cases he would in fact cease to act as a *yuridicheskoye litso* and lose some financial autonomy. It would seem improbable that this would make him happy. The general director would gain, true, but, as we have seen, he gets no or few extra rewards to compensate for the extra responsibility.

Does all this give us ground to assert that managers as a category tend to be predisposed to the *market* type of reform? Not altogether. We can only say that among them must be a sizable group who would benefit from this sort of change and would be willing to accept the risks and inconveniences.

A word about the *technologists and engineers*. Judging from many articles about technological innovation and the quality of machinery, they have reason to be dissatisfied. Another reason for dissatisfaction is the serious loss of relative earnings of these categories *vis-à-vis* the skilled or even semi-skilled worker. Again one imagines that attitudes to reform differ, according to whether the individual is in research institutes or in industry, and whether in a priority sector (e.g. defence) or not.

Which brings one to the complex problem of *the workers* (in this paper I will ignore the peasants). Let us first try to define a working-class interest, as producers. Like most others they desire higher wages. They are probably not too fond of work discipline. They greatly value security of employment. They have little, if any, influence on decision making, outside the sphere of welfare (though the trade union role in labour conflicts cannot be ignored), and none of the proposals for reform seems to make much difference in this respect. (True, as Brus and others have pointed out, the greater the powers of the enterprise, the greater the *possibilities* of self-management at that level, but in the USSR such ideas have little currency.) Some workers, so it is said (by émigrés, for instance) are fed up with the inefficiency of the system. And, of course, as consumers they have much to complain about: availability of goods, quality, queues etc. etc.

I fail to see that the *obyedineniye* reform makes any significant difference to the workers, who are probably indifferent to it. The 'market' reform is quite another matter and requires careful analysis, and a much longer and more thorough one than it can get here.

Many Soviet industries are over-manned, and an effective market reform plus greater cost-consciousness should lead, indeed would be intended to lead, to higher labour productivity by transferring surplus labour to where it is needed: no one doubts that labour is acutely short in some areas and branches, while wastefully used in others. Furthermore, much saving of labour can be made by a more comprehensive, systematic mechanisation, especially of auxiliary processes, and this too is a reform objective.

Plainly, such aims are inconsistent with 'traditional' *job security*.

Some critics raise the spectre of mass unemployment, but this seems to me an overstated danger: the process can be gradual, and unsatisfied demand for labour is great. But none can deny that the jobs done will have to change, there must be retraining, perhaps with a move to another area. As we know from British experience, this causes resistance even if unemployment does not threaten. Many Hungarian colleagues spoke of the same problem: workers want 'one-sided flexibility', as one eminent Hungarian put it. They want to be free to move whenever they wish, but never compelled to move when their services are not needed, or are needed elsewhere.

For some analysts this is decisive: the workers are right to be against, the reform is anti-worker in its nature.

One must agree that workers' attitudes to job security are indeed important. But they are also interested, or should be, in the state of the economy as a whole, since they are beneficiaries from higher output and productivity, and victims of shortages if the economy works badly. If there is relatively full employment (though some are paid who are not fully employed), it follows that new output, factories, construction sites, must be staffed by workers and employees transferred from elsewhere. Many complaints show that the very slow start-up (*osvoyeniye*) of new factories is due in large measure to labour problems (partly, it is true, because the housing projects fall behind schedule). Consequently, flexibility, mobility, retraining, the elimination of featherbedding, are a precondition of improved living standards in the Soviet economy, indeed in any economy. In principle most workers (and most university staffs too!) understand this well enough, so long as it affects others. So the *interests* of the workers in this question are, to put it mildly, not quite clear.

They are affected, of course, by the possible consequences of reform on *income distribution* and inequality. One must distinguish here between the effect of reform as such and the likely effect of other pressures, which may have nothing to do with reform at all. Thus if a research officer with a *kandidat* degree earns 130 rubles a month, a middle-grade engineer 170 and a bus driver or semi-skilled steel worker over 200, there is, naturally, pressure to improve the relative position of the 'technical intelligentsia'. But there is nothing in the reform *as such* which will do this. The market-type reform would link bonuses with profits, making them less dependent on plan fulfilment, but this would not necessarily increase the *average* disparity between worker and director, though it might well enlarge the earnings gap between the successful and less successful director. (I do not enter here into discussions about the adequacy of profits and prices as criteria, this would require another paper.) The 'general director' of an *obyedineniye* seems to need more pay, but this is a relatively minor matter of redefining senior posts. It is probably the case that the whole logic and philosophy of market-type reform place more stress on material incentives and therefore on inequality. But whether *in fact* any greater degree of overall inequality is needed to make the reform function is a moot point. Besides, most workers (unlike certain kinds of intellectuals) are not all that keen on equality: they want more for themselves, being in this respect like other strata of society. Of course they would complain if income is redistributed away from them, as we all would! But, to repeat a point which is so often overlooked, the pressure to improve the lot of the underpaid intelligentsia is not, of itself, connected with reform, especially as some of the worst paid (doctors, teachers etc.) are not in productive industry at all.

This brings one, finally, to *prices* and to the workers' attitudes to price increases.

Here again, on the surface the situation is clear: they are against them. If the reform, any reform, requires prices to be such that a balance is established between supply and demand, and if (as is certainly the case) many prices are below this level, then reform equals price increases, and 'the workers' (and not only they) are against. (The question of *subsidies* is a different one. Thus in Hungary meat is subsidised, in France so is public transport, but there is *enough* for the consumers at these prices. Reform *need* not eliminate subsidies.)

The trouble is that many people (in Britain too) want both higher wages and lower prices, higher state spending and lower taxes, and all this with the goods fully available when wanted in the shops and no ration cards.

Ah, it may be said, but higher prices, at which supply and demand balances, benefit the better-off. Thus meat may seldom be available in Sverdlovsk at 2 rubles per kilo, but, when it is, it goes to those who get to the shop, not necessarily the richest. In fact, according to verbal information from a recent émigré, the Soviet authorities consciously tolerate (or prefer) a situation in which more people have 'the illusion' that goods are within their financial grasp, if only they can be found. Perhaps many workers reason thus, and the Polish events of December 1970 and June 1976 can be cited in support. (But against this, sad Polish planners remarked to me that riots are equally likely if, at the impossibly low official prices, there is no meat to be had.) If the scarcity of goods is not reflected in their price, if demand exceeds supply, the beneficiaries are often not the ordinary worker, but those who have influence, connections, or time to wait in line. Can this really be in the interests of the bulk of the workers?

There is also the Paul Sweezy–Charles Bettelheim 'class struggle' argument: the upper strata (ruling class, state bourgeoisie, elite, what have you) *favour* the market-type reform because it accords with their interests. It enables them better to exploit the masses, acquire more material benefits etc. Their interests are equated with strengthening commodity-money relations.

I have tried to argue already that this is too naive an argument. Indeed some of its protagonists, faced by the obvious fact that the 'elite' successfully *resist* this kind of reform, point to a split among the top stratum, and then discuss along what line the split occurs. It may be argued that older generation party officials see things differently from the more 'modern' technocrats.

This may be so. The passing of the Brezhnev generation of septuagenarians from the scene may clear the decks for change, especially as the urgent *need* for greater efficiency is appreciated by all, even by the septuagenarians.

However, this kind of radical critic is usually unable to see clearly enough the *advantages* to the ruling stratum, or privileged group, that the unreformed system gives. They not only have power and function in relation to resource allocation. They also have privileged access to scarce goods and services unavailable to the masses. *This* privilege is conditional upon their being frequently unobtainable, at the low prices (low, that is, in relation to supplies available). Furthermore, it gives them access to these goods at *low* prices! In terms of crude self-interest, what motive have they to change an arrangement which suits them very well?

So *finally*: the political pressures for reform are unlikely to issue from any powerful group (professional economists do not count!). The pressure for change arises from *circumstances*, from the consciousness that the old way will not, or does not, work. Will this overcome the well-ingrained habits and self-interest of such large and well-entrenched party-state apparatus? Most of the émigré-economists answer this question with a loud 'no'. Yet I wonder if we are not due for some surprises once the Brezhnev generation passes from the scene.

Can Eastern Europe Feed Itself?

The object of this paper is to examine the proposition that the USSR and her European allies are, and will remain, a burden on the world grain market because of the inability of their system to function effectively in agriculture. Obviously this proportion has two parts: that consumption does and will exceed production, *and* that this is due to state and collective farming, implying that some alternative way of organising agricultural production would be more effective.

Let me begin by eliminating certain countries from the discussion, because, in my view, their situation is clear and requires no expenditure of time and ink beyond the paragraphs that follow.

The *GDR* is by any standards a country of intensive and reasonably high yielding agriculture (see Tables 1 to 5). It is clear that the reason for her substantial dependence on imports of grain is the same as Britain's: lack of suitable soil in a densely populated and largely industrial country. Dependence on imports has slowly declined with a steady rise in grain yields.

Bulgarian agriculture has been doing reasonably well, with steep rises in output of grain and meat. Tractor h.p. per 1,000 hectares now actually exceeds that of the USSR and Hungary (though, as might be

Table 1 *Grain Output and Yields*
(All grains, including pulses '000 tons, and quintals per ha respectively)

	1961–5 Output yield average		1966–70 Output yield average		1971–5 Output yield average	
Bulgaria	4,863	19·0	6,454	27·4	7,465	33·1
Hungary	6,905	20·3	8,400	25·4	11,525	35·0
GDR	5,969	25·3	6,991	29·4	8,760	35·7
Poland	15,427	17·0	17,367	19·8	21,241	25·1
Romania	11,101	15·9	12,948	19·3	14,974	24·1
Czechoslovakia	5,658	21·8	7,111	26·6	9,436	33·9
USSR	130,335	10·2	167,562	13·7	181,554	14·7

(*Source*: Comecon statistical annuals for 1975 and 1976)

Reprinted from World Development, *vol. 5, May/June 1977.*

Table 2 *Potatoes: Output and Yields*

	1961–5 Output yield average		1966–70 Output yield average		1971–75 Output yield average	
Bulgaria	400	85	380	114	355	118
Hungary	1,998	79	2,044	105	1,570	117
GDR	12,066	166	12,283	185	10,806	171
Poland	43,682	154	47,906	176	47,083	177
Romania	2,600	85	2,874	93	3,387	114
Czechoslovakia	5,635	114	5,676	151	4,571	153
USSR	81,628	94	94,813	115	89,782	113

(*Source*: Comecon statistical annuals for 1975 and 1976)

Table 3 *Meat (Selected Years, '000 tons)*

	1960	1965	1970	1975
Bulgaria	307	464	476	657
Hungary	816	929	1,040	1,474
GDR	1,021	1,126	1,271	1,718
Poland	1,751	2,012	2,182	3,062
Romania	561	657	857	1,328
Czechoslovakia	802	978	1,098	1,349
USSR	8,681	9,956	12,278	15,060

Table 4 *Production per Capita, 1974 (kg)*

	Grain	of which Wheat and Rye	Potatoes	Meat (live weight)	Milk
Bulgaria	774	338	39·7	65	205
Hungary	1,204	491	152	117*	177
GDR	578	302	792	94	442
Poland	692	424	1,444	91	499
Romania	651	240	196	62	213
Czechoslovakia	712	390	308	89	383
USSR	776	393	321	58	364

*1973

Table 5 *Deliveries of Mineral Fertiliser per ha of Arable Land (kg of Nutrient Content)*

	1960	1965	1970	1975
Bulgaria	36·1	85·5	159	166
Hungary	29·4	63·3	150	276
GDR	188	267	319	370
Poland	48·6	73·1	162	236
Romania	7·9	28·9	66·7	114
Czechoslovakia	94·6	167	230	305
USSR	12·2	28·5	47·0	76·7

expected, it is only half of that of the GDR). (Comecon statistical annual, 1975, p. 214.) Only an unusually poor harvest in 1974 led, exceptionally, to a net import of grain.

Romania is a net exporter of both grain and meat, and has shown a particularly large rise in meat production. Though yields have improved, there seems to be scope for still better results if fertiliser utilisation reaches even Bulgarian, let alone Polish, levels (see Table 5).

Czechoslovakia is second only to the GDR in the intensity of its agriculture (i.e. second both in fertiliser application and in tractor power per unit of land). She imports little meat, but inevitably has a grain deficiency, though the import trend is slightly downwards.

Hungary has done well. Except after bad weather in 1970 she has been a sizable grain and meat exporter, while producing more meat per capita than any other of the countries of Eastern Europe. Yields are high by historic Hungarian and indeed international standards. Livestock exports to the West have been impeded by the Common Agricultural Policy of the EEC, which has also adversely affected Poland.

This brings one to the special case of *Poland*, which requires a more detailed comment.

Poland, alone of the countries analysed here, has predominantly a private smallholder agriculture. This private sector is still comparatively little mechanised, and so Poland in 1974 still had 2,264,000 horses (against only 76,000 in the GDR and 163,000 in Hungary). Horses eat grain. This helps to explain Poland's grain deficit, which, as Table 6 shows, is astonishingly large and continues to grow. Compare production per capita figures in Table 4: Poland has more grain

Table 6   *Foreign trade in grain (Some recent years) ('000 tons)*

		1970	1971	1972	1973	1974	1975
Bulgaria	(export)	462	558	833	367	149	195
	(import)	158	195	—	136	637	653
Hungary	(export)	810	112	505	1,732	1,472	1,285
	(import)	181	808	789	265	390	172
GDR	(import)	3,424	3,066	3,845	2,990	2,770	3,360
Poland	(export)	200	111	208	410	262	104
	(import)	2,484	2,950	3,108	3,263	4,091	3,963
Romania	(export)*	370	702	900	1,026	711	1,163
Czechoslovakia							
	(import)	1,439	2,033	1,550	1,552	1,038	885
USSR**	(export)			4,560	4,853	7,029	3,578
	(import)			15,500	23,900	7,131	15,909

*Wheat plus maize only
**Incredibly, Soviet grain trade data are *omitted* from the source!
   (The figures are taken from the Soviet foreign trade annuals)

Table 7 *Foreign Trade in Meat ('000 tons)*

		1970	1971	1972	1973	1974	1975
Bulgaria	(exports)	65	67	74	65	61	99
Hungary	(exports)	123	163	163	134	201	249
	(imports)	61	16	13	77	25	12
GDR	(imports)	85	56	47	42	24	24
Poland	(exports)	157	174	173	194	234	209
	(imports)	44	153	65	55	6	16
Romania	(exports)	55	55	69	100	133	165
Czechoslovakia							
	(imports)	121	76	45	22	40	32
USSR	(imports)	165	225	131	129	515	515

than the GDR, yet its imports have risen above those of the GDR. Poland has 31·4 per cent of its population engaged in 'agriculture and forestry', the GDR only 11·5 per cent. (Comecon statistical annual, 1975, pp. 393, 394.) Poland also has nearly three times as much sown area as the GDR. It is true that Poland has been expanding meat exports, but domestic consumption has risen faster, indeed demand has risen faster than supply, causing highly embarrassing shortages. Polish meat output per capita is below that of the GDR.

These shortages are due (as also in some other Eastern countries) to a price policy explicable only to politics, and not by economic common sense. Polish money wages have risen in the period 1968–75 by over 60 per cent. Prices of livestock products have been frozen. Attempts to increase them, in December 1970 and June 1976, have been frustrated by mass protest. Income elasticity of demand for meat is high. Evidently, such a price policy as this guarantees trouble. Poland's output of meat has in fact risen impressively. (The most popular meat is pork, which doubtless helps to explain the huge per capita production of potatoes shown in Table 4 – pigs eat potatoes.) Yet demand outpaces supply. It is a very heavily subsidised demand. Relatively to other things, it could be said that meat sells at a price which in contemporary British terms would be of the order of 30 pence a pound, or about a third to a quarter of the price of meat in the West (multiple exchange rates make any precise comparison impossible). The subsidy required to keep food prices at these unreal levels reached 100,000 million zloty, according to official statements at the time of the abortive price rise of June 1976, representing a heavy burden on the budget. It is now (1977) certainly much higher, since state procurement prices were raised in June 1976. To feed the expanded livestock herds requires still more grain imports.

So Poland, with a high proportion of its people still on the land and a relatively modest population density, finds itself a large net grain importer because people eat too much meat (relatively to the general level of economic development) and there are too many horses. Looking at Table 4, one also gets the impression that animals must be eating some sizable share of the bread grains (since wheat and rye output per capita is second only to Hungary, and Hungary is a net *exporter* of grain).

What remedies are there? The traditional nature of smallholder agriculture is a brake upon efficiency. As any visitor to Poland can see, fields are small, many peasant households have 5 hectares of land or less, which is scarcely conducive to mechanisation, and I saw myself literally dozens of peasants sowing by throwing seed into the wind by hand. Productivity per head cannot be other than low, and it is arguable that further gains in yields are improbable without some major structural changes. Against this, Polish peasants clearly detest collectivisation, which in any case is no cure for low yields, as Soviet experience shows, and the government wisely does not use coercion to solve the smallholder problem. Furthermore, the government has itself contributed to technological backwardness by refusing (until 1970) to sell tractors to peasant households, or to make small mechanical tools available, preferring to concentrate tractors and combines in the so-called agricultural circles (*kolki*). Japanese experience points to the very considerable potential of small-scale privately owned farms worked intensively. By reaching grain yields equal to those in Hungary or Czechoslovakia, Poland could be self-sufficient in grain, even with the continuing subsidisation of meat prices (and the resultant high demand for fodder grains). Progress is likely to be both slow and costly. So for the next quinquennium Poland will probably continue to be a net importer, though, if only on balance of payments grounds, the government will clearly do its best to lessen dependence on imported grain and to stimulate exports of meat, subject to the constraints imposed by its fears of the consequences of large and unpopular price rises.

The *USSR*, however, is the key to the entire problem, not only because she has been in some recent years the world's largest importer of grain, but because of her role as a supplier to the grain-deficient East European countries. Thus in 1974 Soviet exports of grain included the following:

	(*'000 tons*)
GDR	1,425
Poland	1,898
Czechoslovakia	669

(*Source*: Soviet foreign trade statistics, 1975)

Consequently we must examine in some detail the performance and potential of Soviet agriculture. A whole book can easily be devoted to this theme. What follows is therefore a necessarily abbreviated summary of the principal factors involved.

In the first place, a glance at Tables 1 and 5 shows the USSR at the bottom of the 'league table' both in yields and in fertiliser supplies. This has, of course, multiple causes. The USSR (like Canada) has a more extensive form of agriculture than Central Europe, and in wide areas the problem is not one of fertiliser so much as of rainfall: a good crop can be obtained (e.g. in North Kazakhstan or the southern Ukraine) if there is no drought. *Climate* is a serious handicap. Thus in the years 1963 and 1975 the weather was outstandingly bad, and most problems would disappear if only the favourable years 1973 and 1976 were to recur regularly. It is also only proper to note that grain yields were far lower ten or twenty years ago, that progress has undoubtedly been made, though at heavy cost to the rest of the economy (investments in agriculture more than doubled between 1966 and 1974).

None the less, there is no doubt that the northern and western areas of the USSR, where moisture is sufficient and soils not naturally fertile, do require *more fertiliser* (and also lime), and there are numerous Soviet official statements to that effect. This, then, represents one remediable cause of low yields, a cause which it is planned to remedy, since fertiliser production is planned to continue its rapid rise. (It is well to recall that in 1960, say, mineral fertiliser was scarcely available at all except for a few priority crops, such as cotton.)

There remain many problems connected with the utilisation of fertiliser. Packaging, transportation, storage are all deficient, and there is sharp criticism of the imbalance between deliveries of fertiliser and the production and supply of machines to spread it. No doubt this can be remedied in time.

Another factor adversely affecting agricultural performance is the *size of farms*. It is perhaps not always realised that they are at once too big and much too small, mechanised (though inadequately) and totally unmechanised, at one and the same time. This requires some words of explanation. *State farms* average 19,000 hectares of agricultural land (6,000 hectares arable), and *Collective farms* (*kolkhozy*) 6,300 and 3,400 hectares respectively. They employ an average of 500 to 700 persons. The level of specialisation is low. Only recently a correspondent in *Pravda* was complaining that *all* the farms of his region were given compulsory plan targets for a wide range of vegetables. Farms usually cultivate a variety of crops, keep most kinds of livestock, and are difficult to administer. There is evidence of diseconomies of scale. These are accentuated by plan orders from bureaucrats and regional party officials, who also launch annual campaigns to fulfil plans for ploughing, sowing, harvesting. This, as will be shown, has unfortunate effects also on the peasant's sense of responsibility and his material incentives.

Side by side with these farms are the *private allotments and animals* of peasants (and of suburban townspeople). These are usually cultivated by spade and hoe, and are often a quarter of a hectare or so in size. These little holdings cannot be disregarded: they produced at least 26 per cent of total agricultural output in 1973 (calculated from figures in the 1973 statistical annual, pp. 456, 469). Individuals own 35 per cent of the cows, produce 32 per cent of meat and milk, 41 per cent of the eggs, 64 per cent of potatoes and negligible quantities of grain. Time is spent on these unmechanised operations, and also in taking produce to the free market in the city. In recent years the pay for collective and state work has substantially improved, and so proportionately less attention is being paid to the private plot and to sales in the market. However, the output of this private sector is slowly rising still, and, owing to the still very inadequate system of rural food shops, these plots and animals still play a vital part in providing for the needs of peasant families.

This leads one to discuss *labour* problems. As in many other countries, the bright lights of the city beckon, and there is a grave shortage of skilled labour, which affects the quality of maintenance and repair of equipment. Despite the apparently very large size of the total rural labour force, there are the most acute shortages of labour at peak periods, necessitating a massive 'import' of workers from the towns plus the help of the army at harvest time. Partly this is due to the lack of interest in extra effort of the peasants on the huge impersonal farms. Partly it is to be explained by inadequacies in mechanisation (of which more in a moment). Lack of effective incentives is ascribed by Soviet commentators to the piecework system on these large farms: thus a tractor driver is paid by the area he ploughs, and finds it easiest to plough shallow. He feels no personal responsibility, moral or material, for the outcome.

'Who does not watch the work of the ploughman: the accountant, the supervisor, the brigadier, the representative of the People's Control, the rural Soviet, the agronomist, the agitator-political-organiser, and even a volunteer quality controller. Yet what sort of a peasant is it, if it is necessary to follow him about to ensure that he ploughs and harrows properly.' (P. Rebrin, *Novy Mir*, no. 4, 1969, p. 156.)

Machinery is often of poor quality, and provided in a 'non-complex' and bureaucratic manner. That is to say, farms often fail to obtain what they ask for, and are allocated what they do not need. Gaps in mechanisation create bottlenecks which contribute to labour problems. (Most forthright criticisms of this state of affairs may be found in G. Dobrynin *VEk*, no. 11, 1974, and many of the same points are repeated in V. Tikhonov, *VEk*, no. 10, 1977.) Livestock raising, vegetable cultivation, loading and materials handling, are poorly mechanised. Spare parts and essential replacements fail to arrive, so that many tractors and combines are out of commission. Very poor roads shorten the lives of lorries.

Distribution of food is inadequate, so that many items are not marketed or are lost. Storage is very scarce. Until a recent drive to build many more grain elevators it was true even of grain. It remains the case for vegetables, fruit, milk: lack of handling equipment, lack of packaging materials, bad roads, insufficient retail outlets and no incentive for the trade network to handle perishables etc. etc. (see, for example, the series on vegetable shortage which was printed in *Pravda* during February 1977).

The specific problems of agriculture are 'concerned with live organisms, affected by a variety of natural including biological factors, as well as by organisational-economic and social conditions'. (Dobrynin, op. cit.) For reasons given above, the system of state and collective farms and of basically centralised planning and party control have given rise to inefficiencies, and have made progress very costly. We have been informed by Glushkov, the head of the state prices committee, that subsidies required to cover the losses on the livestock products sector now reach 19 milliard rubles, or the fantastic sum of 25 milliard (billion) dollars! (Belatedly reported in Pravda, 8 February 1977. The total subsidy bill for 1976–80 is to reach 100 milliard rubles, i.e. 136 billion dollars, according to finance minister Garbuzov.) (*PKh*, no. 8, 1977.) This is *additional* to an investment expenditure which, if one includes investments in industries serving agriculture, takes a third of the total amount invested in the USSR.

It must be stated that output has grown, as a glance at Table 1 will confirm. There are very substantial fluctuations due to weather. One has only to compare the official grain harvest for 1975, 138 million tons, with the record year 1976, 224 million tons, but the trend is upwards. Indeed, there is a problem that must be explained: how is it that the USSR imported hardly any grain in (say) the period 1956–62, when production hovered around 120 million tons, and has become a major importer even when harvests are on average some 60 per cent higher?

This, as in Poland, brings one to questions of price policy in general, prices of livestock products in particular.

In the early 1960s, Khrushchev gave publicity to a campaign to 'overtake the United States in the production of meat and milk'. At that time, Soviet meat output was barely a third of that of the United States. Given the calorie-consciousness of the Americans and the cholesterol scare, it has been possible to reach the (falling) American levels in the consumption of milk products (though fresh milk is often unavailable, owing to lack of means of keeping it fresh and getting it to the customer). It is quite another matter in the case of meat.

American meat production absorbs (or rather the animals absorb) a high proportion of total US production of grains. Maize is especially widely used as a fodder, and this so impressed Khrushchev that he launched a 'maize campaign', insisting on a vast increase in maize growing. Unfortunately, most of the USSR is not well suited to maize, and the effort to grow it for silage in areas in which it could not ripen was a disaster at first, because it was done to order, regardless of availability of labour, machines, fertiliser or experience. Maize silage has become an important contributor to the Soviet fodder balance, but ripe grain, root crops, concentrates and particularly hay are chronically short, especially in years of drought. Yields, as well as the level of mechanisation, are low or appallingly low, as the figures for the fairly normal year 1974 demonstrate.

(quintals per hectare) (1974)

	USSR	Hungary	GDR	Poland	Czechoslovakia
Fodder root crops	240	420	472	315	523
Maize for silage and green fodder	138	186	346	420	282
Hay (annual grasses)	22	27	74	38	34
Hay (perennial grasses)	23	42	77	63	58

(*Source*: Comecon statistical annual, 1975)

Meadows and pastures are in notoriously poor condition. Consequently, livestock is often poorly fed, and the diet is unbalanced, with insufficient protein. All this is well known in the Soviet Union, and decrees have been issued designed to improve matters.

Livestock herds have been built up to the limit of available fodder supplies. A bad harvest can cause a sharp drop in numbers, especially of pigs. Thus the 1963 drought led to a decline (January 1963 to January 1964) from a total of over 70 million head to 41 million. Numbers reached 72 million by January 1975, but the disastrous weather of that year caused another cutback, this time to 45·7 millions. Numbers of cows have been, as a rule, preserved in the bad years, but their numbers rise slowly: thus the increase from 1965 to 1976 was only 7 per cent, or less than the increase in human population, though milk yields per cow rose by over 20 per cent.

Livestock has, on average, been better fed. Supplies of concentrates have almost doubled between 1965 and 1974 (statistical annual, 1974, p. 420). The output of meat has risen faster than the numbers of head – though inevitably the slaughter that followed the 1975 harvest led to a decline in meat output, as the figures from *Pravda*, 23 January 1977, show:

1965	1974	1975	1976
	(million tons)		
10·0	14·6	14·9	13·3

(*Source for 1975 and 1976*: *Pravda*, 23 January 1977)

Obviously the 1977 figures will be better, following the record harvest of 1976.

The essential point, then, is that the effort to increase meat production, and to build up livestock numbers, has literally eaten up the grain supplies. The demand for meat is, as we have seen, heavily subsidised. Glushkov, whom we have already quoted, gave the following information: the price of beef in the shops is 2 rubles per kilogram; the total cost to the state per kilogram is 3·50 rubles. Butter is sold at 3·60 rubles, the cost is 5 rubles. The last increase in prices of meat, butter and milk occurred in 1962 (and led to some disturbances). Since that date, money wages have risen by over 55 per cent. As in Poland, the income-elasticity of demand for meat is much greater than unity. Therefore shortages are inevitable. Endeavours to provide enough meat run repeatedly up against the fodder supply barrier.

This is why the question of the estimated size of the actual or future Soviet grain deficit is, in a real sense, unanswerable. If measured against the declared intention to reach American levels of meat consumption, or to satisfy demand at the present heavily-subsidised price, grain supplies are inadequate even in the most favourable years. One way of roughly calculating the 'deficit' in this sense is to take as a basis the American level of consumption: this calls for roughly one ton of grain per inhabitant per year. (Of course in the United States much less of it is eaten as bread than in the Soviet Union, and much more of it is for livestock.) By this standard, the USSR in 1980 will 'need' something of the order of 265 million tons of grain. Its own declared objective for 1980 (i.e. the five-year plan target for the 'end of the quinquennium') is 235 million tons. This is likely to be reached only if the weather is very kind, and suggests a continued dependence on imports. However, this dependence is bound to be limited on balance of payments grounds, and so the 'gap' suggested by the above figures cannot serve as the basis for an import forecast.

Of course the livestock population will be limited by available supplies of grain, and also of the currency to buy it abroad. So it is within the power of the Soviet authorities to reduce import dependence by reducing the pressure to increase livestock numbers and meat supplies. However, this will mean a continued shortage of meat in the shops, unless prices are raised.

To put the point another way, since demand for livestock products exceeds by a substantial factor the means available to feed the livestock, the projected level of Soviet imports of grain (or, for that matter, meat) in an average-weather year can be as high as deliberate policy, or ability to pay, determine it.

However, this view could be based on an over-pessimistic view of the potential for improvement in the performance of Soviet agriculture. So let us look at the factors which might lead to higher yields, beginning with the Soviet policies which are designed to achieve the planned goal of 235 million tons by the end of the present decade.

Steps actually being taken include large expenditures on 'melioration' (drainage, improvement of pastures, irrigation), more fertiliser, more and better machinery, a large road-building programme. Experts urge much greater attention to seeds, one of them arguing that good seed selection in the USSR and Eastern Europe as a whole could by itself raise yields by 50 per cent. (Yu. Kormnov, in *VEk*, no. 1, 1977, p. 90. 'Kormnov' literally means 'fodder-man'!) Improvements are needed and are possible in livestock breeds, and the same amount of grain can be used for fodder much more efficiently in a more balanced diet (several experts have pointed out that the Soviet use of grain is relatively greater per unit of fattened livestock than the American); this could follow from a much needed increase in Soviet yields of hay, the development of chemical fodder additives and similar planned measures. Also the diet of the people can be improved by increasing the very inadequate provision of vegetables, canned foods etc., thereby perhaps reducing the pressure on meat supplies. (Oddly enough, the USSR appears 'statistically' to consume large quantities of fish, but it is by no means easy to obtain in the shops.)

The point is: the poorer the performance of agriculture is in relation to its possibilities, the greater the *potential* for improvement. Having listed so many evidently remediable deficiencies, have I not in fact argued in favour of the proposition that 235 or even 270 million tons of grain is possible if the correct action is taken? After all, the area sown to grain is around 125 million hectares – it is unlikely to be possible to increase this substantially, given the soil and climate. A steady average yield of 20 quintals per hectare equals 250 million tons. As Table 1 shows, this would still leave the USSR with the lowest yields in Eastern Europe. Why is this impossible? If it *were* possible, then the pessimistic prognostications are baseless. They *can* feed themselves, or rather they *will* be able so to do.

However, this would be, in my view, an unwarranted conclusion. Given (to repeat) the fact that a steady improvement in yields is both possible and probable, there are major obstacles to overcome. One is climatic: no Soviet or Russian government can eliminate drought risk, and irrigation can only help marginally (too much land in relation to the available rivers and underground sources of water).

The other is organisational. The Soviet leadership understands the importance of this aspect, but is locked into the state-farm-collective-farm system. So far its efforts have been in the direction of adapting it by a combination of specialisation and merger: farms are being urged to undertake joint activities, forming many cases an agro-industrial complex (e.g. for processing and canning foods, and also for producing building materials, electricity etc.). Specialised livestock enterprises, based upon modern technique, are being developed. Strong criticism is being directed at inflexible bureaucratic planning.

However, this observer at least is doubtful if the cure might not be worse than the disease. If diseconomies of scale beset the large and clumsy state and collective farms, they will cause trouble also for the merged and joint activities. Perhaps the way out is the one which, so far, has been rejected, and which is in the opposite direction: decomposing some at least of the farms' activities into small autonomous groups, free to arrange their own work schedules and responsible for an entire complex of operations on the particular plot of land, or crop, or animals. In Hungary, this method is intelligently combined with large-scale mechanised cultivation (e.g. of wheat) where technical and soil conditions favour this method. 'Small-scale' care for cows, onions, grapes, may have substantial advantages, and can also utilise the considerable number of unskilled peasants, many of them older women. In addition there is the problem of adapting the clumsy system of supply of machinery and spare parts to the needs of an increasingly complex and more mechanised and specialised agriculture. After all, it has hardly been a secret all these years that tractors need spare parts, workshops and mechanics, and yet articles and cartoons appear which continue to denounce the chronic shortage of all these necessities of mechanised life.

The party's policy seems still to be to approach agriculture as if it were an industrial-manufacturing activity, its problems to be solved by better technique and more intelligent planning. Ideology favours this approach: the 'elimination of differences between town and country', turning peasants into workers, farms into agricultural factories. Of course 'factory farming' does exist, there is ample scope for modern techniques in agriculture. But the best Western models are small scale in respect of the number of human beings employed, which makes for a sense of responsibility and/or the possibility of effective supervision.

So, finally, my estimate remains: that the Soviet Union will continue its slow advance in output, at very high cost to the rest of the economy, but will not reach the target set for 1980 in the yields of grain and fodder crops, and that consequently the USSR itself, and therefore Eastern Europe as a totality, will be net importers of grain and probably also of meat, for the next ten years. After that – well, the world may not last that long, and, even if it does, forecasts purporting to predict the world in 1990 cannot, of their nature, be worth much.

II

Inflation in Communist Countries

There are many communist-ruled countries, and the author's knowledge and time are limited. So, perhaps, is the readers' patience. I shall draw my examples almost exclusively from two countries, the USSR and Poland, but no doubt some interesting variations exist elsewhere. One thinks of China and Cuba, for instance. So this paper does not pretend to exhaust a complex and large subject.

Let me begin with the institutional characteristics of a Soviet-type economy, and the possible manifestations of inflation within it. In the USSR virtually all prices are fixed by state organs, mostly at the centre, though some by the union republics. The only significant exception is the free peasant market (*kolkhoznyi rynok*), in which food may be sold by those who grow it, at prices usually uncontrolled. There are a few other minor legitimate private transactions: the letting of rooms, private medical practice, tutoring, petty craftsmen or seamstresses. There are also a range of illegitimate or downright illegal transactions. But the overwhelming mass of sales is of goods and services provided by state enterprises (or sold by collective farms to state procurement organs) at official prices.

Almost all manufactured goods are made by state enterprises in accordance with the state plan. The plan specifies not only the quantity of various items that should be produced, but will usually attach customers to specific suppliers by a vast and complex scheme of administered material allocation. Consequently, managers are not free to purchase the bulk of their inputs: they need an allocation certificate, which will generally specify the source of the inputs in question. The possession of sums of money therefore does not automatically entitle management to spend it. Indeed all but the pettiest of petty cash must be kept at the state bank, and the bank is under an obligation to disallow payments which are improper (e.g. for an unauthorised purchase, or at the wrong price).

The bank also is under orders to disallow payments of wages and salaries in excess of the enterprise's or institution's 'wages fund', this being the maximum amount payable to labour. There are centrally determined wage scales applicable to each grade of skill, and also for technical and managerial staffs, with rules for payment of bonuses.

Reprinted from David Heathfield, ed., Models and Policy: Perspectives on Inflation, *London, Longman, forthcoming.*

Enterprises sell at prices which normally cover operating costs and leave a profit margin. Most of these profits, plus proceeds of turnover tax, form the largest part of the revenue of the state budget. The budget, as published, shows a small surplus every year. This surplus, and also the increment in savings bank deposits, is added to the state bank's assets, and these are used on a large scale to issue short-term credits to state enterprises; these credits cover the time gap between production and receipt of payment from customers, goods in transit etc. The total volume of short-term credits is planned and limited, to avoid financing excess demand. Investment expenditures are tightly controlled by the centre. With minor exceptions, they are financed out of budgetary grants, retained profits and the depreciation fund. The total volume of investment, and specific investment projects too, are (or should be) related to the availability of the necessary material and human resources.

Therefore demand for producers' goods is a function of the output and investment plan, which determines in considerable detail the levels of administratively authorised demand for resources at the officially set prices. It follows that a balanced plan, i.e. one in which inputs are made available for the required outputs, cannot generate excess demand, and so inflationary pressure is excluded. Similarly, since the state plans the output of the consumers' goods industries, fixes retail prices and determines the level of incomes, demand should equal supply; if it does not, the adjustments can be made in prices and in wages, either in total or in specific categories of goods or workers. The institutional power is there, and there is no (legal) countervailing power, such as is constituted in the West by trade unions, farmers' associations, opposition political parties and the like. (However, most of agriculture is in the hands of private smallholders in Poland.) It

Table 1 *Wholesale Prices of Industry (Excluding Turnover Tax)*
(1949 = 100)

USSR		1955	1965	1970	1975
All industry*		68	70	77	75
of which:	Electricity	74	62	83	83
	Oil	65	63	89	87
	Coal	84	84	152	155
	Ferrous metallurgy	60	60	90	90
	Chemicals	67	66	66	63
	Machinery and metalworking	52	41	39	33
	Light industry	80	81	86	93
	Food industry	91	137	140	144

(*Source*: *Narodnoye Khozyaistvo SSSR* (hereinafter *NKh.*, 1975, p. 231)
*Manufacturing and extractive

180   *Political Economy and Soviet Socialism*

is not surprising to learn that inflation is a greater problem in the West.

Yet is it also a major problem in the 'East'. We will see why in a moment. But before doing so, let us look at the Soviet statistics of prices, concentrating on the past twenty years, see Table 1. (1949 was the year of exceptionally high postwar prices.)

Table 2   *USSR: Retail Price Index (1940 = 100)*

	1958	1965	1970	1975
All products	141	140	139	139
Food	149	152	153	154
(of which: liquor)	(317)	(258)	(262)	(267)
Non-food	133	126	124	122

(*Source*: as Table 1, and *NKh*, 1962. There is no published index for 1955)
(Note different base-years of the two tables)

Of course within these averages one finds very wide differences: thus watches have almost halved in price, while vegetable prices have risen by over 20 per cent since 1965. However, these figures give one no ground for speaking of serious price inflation. True, there were large increases in prices of coal, for instance, but this was due to the impact of higher wages on costs in this very labour-intensive industry. The rise in prices of the food industry's products was due to the (much needed) increase in prices paid to farmers. An overall rise in wholesale prices of a mere 14 per cent in twenty years would turn any Western observer green with envy. As for the retail price index, this shows a remarkable stability – if the official data are to be accepted. Therefore, it might be said, there is no problem, and this article should end *now*. Indeed it should never have been begun.

Wages have, of course, risen, as the figures in Table 3 show.

Table 3   *USSR*

	1955	1965	1970	1975
Average wages and salaries (rbles per month)	71·8	96·5	122·0	145·8

(*Source*: *NKh*, 1975, p. 546)

Incomes of collectivised peasants have risen faster. But the volume of goods and services produced and sold to the population has (according to the official indices) kept pace with this increase. It follows that real wages must have risen by an impressive figure.

The Polish data are given in Table 4.

Table 4 *Poland*

	1960	1965	1970	1975	1976
Retail prices, goods and services	100	106·3	113·5	128·5	134·4
of which: Food	100·0	102·5	109·2	120·7	126·1
(Free market food)	(100·0)	(101·4)	(109·6)	(150·0)	(179·6)
Liquor	100·0	126·2	145·3	184·8	184·8
Non-food goods	100·0	104·3	107·1	121·1	128·4
Services	100·0	111·9	131·3	146·3	149·5

(*Source: Rocznyk Statistyczne*, 1976, p. 389 and *Maly Rocznik*, 1977, p. 226)

Again, there are wide disparities between items: thus meat, bread, macaroni and other basic food items show no price change at all during the entire period, except for the abortive (and brief) attempt to raise some of them in December 1970.

There appears to be no published Polish index of industrial whole-sale prices.

Money incomes in Poland rose much more rapidly than in the USSR after 1970.

Table 5

	1960	1965	1970	1975
Average wages and salaries (zloty per month)	1,560	1,867	2,235	3,562

(*Source: Rocznyk*, 1976, p. 109)

Peasant incomes, derived from sales of produce (mainly to the state) from their (privately owned) smallholdings, rose also. So did the total employed: thus total personal incomes (excluding consumption in kind) rose by over 100 per cent from 1970 to 1975. (*Rocznyk*, 1976, p. 79.)

The inflation, except in the most recent years in Poland, seems mild. But the figures cited above conceal certain phenomena of an infla-tionary kind. These manifest themselves in shortages, queues, grey or black markets, high prices in the legal free markets, unspent or unspendable cash balances in the hands of enterprises or individuals. There are also disguised price increases. Let us first of all examine these phenomena more closely, and then consider their causes and consequences, beginning with the producers' goods (investment goods) sectors.

Here there is one contrast between the USSR and Poland that leaps to the eye. Soviet problems could not be attributed to an un-usually rapid rise in the volume of investment, as the figures in Table 6 show.

Table 6   *USSR. Total Investment in Constant Prices*
(Milliards of Rubles)

1965	1970	1975
57·0	82·0	(114·9)

In Poland, by contrast, the government has proceeded very differently:

Table 7   *Poland. Investment (Milliards of Zloty, 1971 Prices)*

1965	1970	1975
154·2	227·7	529·6

(Source: Roczynk, 1976, p. 123)

The huge increase after 1970 is very noticeable.

In both countries, though not for quite the same reasons, the supply of materials and machines has often fallen short of requirements. In Poland, which relies much more heavily on foreign trade, the shortage shows itself as an excessive payments deficit, which compels cuts in input plans and a sharp downward adjustment in the tempi of investment. This fits into an analysis in terms of a 'political trade cycle': the government tries to go too fast, to adopt over-ambitious plans, then has to jam on the brakes, until enough material and currency reserves are accumulated to start the process over again. Similar trends have been noted in Czechoslovakia and Hungary in previous decades. (See e.g. Goldman, 1964, and Gacs and Lacko, 1973.) This, then, is the generation of excess demand by over-taut plans, which require more resources than exist or can be paid for.

The Soviet pattern is not cyclical, but is rather one of chronic, persistent shortage. Year after year one reads of delays in construction for lack of means to complete the work, and of constant worries of managers about the non-receipt of essential inputs, even when these are planned and allocation certificates issued. This is consistent with two hypotheses: either the planned utilisation exceeds the total resources available (i.e. there is persistent macro-imbalance between output and inputs), or the planners fail to match supply and demand in detail, i.e. there are micro-imbalances within possibly balanced aggregate totals. There is a sizable literature about this whole problem in the Soviet Union, and the most convincing explanation appears to me to be along two mutually reinforcing lines. In the first place, the endeavour to achieve full utilisation of resources, in the interests of rapid growth, leaves no spare capacity with which to correct the inevitable failures to match supply precisely with requirements. Secondly, from all levels below the centre there emerges an intense pressure for more investment resources for the given sector: an enterprise, an industry, a republic or province or city, the department responsible for artillery, or scientific research, or public health, exert pressure through the state and party machine within which they operate.

Let us now look at how these two factors help to explain the generation of excess demand. Why are micro-imbalances *inevitable*? Because of the overwhelming complexity of centralised planning. One can plan and more or less accurately forecast the total requirements for steel, cement and acricultural machinery (for instance), but it is quite another matter when it comes to ensuring the prompt delivery (at the right date) of constructional steel of a given specification, or of the right size of prefabricated cement blocks, or the required spare parts for a specific combine-harvester, to the factory, construction site or farm that actually needs them. This is but one example of perhaps *the* major problem of Soviet operational planning: the necessity and impossibility of disaggregation. So one can easily encounter a situation in which some resources are unutilised while others are short, creating bottlenecks and delays which have a cumulative effect. A further problem arises over the central allocation of investment funds: the cash that is issued is deliberately limited so as to avoid excess demand in total, but obviously those who administer financial flows must sit in a different office from those officials who allocate materials, who in turn are separated by departmental barriers from those who issue orders to those who produce or construct. It is thus quite possible (indeed it is frequently reported) that those who have the money cannot obtain the materials, while others who could obtain the materials are short of money. A network of unofficial supply agents, expediters ('pushers', *tolkachi*) try to overcome persistent shortages of materials in a variety of semi-legal ways. In sum, no Soviet manager, planner or economist would deny that material procurements are a perpetual source of worry and frustration, leading also to a tendency to hoard materials and to over-apply for allocation certificates. Is any of this to be correctly labelled 'inflation', or 'repressed inflation'? This must be a matter of opinion or of definition. But no one doubts that, if prices were freed, many producers' goods would cost more. Indeed, this is advanced as a principal reason for retaining strict control over prices.

Turning now to the pressures for more resources which, of course, exist in all countries, this pressure is reinforced by the fact that capital seems free to the recipient. Again, in part this is universal: thus if my own university obtained the much needed sums to complete its new library complex, this would be an outright grant. This, however, tends to be so in the USSR also in the more strictly economic sphere. As already noted, the enterprise will either receive grants from the budget or will be allowed to retain profits (for an approved purpose) which would otherwise go to the budget. But it would be wrong to suppose, given the nature of the system, that even a stiff interest rate would make much difference. There is, indeed, a capital charge levied since 1967 (averaging 6 per cent), but prices were altered accordingly, and, since plan fulfilment is measured (*inter alia*) in terms of the gross value of turnover (sales), anything that results in the fixing of a higher price is no disincentive, rather the contrary. The ambitions of ministries, managers and localities manifest themselves not only in over-application for capital investment authorisations, but also in two other much documented and much criticised patterns of behaviour. One is to start as many new projects as possible, because an unfinished project is more likely to attract additional grants from the centre. The other is to underestimate the costs of the project. There is thus a constant battle, or tug-of-war, between the officials pursuing sectional interest and the plan-co-ordination agencies (above all *Gosplan*), whose job is to cut the coat according to the cloth. Out of all these factors combined there arises an over-taut plan, too many planned demands in relation to resources. Among the scarce resources is labour: in an economy with little or no unemployment, it is often hard to man new factories, a fact which is advanced as one of the explanations for delays in bringing new capacity into operation, thus contributing to shortage of material inputs.

There is one other point to be made, which will have to be made again when we come to consider consumers' goods: the price index in Table 1 almost certainly understates the increase in prices. This is best seen by examining the index for machinery and metal-working. Is it likely to show a decline in price between 1965 and 1970, for instance, in the face of substantial increases in the prices of fuel and metal, and a 25 per cent increase in wages? This is a sector in which there are many new products, and there are plenty of complaints to the effect that new machines are dearer than the ones they replace. Needless to say, the pricing of new products, and their treatment in computing a price or volume index through time, is a problem for statisticians the world over. 'Accuracy' is out of the question. The reason for suspecting the Soviet index is that there is official pressure to prevent price increases, and therefore a tendency to evade price controls by introducing 'new' products which are just 'new' enough not to be comparable with the old. By contrast, the price index is affected by the (authentic) fall in costs and prices of machines which were new in the base-year and have since entered the mass production stage. The resultant 'deflation' of the price index has as one effect the 'inflation' of the growth rate, which pleases everyone.

Now what of consumers' goods and the citizens' purchasing power? We have seen that wage control in the Soviet Union appears to be more effective than in Poland, at least since 1970. The explanation must be primarily political. In the quinquennium 1966–70 Soviet average wages rose by 26 per cent, against an announced planned rise of 20 per cent. In the same five years, the average in Poland rose by 20 per cent. However, the outburst of rioting which began in December 1970 and led to the fall of Gomulka changed the political situation, and this was followed by a policy of all-out growth of both investment and consumption in Poland, which, as we have seen, led to a mini-wage-explosion: a rise in money wages in five years by over 60 per cent in 1971–5. Whereas in the USSR the relatively modest plan for a rise by 22 per cent in average wages was actually under-fulfilled, the increase being 20 per cent. The institutional means of wage control being similar in the two countries, the difference can only have been due to the will of the political leadership and to pressures from below.

Let us look first at the Soviet case. Here one must note that the under-fulfilment of the consumers' goods production plan, and also of the agricultural output plan, was substantial even according to official statistics. Shortages of many goods can therefore be ascribed to this. These shortages can be shown to have increased in intensity by observing the growing gap (also in Poland, see Table 4) between official and free (peasant) market prices for foodstuffs. Soviet statistical annuals have ceased printing a price index for this free market. It can, however, be calculated roughly from two series, one giving the share of the free market in food sales in volume, the other in value. The figures look like this:

Table 8   *USSR. Share of Free Market in Total Trade in Food, per cent (a)*

	1950	*1965*	*1970*	*1973*	*1975*	*1976*
In actual prices of sale	28·7	10·0	8·5	7·9	7·8	8·4
At official retail prices	27·6	7·3	5·5	4·8	4·4	4·4
Free market prices (official prices = 100)	104	137	154·5	164·5	177·3	190

(a) 'Comparable items' (i.e. presumably excluding bread, for instance)
(*Source: NKh*, 1973, p. 652, and *NKh*, 1975 and 1976)

Another way of measuring surplus purchasing power is to look at the growth of savings bank deposits: for both the USSR and Poland these show very large rises:

Table 9   *Total Deposits*

	1965	*1970*	*1975*	*1976*
USSR (milliard rbles)	18·7	46·6	91·0	103·0
Poland (milliard zloty)	51·3	114·8	302·8	

(*Sources: NKh*, 1975, p. 597, *Rocznyk*, 1976, p. xlviii.)

Since hire purchase is poorly developed, and there have been increases in production of such expensive items as cars, and also so-called co-operative housing (which requires large amounts of cash down), the incentive to save has grown, so that the savers will have the cash to put down if and when the car or the apartment becomes available. (In Hungary savings greatly increased with greater availability, after 1968, of cars and housing (see Lacko, 1975).) However, one has only to relate the total sums deposited in the savings banks with the total annual turnover of state and co-operative trade (178,000 million rubles in 1974) to see what a large overhang of surplus purchasing power now exists. It helps to explain the readily observable fact, especially in the provinces, of persistent shortages of a wide variety of goods and services. No doubt the psychology of a seller's market, continued with little respite for sixty years, contributes to the tendency to hoard and to rush to buy whatever *might* become hard to find, thus ensuring that it does indeed become hard to find. This cannot be quantified, and some purists would treat the evidence as 'anecdotal'. Others might, with more reason, point out that if this has been a chronic tendency for sixty years, this does not show a tendency to inflation, unless the *degree* of shortage has increased. I have suggested already two reasons for considering that shortages (at the official prices) have grown worse. A further point, again, alas, only to be supported by 'anecdotal' evidence, is the growth of black market transactions: thus several (unofficial) sources have asserted that, in order to obtain a suite of furniture priced at 1,000 rubles one must expend 500 rubles on bribes (and even then, according to one informant, there is no choice as to what actual furniture will arrive – 'We just wait and see'). Under such conditions of frequent non-availability and payments on the side, the official price index may be misleading.

It is misleading for another reason, already referred to earlier in discussing producers' goods, the appearance of new or allegedly new goods at higher prices, while the cheaper brands or varieties vanish. This is particularly apt to happen in the case of manufactures, since new varieties of skirts, suits, television sets, bicycles, watches, are a common occurrence whereas (say) bread or milk is of standard type and is more proof against evasion of price control. Such price drift is also hard to resist or indeed to detect in catering: if a cheap dish is replaced by a dearer one in a restaurant, this may or may not be an authentic improvement in quality. Note that, throughout the whole range of goods and services, the replacement of an inferior by a *better* model at a higher price is *not* evidence of a rise in the overall level of prices, if the citizen prefers the better model. It is equally evident that *some* of the new products on sale in Soviet shops really are better than those they replace. It is, however, the universal belief that disguised price rises occur. Nor is this just a matter of folk prejudice or anecdotes:

it can be shown quite rigorously that when there is a wide range of choice as to product mix, plus price control, plus plans expressed in terms of gross rubles or zloty, this *must* encourage management to disguise price increases, especially as price increases are usually forbidden.

One is sometimes asked: if the official Soviet index claims an increase of retail prices by zero per cent in fifteen years, what is the 'real', or 'correct' figure? The question is unanswerable, not only by a Western scholar but also (I strongly suspect) by the Soviet central statistical office. It is the equivalent to asking it to provide information on unrecorded transactions, which by definition are not known to it. (There may, it is true, be instances of disguised increases for which the central government is itself reponsible: one example often cited is the disappearance of the cheapest brands of vodka after 1972.) In Poland no secret was made of the existence of this sort of unrecorded price inflation: even officials told this foreigner: 'The official index admits to an increase of (say) 8 per cent, which means roughly 12 per cent' (referring to the year 1975). But there is no pretence that this is anything other than a rough order of magnitude.

Errors due to failure to incorporate micro-variations in consumer demand into production and distribution plans are common and certainly contribute to the widespread shortages. As in the case of producers' goods, one is never quite sure whether what one is seeing is a macro-imbalance (total demand exceeds total supply) or a series of micro-imbalances (with some goods in excess supply while others are short). In the case of Poland, one can assert with confidence that the wage increases in 1971–5, even after allowance for the increase in prices in these years, exceeded any possible increase in supply of consumers' goods and services (unless these were sustained by massive foreign borrowing, which could only be temporary). One has only to refer to Tables 4 and 5 above. But this has not been so obviously the case in the Soviet Union. In any event, excess demand and shortage (which in the case of producers' goods can be a matter of input-output necessity, independent of relative prices) cannot be analysed without reference to the peculiar distortions of the retail prices system, typical of both the USSR and Poland.

In both countries prices tend to be sticky, for two reasons. One is the sheer administrative burden of altering prices, millions of prices, which totally excludes flexible adjustment to ensure the balance between demand and supply. Matters are not helped by the fact that goods in heavy demand, even if retail prices are moved upwards, may not be profitable to produce, since industrial wholesale prices are related to cost and not to demand, and the gap between the wholesale and the retail price is absorbed by turnover tax. The second reason, however, is the conscious price policy of the government. Higher prices are seen as politically dangerous, higher prices of necessities, especially of food, as very dangerous indeed. One has only to recall the effects of two attempts to raise prices of livestock products in Poland: in December 1970 there were riots and the increase had to be rescinded after the removal of Gomulka from the leadership. In June 1976 the party leader, Gierek, survived, but the proposals had to be hastily withdrawn. In the USSR the last (open) increase in the price of (non-luxury) foodstuffs was in 1962.

The effect of such a price policy has been to create major (and predictable) disequilibria between demand and supply of livestock products, especially meat. Meat is, everywhere, a product with a high income-elasticity of demand. Average wages and salaries in the USSR have increased from 1962 to 1975 by 70 per cent and total disposable incomes have increased by more than this (allowing for the increase in the labour force, higher peasant incomes and some tax cuts), let us say by roughly 85 per cent. Output of meat has risen in the same period by 60 per cent. (It fell in 1976, after the bad harvest of 1975.) But demand has plainly risen much faster, as Soviet calculations show an increase-elasticity of over 1·4. 'Revealed preference' can tell us nothing about demand, when a frustrated customer cannot reveal how she would spend her rubles because what she prefers cannot be obtained.

In Poland the position is equally striking. In just the five years 1971–5 average money wages rose by over 60 per cent, as we have seen. Meat output could not possibly keep pace with demand. (The principal bottleneck is fodder for livestock.) While prices paid to farms have risen to encourage higher output, retail prices have been frozen, and so livestock products now attract some of the highest subsidies known in human history: 19 milliard rubles in the USSR (Glushkov, *Pravda*, 8 February 1977) – over \$25 billion at the not unrealistic official exchange rate (a Russian milliard is an American billion); well over 100 milliard zloty in Poland (possibly \$5 billion in terms of purchasing power: there are many dollar-zloty exchange rates). (The figure for Poland is taken from a speech by Jaroszewicz to the Sejm (parliament) in June 1976).

So one has a heavy burden on the budget to subsidise a price at which demand and supply could not possibly balance. Evidently, then, politics as well as the complexities of price control have totally frustrated any attempt at market-clearing retail prices, and both the USSR and Poland are suffering from this. This fear of higher prices and their political consequences did not operate in Stalin's time: prices of essentials were multiplied in the early thirties, and also in 1946–7. But the Stalin terror is no more.

Space forbids more than a bare mention of other East European countries. They (Poland too) have also had to contend with the dangers of imported inflation, especially in and after 1973. The greatest stability, accompanied by little evidence of physical shortage, has been achieved by the GDR, thus showing the two Germanies out in front in both their halves of Europe. In Hungary, where some progress was made towards aligning domestic and world prices, as part of a market-oriented economic reform, skilful demand management kept the rise in prices to quite modest levels: about 2 per cent per annum in 1968–73 (*Statistical Yearbook* (Budapest, in English), 1976, p. 23), and this despite the fact that a large number of prices were decontrolled. However, the large increase in world prices after 1972 placed severe burdens on the Hungarian economy, and led to a realignment of prices and wages (including a rise in meat prices by 35 per cent in 1976). One can fairly say that these difficulties were due primarily to external factors over which the Hungarian authorities had no control.

The very high rates of inflation in Yugoslavia, accompanied by high unemployment, raise other important questions, which cannot be pursued here.

So returning to the USSR and to Poland, what conclusions can one draw from the evidence presented, which may (or may not) help us to understand the causes and cures of inflation?

The following points seem to be sufficiently significant to justify further consideration.

In the first place, allowing for the important institutional differences, it seems clear that inflationary pressures do exist in Soviet-type economies, and that they too have to wage a constant struggle to restrain excess demand, a struggle which is not always successful.

Secondly, the causes of this excess certainly include pressures from various social groups, exercised through the party-state machine (e.g. by ministers, generals, regional party secretaries etc. etc.), but also more 'passively' from below (e.g. threat of riot if prices rise). Those who, in analysing the causes of Western inflation, lay stress on social pressures in a pluralist society, should note that these pressures (for more than can be provided) exist also in societies thought to be totalitarian. One can speak in fact of their economies as characterised by a kind of 'centralised pluralism'.

Thirdly, control over incomes in the Soviet Union – but not in Poland after 1970 – seems to have been effective, certainly much more effective than in the West. However, the one effective method of control has been over the total wages bill (the 'wages fund'). With widespread bonus and piecerate schemes, and the possibility of evasion through promotion and regrading, no control of individual take-home pay could be effectively applied. Chronic shortage of labour in many areas leads to a built-in tendency to overpay labour, and to evade rules designed to counteract this tendency, except the crude rule which specifies how much the total wages bill should be. This rule does, however, cause serious inconvenience to management: necessary tasks requiring the taking on of extra workers cannot be carried out except after a long and complex procedure for authorisation of additional payments.

Fourthly, price control can be seen to present two kinds of difficulties. The first is political: necessary price increases turn out to be a menace to security and order and are thus avoided or, as in Poland, reversed. The second is technical: it is simply impracticable to amend extremely long price schedules, and to collect reliable information upon which such amendments must depend, without creating a multitude of contradictions and anomalies. (Thus any relationship between demand and scarcity on the one hand and profitability on the other is purely coincidental.) As we have also seen, it is also impossible to prevent disguised price increases via the introduction of 'new' products.

Finally, there is the role of money supply in 'Eastern' inflation. Here it is necessary to distinguish, in the Soviet model, between producers' goods and consumers' goods. Producers' goods are in a real sense rationed, demand is 'authorised' by the plan, dependent on allocation certificates. The money flows, especially of short-term credits, are supposed to match the availability of resources, but there are frequent instances when an enterprise's bank balance cannot be used because the resources that are needed have not been administratively allocated to this enterprise. Therefore most of the 'inflationary' phenomena in *this* field are due to over-ambitious plans, often quantitative plans, or to sectoral imbalances, with money supply playing a subordinate role as a causal factor. It is worth noting that attempts to control credits, if accompanied by over-ambitious obligatory plan targets, have little chance of success. As the work of T. Podolski shows, such attempts in Poland led to the expansion of 'involuntary' suppliers' credits, i.e. delays in payment of debts (though in principle the rules bar the granting of credits by enterprises to one other). (Podolski, 1972.)

In the case of consumers' goods, however, it is possible to speak of excess supply of cash and savings deposits in the hands of the population, though, as has been stressed, it is difficult to distinguish the consequences of 'macro' excess of purchasing power from those of price irrationalities and planning errors and the resultant shortages of many goods (together with excess stocks of others).

The USSR and most of its allies seem better able than most Western countries to keep inflation under control. But the methods used to achieve this end, especially the tight control over material allocation and prices, cause much inefficiency through delays and inflexibilities, the discouragement of initiative and so of innovation. Reformers have been proposing a relaxation of these controls, which would have the effect of increasing the scope of inflationary pressures: thus any measure designed to provide an active role for prices within a more market-orientated economy would lead to a sharp rise in prices, *unless,* as in Hungary in 1968–72, monetary and credit policy plus wage controls can eliminate excess demand.

There is no simple solution anywhere.

ADDENDUM

After the paper was written and sent off to the publishers, I read an article by Richard Portes on 'Control of inflation: lessons from East European experience', which appeared in *Economica* in May 1977. Its conclusions differ very considerably from those of the present paper, and are in certain respects surprising in so far as they relate to the USSR. He denies that repressed inflation can be shown to exist, even in the USSR. It is certainly arguable that a reasonable balance between the cash incomes of the population and the goods and services available has been achieved in Hungary. This is easy to observe from the absence of queues and black-markets. However, it seems totally improper to dismiss the repeated complaints about non-availability of the desired products in the USSR as just 'anecdotal' and to assert that there is no sellers' market! Apart from the plain evidence of the *growing* disparity between official and free market prices for food, documented above, the evidence of shortage is massive. Hungarians travelling to the Soviet Union and Soviet citizens travelling to Hungary (or Czechoslovakia, or East Germany) never fail to notice the contrast in availability, choice and ease of shopping. Whenever the question of the relaxation of price control is raised in the Soviet Union, one of the most frequently cited arguments against such relaxation is that prices would at once rise. It must be accepted, of course, that a considerable part of the phenomenon of shortage is caused by the mismatching between supply and demand for specific products, rather than by a macro-imbalance between total demand and total supply. One cause for such mismatching is cited in Portes's own article: the remarkable stability of most prices over long periods, despite widely different demand and supply elasticities. One consequence is that when price adjustments are made, they are usually very big, as in the case of petrol and coffee in the Soviet Union in February 1978. Would Portes apply the pejorative term 'anecedotal' to the repeated stories from correspondents and others about visible shortage of both petrol and coffee in the period before the price rise?

Finally, a word on savings bank deposits. By themselves they do not provide conclusive evidence of suppressed inflation, except in the sense that the effort to save to obtain cars and co-operative apartments which are not now available does at least prove that they are not available! However, we have no ground for supposing that savings bank deposits represent the totality, or even a major part of stocks of money in the hands of the population.

Part Four
Soviet Studies

12

Is There a Ruling Class in the USSR?

This is a discussion article, not an inclusive survey of all, or even most, of the issues raised when one examines the Soviet social structure. Thus I will deliberately ignore so important a question as nationalities policy, and touch only briefly on problems of social mobility. This is not because they are either uninteresting or irrelevant, but because I wish to concentrate here on something else, which can be formulated as follows: *given* the existence of a ruling stratum, class or elite, why did it establish so dominant a position, and what should one call a stratum of this kind, a society so constituted? The last point is, for this article, the vital one.

There will probably be no major disagreement about the basic facts, though there may certainly be differences of interpretation. We are analysing a society in which almost all the means of production are owned by the state. (At the present level of generality, let us ignore the *kolkhozy*.) These means of production, and also the administrative, judicial, cultural and social institutions of the USSR, are controlled, managed, dominated, by a party which is itself a centralised and disciplined body. The party selects and appoints cadres, this function (*podbor i rasstanovka kadrov*) being carried out by the personnel or establishment department of the central committee – for more junior appointments the republican committees. Rank-and-file party members have very limited means of influencing affairs. The ruling stratum could perhaps be formally defined as all those persons holding appointments deemed to be significant enough to figure on the central committee's establishment nomenclature of such appointments, i.e. who are on the *nomenklatura*. They are, literally, the 'establishment'. As pointed out in an earlier article relating to this theme (see pp. 10*ff.*), this covers all spheres of economic, social, cultural or political significance. It is this which distinguishes the Soviet Union from other bureaucratic or authoritarian societies: in a significant sense there is one centrally administered hierarchy. Of course, within it there are not only gradations but differences of interest. Thus the subhierarchy concerned with primary education or with Kazakhstan may press for resources which officials responsible for artillery or the Leningrad *oblast* might desire to direct for *their* purposes, and such differences are

Reprinted from Soviet Studies, *vol. 27, no. 4, October 1975.*

reconciled at higher administrative levels. But few will disagree that the Soviet system has evolved into a hierarchical society within which status and power depend decisively on rank.

Indeed, one could, without too much exaggeration, fit Soviet society into a 'universal civil and military service' model. Everyone (almost) is employed by the state and party or one of their organisations, doing the work and getting the pay laid down for the rank they occupy. The questions we will have to ask are: What are the upper strata of such a society? What should they be called? Is Marxist 'class' analysis applicable to such a system? If not, what is?

To avoid misunderstandings, let it be said at once that the existence of the hierarchical structure, though certainly a fact, does not imply that everyone obeys his superior passively, nor yet that there is no upward pressure exerted upon the top leadership. No student of Soviet planning can fail to notice that instructions are often ambiguous, or contradictory, or evaded, and that the content of orders received is often influenced by the recipients of the orders. Interest and pressure groups exist, as already noted. Even ordinary workers and peasants can affect plans and income schedules, e.g. by 'voting with their feet' (by leaving occupations and areas where pay is poor or by not going where the authorities wish them to go unless there are sufficient inducements). Mass terror and forced labour cannot now provide a labour force for East Siberia, for instance. However, no autonomous organisations are allowed to exist, no effective trade unions, no uncontrolled organs of the press, and the KGB is active. The structure still accords with a basically unihierarchical model.

Is the elite hereditary, or perhaps becoming such? This is certainly an important question, and one highly relevant to the issue as to whether it is becoming a class or caste. Before considering any of the evidence, it is important to define who it is one has in mind. If by 'elite' is meant the apex of the state- and party-bureaucracy, say, the top 20,000, then one can assert with fair confidence that they are *not* hereditary. Indeed, it is hard to find a single instance of any member of the central committee, minister or party secretary whose father held any of these ranks.

It is another matter if one extends one's attention to the privileged, a much larger group, defined perhaps by family income. (These include successful artists, dancers, professors of philology, and other well-paid persons who exercise no political, social or economic authority, and may be on no one's *nomenklatura*.) There is indeed downward immobility, in the sense that the children not only of the elite narrowly defined but also of other privileged strata tend to receive higher education and to find jobs with reasonably good status, in scientific research institutes, for instance. Statistics in this field are, however, liable to misuse because some analysts shift their attention to yet another group, much larger than the upper elite or the *nomenklatura* officials, or the privileged strata, and use figures relating to the so-called 'intelligentsia' in its Soviet definition. This 'intelligentsia' (officially a stratum – *prosloika*) can include everyone who is not either a worker by hand or a peasant. Teachers, librarians, bookkeepers, hospital nurses, as well as senior officials, fall within this remarkably wide and socially meaningless definition. It includes a great many badly paid persons (many women among them), who could not in any circumstances be described as privileged, or influential or elite. Movement into the elite proper out of the 'lower' intelligentsia so defined is plainly a form of upward social mobility.

This said, it must be stressed that higher education has now almost become a necessary (though not sufficient) condition to get into *nomenklatura* and into senior positions generally. Virtually every party leader or secretary of significance, nearly every industrial manager or minister, has a degree, most usually in engineering or technology. Consequently, access to higher education is vital for advancement. This is difficult for peasants, because of the persistent inadequacy of rural schooling and the low cultural level prevailing in rural areas, and efforts to remedy this have still borne little fruit. Talented children of workers have better opportunities, but the figures show quite clearly that a disproportionate number of places in higher education are occupied by children of the so-called intelligentsia. This whole subject is too complex to pursue here in any analytical and statistical detail, but a very few remarks are in order. The first is again to stress that many of the families of this 'intelligentsia' are not materially privileged. The majority of the group earn less, often very much less, than skilled workers. The second is that, owing to the very large expansion of higher education since 1928, the relative and absolute number of children of persons already educated is now much larger, as is obvious and natural. The third point is that, as our own experience demonstrates, children from educated homes have a clear 'academic' advantage in competition with children from a less cultured environment. We are all familiar with the reasons (books and conversation in the home, parental encouragement, greater motivation, coaching from parents or friends, and so on). But in recent years there has been a notable increase in the intensity of the scramble for higher education places, owing to the fact that full secondary education has expanded much more rapidly than have institutions of university status (demonstrated by the figures for 1960 and 1972) so that a greater number of students qualified through completing secondary school cannot find places. The shortage is, naturally, greatest in prestigious institutions. The use of backstairs methods and string-pulling via influence has therefore become more important, and here the *nomenklatura* officials and their hangers-on have evident advantages, especially as abuses they commit

	1960	1972
	(millions)	
Forms 9–10 (II) in secondary schools	1·5	5·1
Full-time students in higher education	1·2	2·4

(Source: NKh, 1973, pp. 629, 637)

seldom attract publicity. (Khrushchev's efforts to repress these abuses in the 1958 educational reforms were among his less successful actions.)

One needs more evidence before coming to any definite conclusion about recruitment of talent from below into the educational system, and ultimately co-option into the *nomenklatura* ranks, which might enable us to answer the question of whether it is an imperfect meritocracy or a closed corporation. An important point is that, while competitive entrance examinations are held for entry into higher education, recruitment to public and party office is almost always a process hidden from any public eye, and is essentially appointment from above, or co-option. (I abstract here from complications arising out of nationality, which can be very significant. String-pulling and influence have been mentioned already.) Roy Medvedev, in his excellent book, complains that selection pays far too much attention to incidental factors such as personal acquaintance and connections, and far too little to efficiency, but this too we shall leave aside. (Medvedev, 1972, especially p. 352.)

Finally, one must mention one feature of the system in its most recent evolution: the growth of job security in the *nomenklatura*. Under Stalin in the thirties there was a high death and arrest rate, though survivors of the Great Purge proved durable. Even under Khrushchev a fair number of officials were demoted. Since then, the 'civil service' habits familiar in the bureaucracies have become more firmly established, and the vast majority of *nomenklatura* officials are promoted or transferred in a routine manner, save in cases of quite outstanding failure or success. This is no more than to say that the bureaucratic machine functions in accordance with its own rules and habits, with less interference and disruption from a despotic ruler.

One objection to the use of the *nomenklatura* as a means of defining the ruling class or group is that we know little about it, apart from its existence and general function. Details and figures are unpublished in any systematic way. Consequently, even if accepting the *nomenklatura* in theoretical terms, we cannot readily translate it into concrete analysis. Does the central committee's list number 10,000 or 100,000? Just whom does it cover, or leave out? Faced with this problem, Mervyn Matthews, in an unpublished paper, tried to define what he called the 'elite' in terms of a combination of three indicators: income (including the value of 'extras') of over 500 rubles a month, the holding of a *nomenklatura* post, and access to various specific privileges (i.e. to the 'extras' just referred to). We may not wholly agree about concepts or numbers, but clearly Dr Matthews was seeking to define the same sort of group as is here being discussed.

Such a system is not quite the kind of thing the original revolutionaries had in mind. It is a result of a historical evolution, from the libertarian enthusiasm of 1917 to the ordered 'establishment' of today. The causes of this development have been much debated, usually in the context of explaining the rise of Stalinism. Stalin did much to create the hierarchical-bureaucratic system, true enough, but it is proving durable long after his death. I will confine myself here to a bare listing of explanatory factors, each of which could be the subject of a long paper in itself.

First, there is the fact that this was Russia, with its autocratic-bureaucratic tradition and hypertrophy of the state, and relative weakness of spontaneous social forces, repeatedly noted by historians of many different ideologies and backgrounds. This could be expected to affect rulers and ruled, inclining the former to use traditional methods and the latter to accept the methods to which they were accustomed.

Secondly, one must mention the entire logic of change from above, inherent in a socialist-led revolution in a predominantly peasant country. A prolonged period of administered change, imposed upon a peasant majority (the 'petty-bourgeois morass', or *stikhiya*, so often referred to by Bolsheviks in the early twenties), had powerful bureaucratic implications. So did the one-party state, required to maintain Bolshevik rule in such an uncongenial environment. This point is too familiar to require elaboration.

Thirdly, the general low level of education, culture, consciousness, the exhaustion after years of civil war. The few reliable and effective Bolsheviks had to be disposed in key sectors, subject to the discipline of their party superiors. This was when the *podbor i rasstanovka kadrov* was born. Fourthly, there was Soviet Russia's isolation in a largely hostile world, a point which is again too well known to pursue here.

Roy Medvedev put the argument as follows:

'In a vast country such as Russia with its mainly peasant and petty-bourgeois population, its economic backwardness and ignorance . . . in such a country after a socialist revolution a mainly authoritarian regime was inevitable, and not only the old tsarist officials and specialists, who had perforce to be utilised by the new regime, were bureaucrats. Even yesterday's proletarian revolutionaries had to use authoritarian methods, to issue orders, i.e. adopt bureaucratic procedures. Sometimes it is said that the first generation of proletarian revolutionaries could not be bureaucrats. Just the opposite is true. In the conditions of Russia, they *had* to a considerable extent to be bureaucrats.' (Medvedev, 1972, p. 340).

Without the benefit of historical hindsight, Bukharin saw the danger, as early as 1922:

'Even proletarian origin, even the most calloused hands . . . are no guarantee against turning into a new class. For if we imagine that a section of those who have risen out of the working class becomes detached from the mass of the workers and congeals into a monopoly position in its capacity of ex-workers, they too could become a species of caste, which could also become a "new class".'

He noted the existence of 'worker bureaucrats' in Western trade unions, but saw particular dangers in Russia, because, in his words:

'the cultural backwardness of the working masses, especially in conditions of general misery, when *nolens volens* the administrative and leadership apparatus has to receive many more consumer goods than the ordinary worker, gives rise to the danger of a very substantial divorce from the masses even of that part of the cadres which emerged from the working masses themselves . . . . An appeal to working-class origin and proletarian goodness is not itself an argument against the existence of this danger.'

He saw here the germ of a 'new ruling class'. (Heitman, 1970, p. 168. *Burzhuaznaya revolyutsiya proletarskaya*, 1922).
   'Note in passing his use in this context, interchangeably, of the words 'class' and 'caste', reflecting a perplexity which still bothers us today in analysing these phenomena.)
   Rakovsky, when in exile in 1929, noted that the new rulers had changed to such an extent that they had ceased, not only 'objectively' but 'subjectively', not only physically but morally, to be members of the working class, and that 'the Soviet and party bureaucracy is a phenomenon of a new order'. (Carr, 1971, p. 433. For a fuller account of Rakovsky's views see Chapter 3 of this volume, *passim*.)
   We need not enter here into the argument as to whether the bureaucratisation which occurred was inevitable. We can surely all of us accept that the danger was there and the tendencies towards it were inherent in the situation, unless very strongly combated. Far from strongly combating them, Stalin and his faction utilised these trends for their own advantage, thereby providing a powerful additional impetus to the domination of the apparatus.
   Then, next on the list of relevant factors must be the functional logic of a centrally planned economy. With the elimination of almost all

private enterprise, and the imposition through the state planning system of centrally determined priorities, the trends towards comprehensive bureaucratisation were powerfully reinforced. This was not only because, by placing economic management within the party-state machine, its power and control were enhanced. It is also that the *modus operandi* of this species of centralised planning is inherently bureaucratic in nature. The replacement of the largely market economy of NEP by the directive planning of the thirties meant that decisions on resource allocation, production, investment, required to be consciously made and co-ordinated. A complex official apparatus issued the necessary instructions. In practice, the major part of the party-state apparatus, and most of the *nomenklatura* officials, have been engaged in operating some aspect of the economy.

I am, of course, aware that a school of thought exists which claims that central planning can be operated by the 'associated producers' (Mandel's phrase) or by workers' democracy without the great bureaucratic machine which, in actual Soviet history, in fact operated it. I have argued my own view on this matter elsewhere (see Chapter 7). In *this* context it is surely enough to assert that the Soviet way of running the economy was, and is, bureaucratic, and that this is a very important part of any explanation of the all-pervasiveness and completeness of the bureaucratic-hierarchical system as a whole.

While competitive capitalism operates through conflict (for competition is conflict), a centrally planned economy requires hierarchy to ensure consistency and to resolve conflicting claims on resources by administrative decision. In this connection, the French left-wing theorist Claude Lefort is worth citing. His argument is interesting and (at least to English-speaking readers) little known.

'If the productive apparatus did not allow, permit, demand its unification, the role of the political apparatus would be inconceivable. Conversely, if the cadres of the old society had not been destroyed by the party, if a new social stratum had not been promoted to directing functions in all sectors, the transformation of productive relations would have been impossible . . . .' Stalinism made a 'new formation out of elements taken from all classes and pitilessly subordinated them to the task of direction (management) which the new economic system gave them . . .' Whatever their social origin, they form part 'of a new hierarchy, whose common denominator is that it directs, controls, organises at all levels of its functioning the apparatus of production and the living work force, that of the exploited classes'. (Lefort, 1971, pp. 145, 147.) Terror is seen by Lefort as an essential part of the process of destroying the remnants of the older classes, disciplining the workers and peasants and disciplining also the new class so that it could fulfil its functions.

'The bourgeois class grows and develops as a *consequence* of the actions of individual capitalists, economically determined, whatever the conflicts among the actors . . . The division of labour among capitalists, and the market, make capitalists dependent upon one another and act collectively *vis-à-vis* the labour force. By contrast, the bureaucrats form a class only by reason of the fact that their functions and their rules differentiate them collectively from the exploited classes, only because they are interlinked with a directing centre which decides what is produced . . .'

It is because production relations are dominated by the state, with the workers reduced to 'simple executants' of orders received, that the bureaucrats have a class position.

'It is not as individual actors that they weave the network of class relations; it is the bureaucratic class in its generality . . . by reason of the existing structure of production which converts the activities of individual bureaucrats (privileged activities among other such) into class activities . . . The bureaucratic community is not guaranteed by the mechanism of economic activities; it is established by the integration of the bureaucrats around the state, in the total discipline with regard to the directing apparatus. Without this state, without this apparatus, the bureaucracy is nothing'. (ibid., pp. 150–1).

Clearly there *is* something to the proposition that the nature of the central planning system is both a functional justification of the great hierarchy and a precondition of its all-embracing nature. Let me illustrate this with the simplest of examples. In a competitive economy materials are 'allocated' in an unco-ordinated way through a market, and entrepreneurs who find the price too high will switch to another material or another line of business, guided by profit considerations. The outcome may or may not be optimal, but no hierarchical-bureaucratic structure is needed. (Yes, I know that large Western corporations also have bureaucracies. The point still has validity.) In a centralised planning system, however, the decision as to who is to receive the materials requires to be taken at a level *above* that of the factories which are seeking to obtain them, in the light of social priorities, or of input-output consequences of prior policy decisions, i.e. of questions which cannot be resolved at factory management levels – or indeed by those factories' workers. Hence the need for subordination, or hierarchy. I do not share Lefort's basic philosophy, but he surely has a point. In his interpretation, a supreme despot of the Stalin type is required by this economic system, and he argues that the party-state bureaucracy understood this, however much they may have deplored (as individuals) being shot on Stalin's orders.

One other feature, particularly of Stalinism, is worth a brief mention. This is the often brutal and crude relations between superior and subordinate in all spheres of life. The attitude became known as *Borzovshchina*, after a fictional rural official, Borzov, who bulldozed his way through the pages of Ovechkin's stories. In one sense this ruthless disregard of one's subordinates' feelings and interests seems to contradict the entire spirit and purpose of the Bolshevik revolution. But in another it is one consequence of promoting men of little culture into positions of authority, a process which was an integral part of the revolution. One requires to be a starry-eyed idealist indeed to imagine that working-class origin endows individuals with virtue. The civil war brought to the fore those who could get things done in the face of appalling obstacles and much resistance. The 'sergeant-major' type, well known in many armies, is not rendered less authoritarian by the fact that almost every sergeant-major rose from the ranks. It is, indeed, an elementary social observation that first-generation promotees tend to value greatly the privileges which promotion gives them. How well Stalin knew this! He certainly utilised these aspirations in his climb to power. Much of the urban labour force consisted of ex-peasants lacking both 'revolutionary initiative and power of resistance to authority', to cite Carr (1971, vol. 2, p. 432).

An illustration of the psychology of the rising class or stratum of rulers may be found in V. Maksimov's remarkable novel, *Sem' dnei tvoreniya*. The hero, Lashkov, is an honest worker-communist, and he is in conversation with the commissar on the make, in a provincial town in the twenties.

'You live poorly, Lashkov.'
'Like everyone; these are hard times.'
'Like everyone? he mocked, 'We did not seize power to live like everyone! We take what is ours, that belongs to us by right of victory! Let's leave asceticism to the Geneva idealists. Let them swallow their bread ration. We've had enough of this in tsarist prisons. We are men of flesh and blood and do not intend to play at naive communes . . . Money is rubbish (*den'gi dryan'*). Power gives the right to everything. Now women come to me . . .'

The phrase *den'gi dryan'* reflects, by the way, the contemptuous attitude to the market and to money-making, typical of party men of the period, who saw their power as opposed by the power of the market.

There are other points which could be made, including the dominance for long periods of military considerations, which affected both economic priorities and organisational-disciplinary methods. But I think enough has been said in the present context. One has only to add a rather obvious corollary: that the apparatus, once in existence, develops a strong vested interest in its own continuance, and, especially under conditions in which it is tightly in control of communications media, it is in a strong position to abuse its power by allocating to itself material and other privileges. It tends, like other rulers, to identify its interests with those of the people as a whole, and uses its monopoly role of interpreter of the ideology to defend its power. It mobilises millions not only to vote at 'elections', but also to participate in low-level execution of policies decided in the upper echelons of the apparatus, as is demonstrated by the numbers engaged in local soviets and social organisations and committees, under the control and supervision of the appropriate party organs.

Let us now suppose that Soviet society is of the type described in the preceding pages, for the reasons there given. What should such a society be called? Does it possess a ruling *class*?

The official Soviet answer is that there are two classes, workers and peasants, and a *prosloika* (stratum) – the intelligensia. We have noted the uselessness of such labels as these, especially as their applicability to the Soviet economic and political structure is never discussed in Soviet publications.

In the West, David Lane has argued for the concept of a 'uni-class state', socialist because of state ownership of means of production, but 'bourgeois' because distribution is unequal. In this conception, everyone is a species of worker (hence 'uni-class'), indeed it is a workers' state, but there is inequality and privilege. (Lane, 1976). My belief is that this conception is misleading, because it obscures the qualitative distinction between (so to speak) officers and other ranks, between 'we' and 'they', between rulers and ruled, which not only exists in reality but also impregnates people's consciousness in the Soviet Union itself.

Another conception has a long historical lineage: this is the 'degenerated workers' state', which Trotsky favoured and to which some Trotskyists still cling. If by this is meant that there was once a workers' state and that it degenerated, it is an arguable position. E. H. Carr was more sceptical about a workers' state ever existing (Carr, 1971, vol. 2, pp. 429–33), and so am I, since any worker appointed to run any part of the state apparatus ceases to be a worker. To this it can be objected that a workers' state no more requires workers to run it than a state in a capitalist society is run by capitalists, but this argument contains a fallacy. In the 'bourgeois state' model it matters little who the actual ministers or senior civil servants are; so long as the great capitalists and landlords own the bulk of property, they exercise power by virtue of the fact of owner-ship. This is not so in the 'workers' state' model; the workers have no power by the mere virtue of being workers, and can exercise it only through their control over their representatives who run the state (and economic) machine. If this control lapses, so does their influence on affairs. Surely no Trotskyist doubts that it has lapsed, and long ago. They can, and do, argue that something which could be called a workers' state existed in (say) 1920. Trotsky could claim that it had degenerated by the time of his own defeat. Now, fifty years after, is the *present* Soviet state really to be described as a workers' state, albeit a degenerate one? My own answer is in the negative.

A whole number of analysts assert the existence of a new class, or a new bourgeoisie. The most familiar argument is probably that of Milovan Djilas:

'Ownership is nothing other than the right of profit and control. If one defines class benefits by this right, the communist states have seen, in the final analysis, the origin of a new form of ownership or of a new ruling and exploiting class . . . The new class may be said to be made up of those who have special privileges and economic pre-ferences because of the administrative monopoly they hold . . . Membership in the new party class or political bureaucracy is reflected in larger economic and material goods and privileges than society should normally grant for such functions. In practice the ownership privilege of the new class manifests itself as an exclusive right, as a party monopoly for the political bureaucrat to distribute the national income, to set wages, direct economic development and dispose of nationalised and other property . . . The so-called social ownership is a disguise for real ownership by the political bureaucracy.' (Djilas 1957.)

The essence of the case rests on the proposition that what matters is *control*, and that the upper strata are in control; they decide what should be done with nationalised means of production. This too is the basis of Bettelheim's claim that there is a 'state bourgeoisie' which runs the Soviet Union. Bettelheim is, of course, aware that there is both state ownership and planning, but for him these are necessary but not sufficient preconditions for a socialist transformation; essential for progress towards socialism is the domination of the workers. (More will be said in a moment as to what he and others consider to be socialism.) Instead, there is domination over the workers, the means of production and the product by a *class*. (See e.g. his letter to Sweezy, in Bettelheim, 1969.)

A variant of this approach is that of Castoriadis. He argues that the productive process has a class character because of 'the effective possession of the productive apparatus by the bureaucracy, which is in full charge of it, while the proletariat is fully dispossessed'. In common with Djilas, he argues that the bureaucracy enjoys 'surplus revenue', which is unjustified by its productive contribution to society and determined by the position of any given individual in the bureaucratic pyramid. This, according to him, is a form of exploitation of the masses. He asserts that 'bureaucratic property is neither individual nor collective; it is private property in so far as it exists only for the bureaucracy while the rest of society is dispossessed; it is private property managed in common by a class and collective within this class . . . In this sense one can briefly define it as private collective property.' (Castoriadis, 1973, pp. 84–5.)

He concludes: 'it is not capitalism, it is not socialism, it is not even on its way to either of these two forms; the Soviet economy represents a historically new type, and its name matters little if its essential features are understood.' (ibid., p. 67.)

Lefort, whom we have already quoted and who is an ally of Castoriadis in the *Socialisme ou Barbarie* group, also speaks of a 'collective apparatus of appropriation' exercised by a 'new class' which does not dominate through *private* appropriation. For reasons which, as already shown, he finds within the relations of production, there takes place (in his view) a 'fusion of all the strata of the bureaucracy in the mould of a new directing class', whose unity is linked with 'the collective appropriation of surplus'. (Lefort, 1971, pp. 148, 151.)

Chinese criticisms, usually worded in very strident terms, also tend to identify a new oppressive class in the USSR, which appropriates and exploits. (In sources available to me at least, this is backed by no serious historical and social analysis, and the allegation that this class came to power after the death of Stalin is absurd.)

All this raises some awkward questions, though it is none the worse for that: we may be facing a qualitatively new phenomenon for which our customary categories (whether derived from Marx or from Parsons) may require substantial modification.

But before pursuing the argument further let us halt for a moment and consider the relationship of the *namenklatura*-rulers to the means of production. They are in command of them. Marxists will then turn their attention to the *surplus* which they should be extracting. Do they derive an exploitation income? If so, in what does it consist? It is clear that, *qua* individuals (as Castoriadis duly noted), they do not pocket the profits.

The question of surplus in the Soviet economy can be handled basically in two different ways. One may assert that the surplus is equal to what the Soviet leaders themselves describe as the surplus product, or 'product for society', i.e. the total profit (including turnover tax etc.) generated by productive labour and appropriated by the state or its enterprises. It is used for a variety of purposes:

hospitals, schools, investments of all kinds, administration, defence, and so on. Plainly, a part of these expenditures (Brezhnev would say: all) is for the common weal. There are those who assert both that the USSR is an autocracy which pays no attention to people's needs *and* that the masses have no means of exerting pressure. If, then, there is an increase in minimum wages and old age pensions, this must upset these assumptions: either the leaders *are* paying attention to people's needs, or they respond to pressure from below in their own self-interest (in which case such pressure does exist). In practice, surely, both these things are true. The leaders would like the citizens to live better, *and* it would be dangerous for their political security if there were no improvements. The essential point in the present context is that the surplus is disposed of by the *nomenklatura*-apparatus; it decides what happens to it. Naturally, some part of it benefits ordinary citizens, in their capacity as pensioners, patients, students, scientists etc. etc. The 'collective owners' of Castoriadis's conception 'appropriate' *this* surplus in the sense of deciding on its use. They control it.

A different approach is contained in the quotation from Djilas. The 'new class' is held to divert for *its own use* 'a larger income in material goods and privileges than society should normally grant for such functions'. By this criterion, they appropriate an amount equal to the notional excess of what they earn (and receive in the form of 'perks') over what they ought to have received, an excess which control over the means of production enables them to acquire. I shall not discuss this further, but of course one must point out that *this* sense of surplus is statistically and conceptually quite different from, and much smaller than, the surplus product referred to above.

Anyhow, it behoves those who speak of a 'new class' to adopt one or other of these definitions of what it is that this class appropriates. (My own preference is for the second definition, though it too presents difficulties.)

The doctrine of 'state capitalism' should, in my view, be seen as a variant of the above. In a functional sense, it is quite proper to speak of the state carrying out the role of capitalists, especially in growth and development. Presumably, this interpretation lends itself well to the notion that the ruling stratum that controls the state is, collectively, the equivalent of the capitalist class. It is all a question of how useful it is to use this term, whether it helps to clarify more than to confuse. Can one have state capitalism and no capitalists? Or can one call the ruling stratum 'collective capitalists'? This seems wrong to me. Lenin used to refer to state capitalism, but this term led to much misunderstanding among his comrades. Mao interprets it as referring to a workers' state domination over surviving capitalists. (Mao Tse-tung, in 'Miscellany of Mao Tse-tung Thought (1949–68)', parts 1 and 2, reference no. JPRS 61269/1/2, p. 308.

Popular among some neo-Marxists is the view that there is no ruling class in the Soviet Union, but that the USSR is a 'transitional society'. Let us examine this conception, of which Mandel is a well-known representative.

It is based on the belief that a society can be either capitalist or socialist, and that the Soviet system contains some elements of both and is neither. It has a centrally planned economy, the 'law of value' is severely constrained. There are no capitalists. However, it is not a workers' state, workers do not control the means of production, the plan contains many lacunae, and there is pressure to strengthen market elements, pressure which (on this interpretation) could lead to the restoration of capitalism. Alternatively, the assertion of the power of the working masses could or would lead on to socialism. Meanwhile, it is a transitional, mixed system, which must go one way or the other.

Mandel's view of socialism is a common one among the New Left: it is close to, if not identical with, Marx's vision of communism. In such a society, the market would vanish along with commodity relations, the state would wither away and so would money, wages, the disparity between mental and physical labour; there would be no scarcity: we would have 'from each according to his abilities, to each according to his needs. I have expressed elsewhere my scepticism about this conception of socialism, and this is not the place to pursue the matter. It is enough to assert, with (presumably) Mandel's agreement, that such a socialism is not immediately practicable, and that in any case there is no sign that Soviet society is in process of transition towards it. (Presumably, Mandel takes the position that a revolutionary overthrow of the ruling 'elite' is a prerequisite of progress in that direction.) Bettelheim adopts a less fundamentalist definition of socialism: in his letter to Sweezy he argues that socialism is characterised not by the presence or absence of commodity relations, money and prices, but by the existence of the domination of the proletariat. He therefore lays special stress on the decisive role of power. It is because in the Soviet Union power resides with what he calls the new bourgeoisie that he regards the Soviet Union as not socialist, and not because they use money, pay wages etc. It must be added that Sweezy's reply includes the following sentence: 'My conception is that market relationships (which of course imply money and prices) are *inevitable* under socialism for a long time, but that they constitute a standing danger to the system . . .' (Bettelheim, 1969.) He too, then, has problems with defining the relationship to production of the managerial elite, which also in his eyes is tending to develop into a new type of bourgeoisie. He sees a conflict between this managerial elite and the old party bureaucracy. He fears that this might lead to a restoration of capitalism.

If socialism is not on the agenda, why should capitalism be restored? Why, indeed, not assume that the existing system is as durable and stable as any other in a rapidly changing world? Mandel's answer, if I understand it correctly, is that it is in the interests of the elite, or of an important segment of the elite, to strengthen market relations. All reform proposals in Eastern Europe tend in that direction. The implication of a market system is that there will be capitalists; managers will seek the advantages and security which ownership would bring. The 'law of value' re-enthroned will restore capitalist relations.

Is this a likely outcome? All things are possible, but I would like to question the assumption that administrators of state property have a predisposition to wish to own it. Is this so? Analysis of the interests of industrial managers can provide evidence for their desire for security and non-interference, for more autonomy (though some managers fear responsibility and like being given orders) and higher incomes. But ownership? Why is this in their interests as they conceive them? They are privileged members of the hierarchy. They see their own promotion as taking place within it. Thus, let us say, the manager of a medium-sized factory aims not so much at owning it as at being advanced to a managership of a larger factory, or to the rank of deputy minister of 'his' industry. Indeed, most industrial deputy ministers are senior managers, who can scarcely aspire to 'own' their ministry! This whole conception, like that of Burnham, over-concentrates on the factory manager: this level of the hierarchy is important, but it is only part of a complex whole.

The factor of ownership is surely crucial if capitalism is to be restored by the 'Mandel' route. 'Market' type reforms (*à la* Budapest, for instance) are not of themselves enough. It is also worth stressing that, with all their imperfections, market forces may express the desires of the masses more effectively than the plan, if the plan is drafted by a remote and irresponsible oligarchy. It is, surely, as foolish (in the Soviet context) to assume that the plan is right as against the market as to assume the opposite. We all know how often planners' programmes have failed to match consumer preferences, and indeed how often the actual product mix fails to reflect the original intentions of the planners. (See Chapter 6, pp. 100–11.)

Where has all this got us? One could go on citing other interpretations, but perhaps the heart of the matter is in the significance of *control* through a hierarchy, and the relation of this to the traditional Marxian analysis of class. Control relates to power, and power resides in ownership, so Marxists naturally look at property relations as a key to identifying a ruling class. This is a useful model for analysing capitalism. But what of other social formations?

Danilova, a Soviet anthropologist, boldly grappled with this question. Ernest Gellner should be thanked for drawing attention to her ideas, which are highly germane to the fundamental question just raised. (E. Gellner, 1974, citing L. V. Danilova's writing on pre-capitalist societies.)

'Does the ownership of the means of production constitute the determining element in all societies? Is it correct to extend the primacy of production relations to all stages of human history . . .? Contrary to the viewpoint widely diffused in Soviet science, the relations of domination-subjection conditioned by the development of the division of labour are themselves by no means relations of production. The dominant relationships in all pre-capitalist structures are non-economic ones.'

In her view, 'the absolutisation of the economic factor in due time became an obstacle to solving serious theoretical problems, notably the problem of socialist and pre-capitalist societies'. Gellner commented: The absolutisation of the economic factor is applicable to the capitalist period only. Elsewhere, before and since, we must look to relations of domination-subjection.'

This, surely, means that there are circumstances in which power ('domination-subordination') determines relations of production rather than vice versa. The mention by Danilova in this connection of 'socialism' (which her readers would construe as the Soviet system) is, of course, most important. A similar or related point was made by Wlodzimierz Brus:

'In my opinion, the traditionally accepted relationship between economy and policy as 'base' on the one hand and 'superstructure' on the other, and hence as 'in the last resort' the determining factor and the determined factor, needs, with respect to socialism, fundamental modification. Economy and politics are so intimately intertwined, especially when considered dynamically, that the continued use of the old conceptual apparatus of 'base' and 'superstructure' becomes more and more inadequate.'

He goes on to stress the 'dependence of further development of socialist relations of production, and hence of the evolution of the "economic base" . . . on changes in the political power system'. He continues:

'Marxist literature . . . has never been satisfied with the definition of social ownership as public ownership. Public ownership (especially state ownership) is not considered to be social ownership if it occurs in a capitalist state. The socialist character of the state is a necessary condition of public ownership as social ownership. Hence, in this case, the *character* of the state – a political institution, an element of the superstructure – is considered to be a factor determining a basic relation of production – the nature of the ownership of the means of production'. (Brus, 1973, p. 88)

This raises a historical-philosophical issue, which causes difficulties for Marxists and concerns the meaning to be attached to the relationship between basis and superstructure. One recalls arguments concerning the class or above-class nature of the tsarist autocracy, and also Menshevik critique (and the Bolshevik view) of the October revolution. In a recent article, Gerschenkron cited a Soviet historian who put forward the concept of *operezhenie*, i.e. that political (superstructure) changes can get ahead of the economic base and alter it. The orthodox historian Nechkina retorted that the political system would then 'hang in the air', deprived of its (economic) base, and Gerschenkron points out that this is an example of a dead metaphor (infrastructure – superstructure) coming awkwardly to life and obstructing scholarly discussion. (Gerschenkron, 1974, p. 441. A 'dead' metaphor is not a pejorative term. They abound, legitimately, in everyday scholarly useage.)

Trotsky wrote long ago, in relation to the Soviet system, that 'the character of the economy as a whole thus depends upon the character of state power'. (Trotsky, 1937, p. 237.)

Even longer ago Lenin wrote: 'Politics cannot but have dominance over economics. To argue otherwise is to forget the ABC of Marxism.' What, then, is the name to attach to an identifiable group which exercises state power, and achieves political and economic domination?

Let us attempt a few generalisations based upon the considerations set out above.

1 If the state owns the means of production, the nature of the state, its political processes, its power relations, are essential determinants of production relations.
2 If such a state is in some sense a workers' state, i.e. the masses have a strong and continuous influence on public affairs and on economic policy, *and* if planning dominates in large-scale economic decision making, I for one would accept that the system could be described as socialist. Probably, I would have Bettelheim, Brus and some other Marxist theorists on my side in doing so. There will certainly be others who regard the survival of *any* market (even if confined to micro-economic links between customers and producers, even for trousers, fish and chips and books) as inherently inconsistent with any socialism, and would label the society as transitional. They are entitled to their views, and to the quotations from Marxist holy writ on which they base them, though this lands

them in a predicament: they would be using the same term ('transitional') to describe the Soviet system of today, in which, as they loudly and rightly assert, the state is *not* any sort of workers' state.

3 If the Soviet state machine, the process of production and the producers, are directed by the party-state *nomenklatura* officials, who recruit by co-option from among the beneficiaries of higher education, and who in various ways benefit from privilege, it follows that this ruling stratum has *some* of the characteristics of a *ruling* class, though not that of ownership, except possibly in some collective sense (cf. Castoriadis). Medvedev argues, however, that 'it is evident that they are not owners of the means of production, do not possess lands and cannot bequeath their rights and their ranks (*dolzhnosti*) to their children'. He claims that, though their power is 'very great', none the less 'the position of these men is in many ways less secure than that of high officials of a church hierarchy, for instance the Catholic one'. (Medvedev, 1972, p. 347.) He prefers to regard the leadership as in a position analogous to that of a trustee, administering the property of a minor: while appearing to be in full charge, 'the trustee is not the owner of the property he controls. True, some trustees can succeed in prolonging the trusteeship even after the real proprietor comes of age. None the less the trustee is still only a trustee, the administrator and not the boss, not the owner. This is known . . . by all society'. Medvedev quotes the view that 'the bureaucrats' power rests only on political equilibrium, and this is a much more fragile basis for a superior position in society than any of the known structures of property relations, hallowed by law, religion and tradition'. (ibid., pp. 347–8.) This is indeed a serious argument, though surely it is only the power of the individual bureaucrat which rests on 'political equilibrium', rather than the power of the ruling group as a collectivity. It still leaves one perplexed about how to define the ruling stratum.

An (anonymous) Soviet commentator, also cited by Medvedev, puts the dilemma in another way, very close to the ideas of Medvedev himself (and of the author of this article too). He notes a

'contradition between the socialist form of production relations and the bureaucratic system of control . . . For a scientist the question of the social nature of our bureaucracy is a vital and fundamental question. The Stalin and post-Stalin periods formed the bureaucracy into a separate social group, a separate stratum . . . Of course our bureaucracy is not a new exploiting class, representing state capitalism etc. But then what is it? It seems that we need more subtle intermediate categories, different from [conventional Marxist] social-economic

formations – although we note in parenthesis that the fact of the appropriation of a part of the surplus product [by this stratum] is undeniable. It is not enough to talk of "elements of caste", when power is in
the hands of a social group standing above society, self-sufficient,
closed, which retains power in the hands of these same people. New
recruits . . . enter only from the ranks of the "reliables", who satisfy
the social requirements of the bureaucracy'. (Medvedev, 1972,
pp. 349–50)

Here again the search is for new categories, new labels to attach to a
phenomenon which Marx did not analyse.

Rolf Dahrendorf distinguished 'class' and 'stratum' (*Schicht*): 'The
concept class is an analytical tool that can only make sense in the
context of a class theory. "Classes" are major interest groupings
emerging from specific structural circumstances, which intervene as
such in social conflicts and play a part in changes of social structure.'
Whereas a 'stratum' is merely an analytical category, identifying
persons of a similar situation in the social hierarchy, who share some
situational identities such as 'income, prestige, style of living etc . . .'
So for him *classes* relate to groups which act together in a power
context, about which one speaks in terms of 'inclusion or exclusion
from positions of power'. (Dahrendorf, 1957, pp. ix, 139 (translation
mine). Thanks are due to H. Adomeit for drawing my attention to
these passages.) Ownership is, of course, one means of acquiring
power, but Dahrendorf, if I understand him correctly, would certainly
not confine his definition of a ruling (or any other) class to any specific
property relationship: there could be ownership with little power, or
more commonly, power without ownership. In these terms, the Soviet
'establishment' would seem to qualify as a 'class'. This appears to be
not Marxist, but then we are trying to deal with a society unlike any
that Marx described.

Is the term 'power elite', associated with C. Wright Mills, more
suitable? There is no doubt that it *can* be used to describe the Soviet
dominant stratum. However, the term is most usually applied to the
group that exercises power within a Western class society: thus it
may consist of top officials, generals, senior advisers, a few influential
industrialists and bankers, even some trade union officials. The
common denominator is that they all have their hands on the levers
of power. Yet in this society there are a great many others who may
have as much (or more) wealth or social prestige, and the power elite
itself lacks social cohesion or any definite relationship to the means of
production. This is not to criticise Mills's use of the term, but merely
to underline that the Soviet case is different: the rulers ('power
elite') are at the same time the controllers of the bulk of state property, of almost all means of production, and can determine to a great

extent the status, earnings and social position of various sub-groups in society. Thus in America there is a power elite *and* a class structure, while in the USSR the power elite *is* the class structure, or rather its apex. The use of the same term for these two distinct formations may mislead.

The word 'caste' is unsuitable because it suggests fixed hereditary status. So does the old Russian word *soslovie*, or 'estate', though the *dvoryanskoe soslovie* could be entered under tsarism by promotion in the civil and military service (Lenin's father was one of many). But some would argue that the term 'class' also implies heredity. Thus Bukharin wrote of the ancient Inca state, in which there was 'a gentry-priesthood *class* . . . which controlled everything, ran everything and operated the *state* economy as a dominant *class*, sitting on top of all the others'. (Bukharin, 1921, p. 69. Emphasis added.) Note that Bukharin used 'class' in relation to a society without private *ownership*, but presumably the 'gentry-priesthood' were hereditary. We have seen that, despite some evident advantages in being well born, the Soviet 'ruling class' is not hereditary. Does this destroy the validity of the 'class' label? I think not, though I see the force of objections to my position. Other labels have their own weaknesses. The term 'elite' is used so indiscriminately, along with the pejorative jargon-word 'elitism', as to deprive it of meaning, except just that some people control and others are controlled, which is no doubt true in all societies. (Defined more precisely, with special reference to its peculiarly Soviet features, the term 'elite' is certainly usable, however.) Also vague and unsatisfactory is the equally popular word 'bureaucracy', again used pejoratively with the minimum functional analysis, and with no attempt at all to define and limit the concept: thus, is a junior official who allocates ball-bearings in Uzbekistan a 'bureaucrat'? Functionally yes, but he is not well paid and has very little influence indeed (is he 'elite'?). Is the well-paid manager of a soccer team a 'bureaucrat'? Or, indeed, is the manager of a construction project in North-East Siberia a bureaucrat? Or an academician-physicist who heads a research team? Many jobs of importance *are* rightly to be described as 'bureaucratic', their holders as bureaucrats, but the indiscriminate use of the term, especially interchangeably with 'elite', is surely open to severe criticism.

It seems to me not greatly to matter that, in a unihierarchical system, the definition of where to draw the 'class' line is necessarily arbitrary. I do not insist on *nomenklaturnyi rabotnik*. There is no scientific reason why one should include only the top 10,000 or the top million. The point about the *nomenklatura* is that it lists those whom the *system itself* regards as being important enough to require the special attention of the central committee's organisation department. Consequently, unlike vague words about bureaucrats and elite, they represent something not only definable but defined, and defined not by the arbitrary whim of the foreign scholar but by the party machine itself (though this definition is not known to us in detail).

There is another dimension to the problem of 'class' analysis of Soviet society: that of consciousness. Do *they* regard themselves as a sort of class, *sui generis*? Some would certainly argue that they do. The poet-playwright Aleksandr Galich quotes a story of a woman patient at one of the special 'government' hospitals who, eating a smoked salmon sandwich, remarked: 'I visited a school friend, not one of us (*ne iz nashikh*), who gave me tea, and it was awkward to refuse, so I ate some town sausage, and got gastritis.' (Galich, 1974, p. 188.) The two key points are the concept of *iz nashikh*, and access to superior sausages (and smoked salmon) which are simply not on sale to ordinary townspeople. Galich speaks of a special official pass giving access to 'special buffets, smoked fish, caviare, American cigarettes, cheap dinners', and also 'dachas with paintings, Czech crystal, silver cutlery, service personnel', a separate existence with its own access to information ('the white TASS') and to politically spicy and sexy films, luxurious and cheap sanatoria and the opportunity to visit foreign countries. The beneficiaries of such privileges live in a world of their own, to which ordinary mortals are denied access. Surely they have a sense of belonging to some separate and high 'class', and their subordinates, and ordinary workers and peasants, regard them as a privileged group. David Lane argues that the dominant values are in some sense working-class values, but I find this hard to follow. (Lane, 1976.) The *nominal* values of Soviet society indeed stress the working class, but has this more significance than did Christian poverty and humility in relation to a proud, rich, aristocrat-archbishop in Renaissance times? Galich writes sarcastically of the 'people's servants, whom the people elect' in luxurious homes 'cut off from the people by high fences and guards'. (Galich, 1974, p. 188.)

In presenting a paper on this subject in Paris, I used a naval analogy: an admiral belongs to a different *class* from a seaman, even though they are both in the same hierarchy and the admiral does not own any part of the navy. At once came the predictable objection: military and naval analogies are irrelevant, because, like the civil service, they merely reflect indirectly the class structure of society, which is based on ownership of property. It was necessary again to remind the critics that the problem is how to analyse a society which is *based* on a civil and military service (and not, *pace* Burnham, on industrial managers, though they are an important part of it, to be sure). It seems to me that neither political science nor sociology, whether Marxist or non-Marxist, are of much help in devising a suitable conceptual framework.

In functional terms, such a hierarchical structure may well be the only alternative – in a world of scarcity and acquisitiveness – to private ownership or indeed to any predominantly market economy.

A case for the existing Soviet rulers could be made out as follows:

Whatever Marx or Lenin may have said, in the real world ordinary people pursue inconsistent objectives, do not know what is good for them, enter into conflict with competing groups. This is so everywhere, and the disarray of the Western world today is ample proof of the bankruptcy of liberal pluralist ideas, even where they have deep roots in tradition. *A fortiori*, Russia can only be ruled from above, by a disciplined party, which at least avoids the excesses of Stalin's despotic terror, and which tries – by expanding the output of goods and services and mitigating inequalities by minimum wage and social legislation – to improve the material and cultural position of the masses. We claim [says my imaginary Brezhnev-apologist] that our record is one of steady improvement. All this talk of workers' control and freedom to make demands is a recipe for confusion and anarchy, and therefore for a reduction of material standards. We plan and administer the productive process for the good of society, as best we conceive it. The elite's 'take' is small as a percentage of the national product, much smaller than that of the capitalists and landlords in the West. It is a price the people should pay for stability and order, which we ensure. There are abuses, true, but to talk of them openly would be dangerous. You say this is not socialism? Well, it is the best that we can do, and you [the critics] adopt unreal criteria . . . One day we will have much greater material abundance, and then we can talk of communism.

I am unconvinced by the case put by my imaginary Brezhnevite, but it has a more solid basis than some enthusiastic critics (from left *and* right) are prepared to admit. It may not be socialism, but it provides stability, in an increasingly unstable world. Contrary to those who use the term 'transitional society', I am inclined to the view that this unihierarchical system can be durable. True, its leaders could commit grave errors of policy. They may fail to improve living standards, repression could cause trouble in some national republics. (However, nationality problems are largely irrelevant to the unihierarchical *model*, just as the quarrels between Serbs and Croats, though of evident importance, are irrelevant to an analysis of Yugoslav 'workers' self-management' as a model.) If the promotion routes of able and ambitious workers are blocked this could stimulate a challenge from below. Finally, the ruling stratum can weaken itself through inner conflicts. All such things are possible. However, I take seriously the views expressed to me by several bitterly critical recent émigrés from the Soviet Union. They dislike the system, the *nomen-*

klatura, the network of controls, they also dislike their own conclusions, but none the less these conclusions pointed to stability, durability and acceptance, not instability and rebellion. One philosopher-sociologist said – I quote from memory – that 'unfortunately the system that has developed in the USSR is the one that best fits the circumstances of the second half of the twentieth century'.

If I understand him aright, the point is as follows. Our present discontents in the West arise because many people are not prepared to accept the distribution of income and property which the system of private ownership has generated and is reproducing. They make demands which the system cannot meet, which, indeed, cannot be met at all, in that they exceed productive capacity. Hence political instability, inflation, increasing disruption. The Soviet system eliminates almost totally any income from property, decides on wage and salary scales and suppresses any challenge from below, aware that no generally acceptable criteria for income distribution in fact exist. Similarly, it reconciles (more or less) the conflicting demands of all sorts of interest groups, including those which exist among the *nomenklatura* officials themselves. To operate such a system one cannot rely on coercion alone, there must be a fairly widespread acceptance. In the view of these émigrés, such acceptance is in fact widespread, despite the undoubted existence of grievances; all hitherto known societies contain within themselves unsatisfied aspirations, if only for higher incomes and lower prices, and a demonstration that these exist is not evidence of instability or threat to the system. Indeed, the greater ability (compared with the West) of the Soviet unihierarchy to keep demands and aspirations from below under control, ensuring some improvements in living standards the while, is part of its strength. People resent in general terms the privileges of the 'elite', and often imagine that they live like millionaires, a consequence of the secrecy surrounding this question (the salaries and 'perks' of party secretaries and ministers are probably not in fact exceptionally high, but they are hidden from public view and critical scrutiny, so many people assume the worst). However, the willingness of workers and peasants to accept hierarchy and material inequalities may be greater than that of left-wing intellectuals.

The word 'accept' may be too positive, and could perhaps be replaced by 'tolerate'. Most of us 'accept', in the sense of working within, systems which contain many things that we heartily dislike but feel powerless to change. There are indeed forces making for change, particularly those associated with the contradiction between bureaucratic centralisation of the economy and the requirements of a modern industrial structure. The effort to increase expertise among the *nomenklatura* officials can only very partially resolve the problem, which will certainly continue to give trouble. So will nationalism. But enough is enough. This article is not an exercise in futurology, but an attempt to place a complex and evolving reality into some sort of conceptual framework. If anyone does not like it, they are invited to do better.

13

Some Observations on Criteria for the Study of the Soviet Union

Some words are needed in the way of a methodological introduction. Criteria imply judgement. Some may say: it is not for us, as historians, political scientists, economists, to judge. We should describe, analyse the causes of what occurred, or of the situation that exists, and leave judgements to the moralists or to those intellectual inferiors who choose to practise counter-factual history.

For reasons which should be clear, but which still need to be spelt out, this attitude is not only incorrect, but is in fact untenable. Value-judgements, criteria, are constantly used even by those who claim to be free of them. Nor can one really avoid counter-factual history. Let me illustrate, first, with a quotation from Richard Löwenthal: criticising Habermas, he states that he (Habermas) 'measures actual democratic institutions by the yardstick of his utopian-idealist vision of a "substantive" democracy'. (Löwenthal, 1976, p. 257.) This brings one immediately into the heart of the 'realistic criteria' problem. According to Löwenthal, Habermas is explicitly or implicitly comparing (say) West German democratic institutions with an unattainable ideal. Habermas would presumably disagree, and the argument would then turn on the possibility of alternatives, i.e. in a sense on counter-factual history.

Other examples abound. When we analyse (say) the campaign that culminated in the battle of Tannenberg, we inevitably discuss the inactivity of the commander of the Russian 1st Army, implying that General Rennenkampf *could* have acted other than he did, and that this would (or could) have made a difference to German dispositions and to the outcome. When we describe the vigour and efficiency with which Zhukov gathered together a defence force in front of Moscow after the disaster of October 1941, we surely judge his performance by reference both to what he did and what *could* have been done, by him or others, in that critical situation. Indeed the entire discussion of the role of the individual in history always poses the question: what difference did he make to what might otherwise have happened? If this is 'counter-factual', it is inevitably so.

Reprinted from Socialism in Theory and Practice, *Festschrift for Richard Löwenthal, Berlin, Freie Universität, 1978.*

Similarly, discussions on the 'inevitability' of the Russian revolution, the causes and consequences of collectivisation of agriculture, the feasibility of Trotsky's economic programme in 1925, Khrushchev's reorganisations of planning, all imply judgement, about the possible and therefore also about alternatives. Nor are *moral* judgements entirely avoidable. Few human beings exist who can discuss the cold statistics of Stalin's victims without at least suggesting that killing so many (communists, peasants, officers) was not merely unnecessary but also in some sense wrong. While I will not, in this paper, be much concerned with moral judgement, it is worth mentioning that it too is intimately connected with a not strictly deterministic view of history, i.e. one allowing of choices, alternatives and therefore the counter-factual approach. One cannot meaningfully praise or condemn that which necessarily, inevitably, had to be.

This said, I would at the same time stress that a *degree* of determinism can scarcely be denied. Some would demur at the notion of *degrees* of determinism, it might sound like the equivalent of 'partially pure'. Yet this can be a fruitful approach: choices exist, but are limited, by circumstances, by the upbringing and experience of the historical actors, by the existing social, economic or military forces. Some outcomes were or are impossible. Counter-factual history can turn into meaningless 'what if' questions, such as: suppose the Russian revolution had not occurred, suppose the assassins had missed the archduke at Sarajevo, suppose Lenin had been run over by a tramcar in Zürich, or, even more far-fetched, that Russia possessed the institutions and traditions of Western 'bourgeois democracy', or that the Spartacists has been successful in seizing power in Germany. As well imagine the survival into the 1970s of the Austro–Hungarian empire. One recalls a few lines of an old Russian play:

> If, ah if grandma had a beard,
> She would be grandpa.

Similarly, in judging (or describing) events one must take into account the limitations built into the actual situation. Using another military example, whoever commanded the Red Army in 1941 was bound to be severely handicapped by the great shortage of radios and of motor transport, and both these factors contributed to the scale of the disasters. This was something the Soviet commanders could do nothing to alter. In fact poor General Pavlov and his staff doubtless pointed this out to their court-martial before they were shot, but Stalin had no time for realistic criteria; 'objective circumstances have a name and address'. In assessing the problem faced by those who, before 1941, might have ensured a more adequate supply of radios and lorries, no doubt any sensible historian will bear in mind the relative weakness of Russian industry, and the fact that greater effort in this sphere would have caused neglect of another.

Criteria for judgement should relate to the possible. Statesmen and regimes should not be criticised for not doing what in fact they could not do. Of course it is true that one can disagree about the limits of the possible. It is also important to note that much may depend on time-scale, and also on the situation of the given individual or event in the hierarchy of individuals or events. Thus, as Czechoslovakia's tragic experience of 1968 showed, the range of choice is limited in a country in a subordinate position. So 'impossible' could mean that a course of action which is quite feasible as such is prevented by powerful *outside* forces. Still another limitation worth a mention relates to actions barred by ideology. By this I mean that one or more alternatives are not seen to be alternatives, because they conflict with strongly held beliefs or prejudices. Thus to eat a cheese sandwich or a ham sandwich represents alternative choices for most readers of this paper, but not for an orthodox rabbi.

After this perhaps over-long introduction, let us look at various aspects of Soviet experience in the light of various criteria, beginning with the Soviets' own declared objectives and claims.

In examining the Soviet record by reference to the Soviets' own criteria, one is at once confronted by two quite distinct sub-groups of problems. One relates to claims that are simply false or very seriously distorted. The other concerns the unrealisable or utopian elements of the original aims of the revolution. It may well be that the false claims are in some part motivated by the need to claim that the unrealisable has in fact been realised.

In his unusual and highly critical satire, recently published in the West, the Soviet philosopher Alexander Zinoviev cites the following imaginary conversation. 'You do not have a real Ism,' said the Journalist, 'you have state capitalism.' 'Nonsense,' replied the Neurotic, 'this is the delirium of you Ists, who have never visited us. What we have is state feudalism.' 'I cannot agree with this,' said the Dauber. 'We rather have state slave-owning.' 'You also are wrong,' said the Chatterer, 'as you do not take into account the decisive factor. Our country has been invented, and invented on assumptions that could not possibly be realised anywhere. We are the fruit of a sick imagination . . . None of these concepts is applicable to us. Slavery, feudalism, capitalism are categories of civilisation, but we are anti-civilisation. If we really could exist, we would go through the same stages of civilisation, only with a negative sign.' (Zinoviev, 1976, p. 248.)

At a recent seminar, a speaker (it was Michael Ellman) stated that the Soviet regime had failed to eliminate or even to reduce the division of labour. To the objection that the process of industrialisation inevitably extends and deepens the division of labour, Ellman replied that he agreed with this objection, but that it was none the less proper to judge the record of the Soviet regime in relation to its original declared aims. It is, of course, equally possible to note that the state has not withered away, that there still exists a professional bureaucracy, a regular army, a hierarchy. But this part of the original revolutionary objectives has fallen into desuetude. By now Soviet ideology and the bulk of its Soviet critics have explicitly or implicitly recognised the inevitability of the existence of the division of labour, the state, hierarchy etc. So we will leave aside for the present the 'millenarian' critique, and concentrate on what could be called the constructive critics. While, of course, some of the dissidents are anti-socialist, anti-Marxist, some – for instance the Medvedev brothers – try to judge the regime by its own declared standards, i.e. by what it claims to have achieved and to be. They condemn the currently approved histories of the Soviet period for their cowardly evasion of unpleasant and difficult issues, such as Stalinism, or collectivisation; their criterion is historical truth, they resent the false official claim that the published histories of the USSR describe what actually happened. They compare the realities of everyday life with the legal guarantees enacted in the 1936 constitution and re-enacted in 1977: freedom of speech, of religious observance, of the press, the rights of the union republics, and so on, with or without reference to the Helsinki Declaration. They point to the so-called democratic 'elections', and equal political rights for women (with not a single woman minister or senior party official). The list of matters barred by the censorship, including the existence of censorship itself, the 'closed shops' and other privileges of the *nomenklaturnye rabotniki* ('establishment') and their children, is of itself evidence of the gap between what is supposed to exist and the actual reality. Needless to say, in no country is there a coincidence between 'is' and 'ought', all are variously guilty of making exaggerated claims of virtue while concealing vice. However, not only are such habits legitimate targets for criticism, but they can be, often are, freely criticised. It is not that hypocrisy is a peculiarly Russian vice, but systematic officially imposed hypocrisy, reinforced by equally systematic official concealment, such things are particularly well developed in the USSR.

The working class may legitimately contrast the formal rights of workers with the virtual non-existence of any institutions to which workers' representatives could be genuinely elected. Nor, it may be pointed out, is there anything in the Soviet constitution or in the works of Marx about outlawing modern art, obstructing marriages with foreigners, or encouraging the glorification of Russia while preventing the glorification of (say) the Ukraine. Indeed neither Marx nor Lenin wrote anything about the existence and legitimacy of a one-party state. The civil rights movement, Charter 77 in Czechoslovakia, the committee for the defence of workers in Poland, all insist that they observe the formal provisions of the law and insist that the state and party do likewise.

These are, surely, realistic criteria, in the sense that (unlike the elimination of the division of labour) they appear all to be within the bounds of feasibility; indeed one is dealing here with the contrast between what is said to be and what is.

The Soviet leaders might reply that existing institutions and practices are essential for the stability of the regime, and that instability leads to chaos and confusion, to the detriment of the people's interests. Even some émigrés insist that freer access to information, the right to organise an unofficial art exhibition, let alone open criticism of the regime, would present the gravest danger to public order. This contrasts with a view, held by other dissidents, that relaxation would entail little or no risk, and that much that exists can be explained by a tendency to *perestrakhovka* (over-insurance), exaggerated fears, habit, vested interest of the ruling stratum. It is hard for an outsider to judge between these interpretations. Maybe, as Sir William Hayter wrote, 'the Soviet rulers believe, and history provides few arguments to the contrary, that Russia can only be governed as an isolated autocracy' (*The Times*, 7 September 1973). Privately one hears similar arguments from Soviet officials. They should be taken seriously. Thus, even we in the West, with very different traditions, should be conscious of the fact that the untrammelled pursuit of sectional interests can in the end be self-defeating and can lead to acute political and economic problems; one has only to study the recent history of British trade unionism. It would be foolish indeed to assert or imply that the introduction of parliamentary multi-party democracy plus a free market would solve all problems or not create some new ones. None the less, it seems appropriate to judge Soviet reality in relation to its own claims and assertions.

Yet it does seem equally appropriate, in looking at Soviet post-revolutionary history, to recognise the constraints under which the Bolsheviks operated. The great poet Mandel'shtam wrote of the 'twilight of liberty', but also of the 'intolerable burden' (*nevynosimyi gnyot*) of power, which was thrust upon a tearful leader. The idea that Lenin sobbed with dismay when power was thrust upon him may seem comically wrong. Yet the poet's imagination was not altogether wide of the mark. Lenin and his comrades picked up power when it was, so to speak, lying in the gutter, when traditional tsarist authority had collapsed and no one else had the legitimacy and the ruthlessness to reimpose order. Anarchy and disintegration were, quite possibly, the only practicable alternatives to a Bolshevik Russia, and a Bolshevik Russia could survive only by imposing a party despotism on the reluctant or indifferent masses. It is not, in my view, very helpful to understanding to imply that there existed, say in 1918 or 1921, a viable democratic solution, that Martov, or Milyukov, or Spiridonova could have governed Russia. This might be as irrelevant, in the context of the then feasible alternatives, as a free election in the reign of Peter the Great, or in Germany at the time of the Thirty Years War. Needless to say, this does not 'justify' any specific act or institution which existed under Lenin (or Peter the Great, or Wallenstein). It is just that some liberal historians are apt to over-look the limits of the possible in the given historical context.

So, for quite different reasons, are certain liberal economists. Let us now move on to the problem of criteria appropriate to judging the economic performance of the USSR. Two kinds of measures suggest themselves: one is of growth, the other is comparison with an advanced capitalist economy, such as the United States.

I have written at length elsewhere (e.g. Nove, 1977) about the limitations of growth statistics, so let me briefly indicate the essential difficulties. The official volume index (for national income, or indus-trial production) is regarded with suspicion, for good reasons. Western scholars have made noble efforts to recompute growth, and no one can do better than they have done with the available data. However, some data are not available at all (armaments, aircraft, ships, gold, to cite a few examples), some are aggregations of a rapidly changing product mix (e.g. footwear, machine-tools, clothing, lorries), and some relate to new products, whose valuation for purposes of an index is to some extent arbitrary. Then there is the exaggeration arising from the interest of reporting agencies to claim a high rate of aggregate growth and to conceal price increases (e.g. by claiming that a dearer new model is of higher quality). It is virtually impossible to devise a 'correct' index in the face of such obstacles. Thus, to take one example, how can we tell if a new kind of trousers, sausage, plough or furniture is in fact of better quality or only pretends to be? Yet this could affect the price index, and through it the growth rate. This is not intended to deny the fact of impressive economic growth, or that the Soviet economy has grown faster than the American, or British. But when comparison is made with the most dynamic capitalist nations, say postwar Japan, the statistics leave room for much doubt.

Comparisons with foreign countries, in turn, raise several sub-problems. One of these relates to the usual difficulty inherent in index numbers: the outcome depends greatly on the chosen price-base (this applies also to calculations of growth rates, of course). But there is a further problem relating to prices. In Western capitalist economies the statement that some item costs 50 or 500 dollars implies that it is in fact obtainable at that price. In the USSR, however, producers' goods are rationed by the administered allocation system, while many consumers' goods are unavailable, or can be found only occasionally after standing in line (or perhaps paying a bribe). Suppose one knows that a given type of shoe costs 50 dollars in Milwaukee and 42 rubles in Kharkov. This can help us calculate the value of a 'shoe-ruble'. But suppose that, for most of the year, these shoes are not to be found in or near Kharkov. There should then be a downward correction to the shoe-ruble valuation, but no known way exists to calculate an 'unavailability-coefficient', though plainly this is important in comparisons of living standards. (The same difficulty arises in comparing (say) British purchasing power before and after the abolition of rationing.)

However, if and when all these difficulties are overcome, one faces yet another problem: that of identifying those elements in the comparison which are affected by the system, as distinct from the physical and human facts of Russia. Let us suppose that Bergson's careful calculations of factor productivity are not only the best that human ingenuity can make them (which they are), but are literally and absolutely correct, and that factor productivity in the USSR in 1960 was either 34 per cent or 56 per cent of that of the United States, using Soviet and US price weights respectively (Bergson, 1968, p. 26.) What would this tell us – apart from providing us with information of evident interest in itself?

What allowance should be made for land fertility, the location (often highly inconvenient) of mineral resources, the fact that rivers flow in the 'wrong' directions and freeze for half the year, or the extent of drought risk, or the length of the growing season? All of the above would tend to increase the amount of human effort and material expenses required to produce a given volume of final output. None is in any way dependent on the nature of the Soviet regime. All would handicap, relatively to the United States, *any* kind of Russian economy. Though Bergson himself tends to play down these questions (ibid., p. 27), they seem rather important. Thus to take a contemporary example, the fact that Soviet fuel resources are located mainly in remote Siberian regions adds heavily to cost: new towns need to be built in the wilderness, very long pipelines and other transport facilities have to be provided, with evidently adverse effects on capital output ratios and factor productivity. (Indeed I recall the German economist Hans Raupach arguing that an important reason for the role of the state in Russian-Soviet industrialisation was the very big distances between complementary mineral and fuel resources, such as those involved in the Ural-Kuznetsk combine, making such developments unprofitable for private business.) The researches of Robert W. Campbell have shown that the very much lower productivity of the Soviet coal industry, compared with the American, is to a considerable extent due to the accessibility and thickness of coal seams. And so on.

Then, of great importance, is the human factor. Economists are apt to neglect this, partly because it is unquantifiable, partly because it seems more 'scientific' to assume that men react identically to identical stimuli or opportunity. Yet who can doubt that traditional attitudes play their part? Of course, attitudes and responses change. Japanese businessmen do not resemble in their behaviour their sword-carrying Samurai ancestors. Yet no explanation of Japan's remarkable postwar economic performance can omit the uniqueness of the Japanese people. It does not seem very meaningful to criticise Soviet or British governments for not introducing the very successful 'Japanese model' to the USSR or Britain, because, surely, it is not transplantable into such very different environments.

Most of us would probably agree that, in any analysis of the differences in economic performance between West Germany and Great Britain, 'traditional' practices and attitudes of both employers and workers should occupy an important place. The GDR is well ahead in the Eastern European productivity 'league table', followed by Czechoslovakia, with the Soviet Union very considerably behind. Why? Within the Soviet Union itself pride of place goes to Estonia and Latvia, with the Central Asian republics bringing up the rear. Again – why? Can one ignore the human beings and their traditions? Could we implicitly assume that Soviet peasants and American farmers respond similarly, or would have done so but for the Soviet regime and its agricultural policies? While noting the many inadequacies of the Soviet system in the field of technological innovation, could we not readily imagine that the Russian empire, had it survived, would also be importing technology on a large scale from the West?

Also relevant to any comparison of efficiency of systems are two other points. One concerns *objectives,* or the answer to the question: 'Efficiency for what?' Thus the Stalin strategy was one of creating a powerful military-industrial base in the shortest possible time, and not allocative efficiency, which is in any case very difficult to measure or define in a period of rapid structural change. The concentration of resources on priority objectives, which is facilitated by centralised planning, involves a substantial cost: bureaucratic distortions, irrational prices which confuse calculations, and so on. The cost is, in certain circumstances, worth paying. All states are willing to pay it during a war. To take a different example: the Swiss and the Swedes deliberately support a high-cost agriculture on political-social grounds. One's estimate of the effectiveness of their policy cannot abstract from this deliberately chosen objective, even though it is in disaccord with the standard theories of international division of labour and comparative costs.

Mention of costs leads one to consider that *all* systems have costs and various specific forms of waste, and that, in East and West alike, they are not readily ascertainable. Indeed, some of them enter into the national accounts as output. The West spends vastly more on advertising, packaging, salesmanship, uses artificially induced obsolescence. The West has more human and material resources unused for longer periods. The 'East' tends to produce poorer quality output, to waste more materials, to neglect the needs of the user, suffers from bureaucratic delays and supply bottlenecks. Soviet prices are usually irrational or confusing, ours are affected by inflationary instability, which inhibits rational investment decisions. All these pluses and minuses inter-relate. Thus the inflexibility and unresponsiveness of the Soviet system is largely explicable by the full utilisation of resources and the resultant sellers' market. It is the difficulty of finding customers which causes Western firms to pay much more attention to user demand, but also leads to expenditures on advertising and salesmanship, legitimate and illegitimate.

It is pointless to contrast the real Soviet economy with a model of the capitalist market system. The *model* of the Soviet economy is also perfect. Western reality, at present especially, gives rise to many a worry and uncertainty. True enough, there are social as well as economic stresses and strains also in the 'East': one has only to look at Poland. A comparative study of dynamic trends, including the future stability or instability of West and East, would take us far from the subject matter of the present paper, but it is not irrelevant to the assessment of the relative efficiency of systems.

I have no doubt that there are major areas of inefficiency in the Soviet economic system, and I have tried to describe and analyse them for many years. However, to *measure* the difference which the system makes, to identify the specific contribution of 'Soviet socialism', within the comparative statistics, is quite beyond my powers. What we would really like to know is: what *would* have been the output, efficiency and living standards of Russia had there been no Bolshevik revolution? But this, as we have agreed, is an illegitimately far-fetched exercise in counter-factual history. One can scarcely also assume away World War I, while imagining that foreign and domestic capital sustained the trends of the 1900–13 period. One can arrive at a result by simple extrapolation, but what would it all mean?

There is the further complication that the ideology and party which have so greatly affected economic structure and performance are themselves a product of specifically Russian conditions. These conditions included those aspects of Russian historical development which (until very late) inhibited the growth of Russian capitalist enterprise. To some extent the Bolshevik state and economic system, as they emerged, can be seen as a *substitute* for a capitalist road, which Russia had entered by the end of the century (as Lenin pointed out in his *Development of Capitalism in Russia*), but from which she was driven by the revolution.

The final section of the paper will try to deal with the critical stance typical of the 'New Left'. This can be distinguished from the moderate dissidents of the Medvedev type primarily because the Medvedevs operate *within* the system and urge its leaders to observe their own laws and professed beliefs, while the New Left – including its Chinese variant – assails the system as essentially not socialist, or as anti-socialist, or even as some new form of tsarism or social-imperialism, judging it by reference to their definition of socialism.

They claim that this definition is in fact Marx's and conforms to what Lenin and his comrades believed when they made the revolution. It is similar to Marx's 'communism': no commodity production, no markets, no money, no wage relationships, no inequality, 'from each according to his ability, to each according to his need', abundance, changes in human psychology, the withering away of the state, the elimination of all or most national boundaries, and so on. Of course, it is recognised that such a world as this has not been, and is not, immediately practicable. Some recall Marx's reference, in his 'Critique of the Gotha programme', to a 'lower' stage of communist society, in which earnings and distribution depend on work, not yet on need. Some classify the Soviet Union as a 'transitional society', which, therefore, should be judged by reference to whether the basic trend of change is towards socialism as these critics define the word. New Left critics differ about how much could have been achieved, and also on precisely why it was not. They differ also about the role, in any explanation, of Russian economic and cultural backwardness. Thus, for example, Charles Bettelheim, in his *Class Struggles in the USSR*, accuses many of his fellow-leftists of the deviation he calls 'economism', which consists of what he would regard as an impermissible degree of economic determinism (such as the Menshevik view that Russia was not ripe for a socialist revolution, or Trotsky's stress on the importance of state ownership, or Stalin's emphasis on the development of productive forces). For him the key that failed to turn was the class struggle, led and organised by a sort of *deus ex machina* super-party, which could transcend backwardness by following the correct mass line. (Bettelheim, 1976.) Bettelheim clearly imagined that Chinese experience under Mao justified this attitude, though more recent events in China have given him grounds for doubt. There seems to me no doubt that Bettelheim's condemnation of 'economism' would sweep most of Marxism away. (Interestingly, the same idea, in a different way, is propagated by Mihailo Mihajlov, who vigorously attacks the whole notion of an economic basis and a political super-structure, declaring politics to be the 'basic basis'. (*SSSR: demokraticheskiye alternativy*, Achberg, 1976, p. 44.)) The party seems superhuman, with no discernible economic-social base, mysteriously free from what Rakovsky called 'the professional risks of power' and also of the normal human failings of people of all classes (such as self-seeking, ambition, drunkenness, intolerance etc.). Bettelheim, especially in his first volume, typifies a basic weakness of the entire New Left position: considerations of economic effectiveness are almost totally ignored, words such as 'expert', 'technical' and the like are placed between ironic inverted commas, as if consideration of practical feasibility is of quite secondary importance, as against ideological purity and the class struggle. The Red Army, it seems, was organised on the basis of bourgeois or even feudal hierarchical subordination, and not of 'proletarian discipline': the soldiers did not 'control' the officers! It is almost as if the author was unaware of the simple necessities of fighting a war, unaware too of the fact that the Red Army included hundreds of thousands of reluctant conscripts with a high propensity to desert.

This is a good example of 'impossible criteria': one can scarcely condemn Trotsky for insisting on discipline in the Red Army, rather than giving priority to the 'class struggle' and losing the war. Perhaps the psychological explanation of such attitudes lies in a refusal to face the logic of a 'premature revolution', the consequences of immaturity, because to do so implies that perhaps the Mensheviks were right. Other members of the New Left escape from this dilemma by denouncing the policy of socialism in one (backward) country. They imply that, yes, indeed many evil consequences followed from the isolation of Russia, and that the solution was a link-up with revolutions in advanced countries. But – it may be objected – there *was* no revolution in advanced countries. To which this species of critic retorts that the failures of the revolutions in Germany and elsewhere were due in large measure to the errors or worse of the dominant Stalin faction. Errors there of course were – one has only to think of the muddle in Germany in 1923 – but a sober assessment of probabilities of successful communist revolutions in advanced countries does not suggest that a more skilful Comintern leadership would have succeeded. Nor is it really clear that the forces which brought Stalinism to power would have been seriously weakened if a more advanced country *had* had a successful communist revolution.

Unreal criteria are a common feature of many New Left critiques, of past and present alike. These flow, in my view, from the New Left's essential millenarianism. That is to say, while differing from one other in many ways, they share a definition of socialism (and a view as to the road to this socialism) that bears only a remote relation to reality, and furthermore their 'socialism' is one in which the social, economic, political and cultural problems which trouble all hitherto known states are absent *by definition*. Their criticisms are frequently well founded, but their validity is affected by the silent (or not so silent) assumption that the problems are the creation of the bureaucracy, elite or ruling class, and that the power of the workers or the 'mass line' will resolve them.

It is as if criticism of Soviet criminal law procedure was based upon the dogma that, of course, under socialism there would be no crime. Or, to take a more fanciful example, if the (correct) statement that professionalism and financial interest stimulate dirty play on the football field is held to imply that, in a socialist society, there is no need for a referee.

Thus a typical New Left survey of Soviet education stresses that officials use influence to get their children into prestigious institutions, that children of white-collar staff and intelligentsia have a disproportionate share of places in higher education, and that the system is 'elitist'. While the facts bear out most of these criticisms, it is implied that a society can exist today in which those with influence will not use it to secure a good educational start for their children, or that in a socialist society all institutions will be equally prestigious, that resources are available to provide universal higher education, and that the familiar advantages of a cultural environment (parental encouragement, motivation, books in the home etc.) could somehow vanish. As for the word 'elitism', it has become in their hands an almost meaningless prejorative term, unless what is being asserted is that, even in the so-called transitional period, there is no need for leadership, organisers, managers, rectors, and so any training scheme designed to produce persons able to carry out these functions is to be condemned. We shall return to this point in a moment.

Before that, let us look at the criteria appropriate to the position of women in the Soviet Union. Here again there is much to criticise. They do tend to occupy the less well paid positions, their everyday life is difficult (work, then the wearisome task of shopping, little help from menfolk in the home etc. etc.), and their role in politics is small, contrasting with earlier times (Figner, Spiridonova, Zasulich, Kollontai, to name a few), and contrasting also with their major role in the middle echelons of the bureaucracy, But women have made some significant advances, too. Let us take as an example the information that 10 per cent of professors in the USSR are women. This could be (and by one of my militant women students was) interpreted as evidence of discrimination. It could, on the contrary, be contrasted with the statistics of virtually any other country, West or East, and be found to be unusually high. One cannot really expect the attitude to women, and of women, formed by millennia of experience, to alter so radically after a revolution as to make possible equality in this and similar spheres. Indeed, one needs to remember that workers (and peasants) typically have a conservative and conventional view of the role of women in society and the family. It never ceases to surprise me to hear from the New Left, that women's liberation and working-class domination are somehow linked. Indeed it is not surprising that, as has just been noted, the role of women in political leadership has actually diminished since 1917; the women who were then prominent were, with hardly an exception, from the upper or professional classes. The existing party leadership consists of men whose family origins would predispose them to share the conventional attitudes of ordinary people and they are not, and cannot be expected to be, selected by special reference to their views on women.

It is clear that there are indeed criticisms to be made of the Soviet record in this field, so long as it is not implied that a 'real' working-class-dominated society would have solved the problems in question.

Nowhere is the issue of realistic criteria more important than in assessing economic performance and institutions. This relates particularly to the issue of the role of the market and of market-type reforms, and of bureaucracy and hierarchy. Involved too is a view of what constitutes, or can constitute, meaningful mass participation in decision making, and, again, the function of leadership and of elites.

On the whole, the New Left is hostile to market-type reforms. (Sweezy: 'Beware of the market; it is capitalism's secret weapon!') Mostly they are hostile also to the Yugoslav self-management model, because it relies heavily on the market and on material incentives, and for a number of other (often very cogent) reasons, such as the weakness of planning, excessive income inequalities, high unemployment, inflation, and so on. It is hostile also to bureaucracy. However, as several critics have pointed out, this is really a quite untenable position. (See Chapter 7, pp. 111–32; Lindbeck, 1971; Selucky, 1974.) A modern industrial economy is a highly complex inter-related system, which requires a highly complex information-processing and co-ordinatory mechanism if the parts are to operate coherently and chaos is to be avoided. The market model is based on the propostion that coherence and co-ordination can be achieved through the market-place. This view must be modified, taking into account imperfect knowledge, uncertainty, the evident need to *administer* closely related activities, the existence of giant multi-national corporations, and so on. Bureaucratic deformations can and do occur in both East and West. However, it should be clear that any attempt to administer the entire economy from the centre requires a large bureaucracy as a functional necessity. A sizable literature in East and West analyses the economy as a whole as a species of hierarchical system. With no micro-economic market, the sheer overwhelming volume of data collection and decision making, the size and complexity of the bureaucracy, become major causes of inefficiency, for reasons abundantly explored in many works on the Soviet economic system.

Hence the efforts to reform it, by introducing stronger elements of market decentralisation, efforts stoutly resisted by the party-state machine.

The New Left see the inefficiency and the waste, but tend to attribute it to the power of the bureaucracy and the lack of democratic control by whose whom they like to describe as 'the direct producers'. At no point do they analyse how the direct producers are to control the economy. Bettelheim, for instance, asserts the dominance of politics over economics, but by what political process are the direct producers to determine social need, and to 'translate' this into literally thousands of millions of interrelated decisions on production, allocation, distribution, transport? Indeed, in what units should the necessary calculations be made?

This is not for a moment to deny that the greater democratisation of Soviet political life would have profound economic consequences. However, they would surely be limited to 'macro' questions, concerning basic policy priorities, and also to combating blatant abuses. It seems to me that Mihailo Milhajlov went too far when he wrote: 'The liquidation of the monopoly of the party would at once sharply improve the economic situation, because then the party in power, to avoid losing the election, will do everything possible to activate the national economy . . . So that feedback [i.e. of demand on the producer] can be ensured without a market in a politically pluralist society.' (*SSSR: demokraticheskiye alternativy* . . ., p. 46.) Brezhnev also desires to 'sharply improve the economic situation'. *The* problem is how to achieve this while preserving the centralised planning system, with its functionally necessary bureaucracy. Nor can the computer resolve the problem: as the talented Soviet mathematicians well know, the amount of information to be gathered and processed, the definition of the 'objective function', the necessary disaggregation of operational instructions, far transcend the capacity of any known computer. Furthermore, as the Hungarian economist Maria Augustinovics has pointed out, computers, once programmed, are far less flexible than even the most rigid bureaucrat, who can (and does) modify and amend plans in the light of the unexpected and of new information.

The Soviet economist Maiminas wisely noted a characteristic of the modern industrial economy: on the one hand, the extent of systemic inter-relationships leads one to see advantages in centralised planning, in which the interests of the whole can be given precedence over the apparent interests of the part. However, efficient operation and planning require a meaningful initiative by management and labour on the spot, and their remoteness from centralised decision making is a negative factor. (Paraphrased from Maiminas, 1971, p. 46.) For Bettelheim and his comrades this dilemma seems not to exist. The 'mass line' and 'control by the direct procedures' will resolve it. There is not much value in criticism of the undoubted evils of current Soviet practice, and of proposals by various reformers, if it is based upon 'solutions' that are not feasible.

Some critics of this type insist upon the importance of attitudes, of workers and managers alike. If they are alienated, if they do not strive for the common good – as they would do under 'real' socialism – then they are not efficient, they produce spoiled work, they fail to provide accurate information. (For such an argument, see Ticktin, 1973.)

Here again, as so often with New Left critiques, there is some substance alongside the unreality. Human attitudes do matter, do affect productivity, efficiency, the quality of reporting. However:

(1) The problems of central planning without a market are not *primarily* due to negative human attitudes of men or women on the spot.

(2) In all large organisations, information is distorted by the interest of those who provide it. 'Interest' here does not mean pecuniary interest only: all of us tend to identify whatever we are responsible for with the good of society, be it nursery schools, cancer research, medieval history or writing a Festschrift for Richard Löwenthal. This must be a problem *unless* one silently assumes abundance, in the sense of resources for all purposes being infinitely available.

(3) Much of the problem is precisely due to the *unavoidable* remoteness of central planners.

(4) One must agree with Wiles that 'the connection of size with alienation is so extremely obvious that one wonders how at least Marxists living in free countries cannot grasp it . . . For Marx and Marxists the size of society is irrelevant, since everyone under 'full communism' is rational, moral and unanimous. Therefore there is no administrative problem, no conflict, even no need to vote. No one can feel alienated, no matter how large society is. The size problem has been defined out of existence by the perfection of the individual citizens.' (Wiles, 1977, p. 585.)

There is a parallel between the vision of socialism as the New Left sees it and the equally impossible model of general equilibrium, with perfect information and perfect markets, of Western neo-classical textbooks. Be it noted that neither has any role for the entrepreneur, everything can be (or has already been) routinised, the problems of unpredictability, complexity, choice, efficiency, ignorance, have been assumed out of existence. (See Loasby, 1976.) The neo-classical world of static Pareto efficiency is as irrelevant a criterion by which to judge the Western as the Eastern economies.

If any group of workers is able freely to decide about production, then this group is bound to be producing for exchange and not for use; it is bound to be engaged in what Marx called commodity production. There will then be a market. Such a solution will give rise to problems and to distortions, but the only known alternative carries with it, as functional necessities, the bureaucratic structures of Soviet-type economies. The unwillingness of the New Left to face these issues squarely diminishes the impact of their criticisms of Soviet reality. True, as already noted, they do not expect 'full communism' to be achieved already, they speak of a transitional society. But how can it be in transition towards the unattainable?

The New Left usually suffers from a chronic inability to see that virtually any system, or reform, carries with it certain costs, risks, deficiencies, which must be realistically examined. Let me cite two more examples. My colleague Janusz Zielinski, in a paper shortly to be published, points to the fact that the security of employment typical of Eastern Europe (a worker is very seldom dismissed) goes with low productivity and low wages, that a decisive move towards greater efficiency and higher wages must have as its corollary the weeding out and transfer of surplus labour from the sectors and factories where it is to be found. Almost every New Left critic will at once denounce any such move as 'anti-worker', and imply that there exists some painless and costless route to higher wages and higher productivity, which would follow (in some undefined way) the adoption of a mass line, the ending of alienation. Similarly, while the East European reformer will usually urge the adoption of supply-and-demand-balancing prices – which logically require an increase in certain prices, e.g. of meat – the New Left attack this too as anti-worker, benefiting the better-off or the new bourgeoisie. Trotsky at least understood well that those officials who allocate scarce commodities 'never forget *themselves*', and indeed he quite specifically assigned to the phenomenon of shortage an important role in the rise of the Stalinist bureaucracy. (Deutscher, 1964, p. 159.) Yet those who claim to be his followers seek to persuade the workers that there exists some magic formula by which low prices can coexist with higher wages and abundant supplies of goods in the shops. Or rather that such a happy state of affairs would exist if they were able to overthrow the bureaucrats. Interestingly, the bureaucrats seem satisfied with the existing situation and resist the market-type reformers, since their control over the allocative mechanism gives them preferential access to scarce goods at low prices.

The critical Soviet philosopher, Alexander Zinoviev, puts a similar line of thought into the mouth of one of his characters:

'Inventors of utopias all commit the same error, that of failing to take into account the fact that positive and negative aspects of reality arise out of the same order of life . . . It is impossible to eliminate an evil without also eliminating something positive that is linked with it. One cannot create a good quality without bringing into being some negative quality linked with it. Just as in aerodynamics one cannot increase the speed of an aircraft without increasing wind resistance . . . We should establish these dependent relationships and analyse all their logically possible combinations. You will then find no known utopias among them, as utopias are logically contradictory in the very nature of their construction. This is what makes them unrealisable.'

The author went on to claim that a chance to realise human ideals would follow from 'a pitiless analysis of our life today, without under-statement or overstatement, an objective and unbiased description of what we really are'. He added ironically, 'But that is indeed to be utopian'. (Zinoviev, 1976, p. 362.)

Much of the New Left critique, therefore, suffers from their espousal of unreal criteria, from a definition of socialism that is liter-ally out of this world, a view of hierarchy and 'elites' in terms of which one must condemn any government or any authority, including any conceivable government which these same critics would or could set up. But then an essential part of the New Left philosophy, if philosophy it is, involves an almost militant disregard of what they contemptuously refer to as 'empirical facts' and feasibilities. Thus I have never succeeded in interesting a New Leftist in the problems of economic efficiency under socialism. For them Soviet inefficiency is one more proof of the non-socialist nature of that society. Under a real socialism, with a new Man and social harmony, efficiency there would be, and there's an end of the discussion.

In fairness it is necessary to add that many individual members of one or other of the New Left schools have contributed significantly to our understanding of Soviet history and have had much of interest and importance to say about the nature and social structure of the USSR. Therefore, in concentrating on one aspect of their approach to the subject I have been unintentionally less than fair to their academic contribution. In a longer and more complete discussion their more positive contribution would certainly find a more prominent place.

Where does all this leave us? Some readers may conclude that, in drawing attention to the inherent limitations and constraints within which the Soviet regime has operated, I have been undertaking a sophisticated exercise in justification. Others may interpret the preceding pages as anti-revolutionary, because anti-utopian. Such criticisms would not be valid. Taking the last point first, it is undeniable that certain drastic systemic changes have required revolutionary action to remove obstacles, or to overthrow an entrenched ruling oligarchy, or may require such action in the future. It is also true that many revolutionaries have been inspired by 'millenarian' goals, by a striving after an impossible perfect society. But belief in an impossible perfection is surely not a necessary precondition of commitment to revolution. As for so-called justification, against criticism from right and left, one can only say that the recognition of feasibilities and constraints has absolutely no connection with right or wrong, or value-judgements. Exceedingly unpleasant events have occurred in the twentieth century, thereby proving that they were, alas possible.

One aspect of the problem has, perhaps, not been sufficiently stressed so far, though it has been mentioned. This could be called a kind of historical hierarchy of levels. Thus Bolsheviks and Mensheviks debated, with quotations from Marxist classics, whether it was proper to seize state power in the name of socialism in backward Russia. Of course, the *opportunity* was created by antecedent circumstances, but opportunities are not always taken. Once power was seized, a whole new series of possibilities and constraints came into being. Thus if, in the situation of 1921, power was to be retained by the Bolsheviks, the suppression of other parties was essential, whether or not the one-party state was foreseen or advocated by Marx. Given the circumstances of NEP and the ideological commitments of the Bolshevik party, industrialisation required the mobilisation of resources by the state, which was bound to lead to grave social-political difficulties in an overwhelming peasant country. At the same time the kulak solution to the peasant problem was excluded by ideology. We may be sure that non-Bolsheviks would have found a much less drastic and painful solution than collectivisation, so here we have ideological commitment as a constraint on otherwise possible action. And, of course, at any given moment the executants of policy work within constraints set by their superiors. Thus, to return to military parallels, a divisional commander's courses of action are limited by his orders, his resources, and so on. Criteria should also be seen as having a kind of hierarchy, i.e. recognising the limitations applicable at the given level, or constraints set by what has already happened or been assumed: antecedent circumstances are unalterable, existing constraints must be taken into account, whatever the country or system. Thus, to take British examples, Edward Heath showed a grave misjudgement in his policy towards the unions in 1973, Anthony Eden was even more wrong-headed over Suez in 1956, because both chose to neglect the objective limitations on action. Of course it is possible to envisage circumstances in which the Anglo-French military force would have won or the miners were defeated (as they were in 1926). The analyst may (or may not) prefer that Eden and Heath had been successful. In judging them we have the benefit of hindsight. But it will surely be the judgement of historians that the two statesmen blundered, in assessing what was known at the time and indeed was forcefully pointed out to them.

At the same time we must be conscious of the fact that future historians may condemn our statesmen for failure to take action which we know, as contemporaries, was not within their power to take. Or that, in the given situation, a statesman who was thought likely to act in a certain way would not be in power, or would not occupy a leading position in his party. (Thus those who reproach Allende for not seizing power and suppressing right-wing parties should remember that he was confirmed as president by congress only because he was known to be against such actions.)

To what conclusions does the above analysis lead? In what terms is it proper to judge the Soviet Union, or indeed any other country or system? What *are* the appropriate explicit or implicit criteria? Evidently there is a range of choice, depending on the outlook and particular interests of the analyst. This may affect what is regarded as an unrealistic utopia. Thus Levitin-Krasnov's reply to those who say that his Christian-socialist ideal is a 'utopian golden age' is: 'If this ideal of a society with neither rich nor poor, without governors and governed, were unrealisable, then Christ would not have given it to us!' (*SSSR: demokraticheskiye alternativy* . . ., p. 225.) But of course even those who do not invoke the supernatural can differ legitimately about the possible. In passing, it is of importance to be clear about the meaning one attaches to the word 'utopia'. Several thinkers, among them Leszek Kolakowski, defined it as that which cannot be done at the time it is proposed. In *this* sense one can readily agree that every new idea, when first put forward, was utopian, whether it was votes for women or the nationalisation of the coal industry. This is *not* the sense in which I have used the word. The vision of perfect competition and perfect markets, as well as 'full communism', *are* utopias in my sense, something inherently unrealisable (like having your cake and eating it too), without the divine intervention referred to by Levitin-Krasnov. I am not intending for a moment to suggest that sweeping criticisms of the system as a whole are somehow illegitimate, or that only the comparatively modest reform of the Medvedev brothers is 'realistic'. One can recognise (indeed some of the most sweeping critics of the Soviet regime do recognise) the limitations of possible changes *within* the system, which indeed has shown itself incapable of accommodating Medvedev-type reforms. This can lead quite logically to a demand that the system be swept away. This in turn can be followed by a discussion concerning possible future policies and their outcome, avoiding the empty phraseology which, for generations of Russian (and other) radical intellectuals, has served as an alternative to hard-headed realism.

Similarly, it is proper to distinguish between choices made by Bolsheviks (limited by their commitment to Bolshevik ideas) and those which could have been made by governments of different persuasion. Events are not predetermined, choices exist, though some outcomes are excluded. In a lecture, the Yugoslav Marxist Mihajlo Markovic drew two lines on the blackboard, thus:

They indicate the limits of the possible, in the given circumstances, with diminishing probability as one moves away from the centre. Of course it is easier to draw lines on blackboards than to identify their real location in the real world, but it is surely the task of the analyst to try to find them, and to refrain from ignoring their existence in the past or in the present (while it must be recognised that the location of the limits of the possible was probably much less clear to the actors in the drama of history than it might seem to us after the event).

There is evidence of hard-headed thinking among some émigrés, who show that they too would support Richard Löwenthal's criticism of Habermas's political utopianism, cited earlier in this paper. Thus Vadim Belotserkovsky shows himself well aware of the limitations as well as of the advantage of a multi-party system, in the Soviet context especially, and advocates the separation of powers ('we should refrain from combining the legislative and executive functions, as this facilitates the concentration and usurpation of power'), though his notion of 'soviets without parties' may also be quite impracticable: is there to be no function of political leadership? (See *SSSR: demokraticheskiye alternativy* . . ., pp. 85, 89).

Proof that there is serious thinking among the dissidents on this issue may be found in the work already quoted by Alexander Zinoviev, in which the USSR is thinly disguised as Ibansk and the party as the Brotherhood (*Bratiya*):

'The Brotherhood of Ibansk is the essence of state power . . . To understand the Ibansk polity one must understand the essence of the Brotherhood . . . I think that in assessing the role of the Brotherhood the apologists are closer to the truth than its enemies. In Ibansk it really is the case, and not just demagogy and propaganda, that the Brotherhood is the only force capable of maintaining order in society and in some degree able to tame the wild social forces and ensure some sort of progress. It is not the strongest force, it is the *only* force. It is impermissible not to take this into account.' (Zinoviev, 1976, p. 346).

Anyhow, I hope that this perhaps excessively wide-ranging discussion can help to clarify a few aspects of real and unreal criteria for assessing Soviet history, performance and policies. Or, alternatively, that those who disagree with my approach will be stimulated to contradict or to do better than I have been able to do.

References

C. Abramsky and H. Williams (eds) (1974): *Essays in Honour of E. H. Carr*, London.
O. K. Anonov (1965): *Dlya vsekh i dlya sebya*, Moscow.
A. Bergson (1968): *Planning and Productivity under Soviet Socialism*, New York.
C. Bettelheim (1969): *Monthly Review*, March 1969.
C. Bettelheim (1970a): *Calcul économique et formes de propriété*, Paris.
C. Bettelheim (1970b): *Monthly Review*, vol. 22, no. 7.
C. Bettelheim (1976): *Class Struggles in the USSR, First Period 1917–23*, London.
I. Birman (19771): *Metodologiya optimal'nogo planirovaniya*, Moscow.
M. Bornstein (ed.) (1975): *Planning East and West*, Cambridge, Mass.
A. Boyarsky (1962): *Matematiko-ekonomicheskiye ocherki*, Moscow.
W. Brus (1973): *The Economics and Politics of Socialism*, London.
N. I. Bukharin (1917): *Sotsial-demokrat*, no. 5, November 1917, reprinted in *Na podstupakh k oktyabryu*, Moscow (1926).
N. I. Bukharin (1920): *Ekonomika perekhodnogo perioda*, Moscow.
N. I. Bukharin (1921): *Teoriya istoricheskogo materializma*, Moscow.
N. I. Bukharin (1923): *Proletarskaya revolutsiya i kultura*, Petrograd.
N. I. Bukharin (1925a): *Mirovoe khozyaistvo i imperializm*, Moscow, 3rd edn.
N. I. Bukharin (1925b): *Put' k sotsializmu i rabochi-krestyanski soyuz*, Moscow.
N. I. Bukharin (1925c): *K voprosu o trotskizme*, Moscow.
N. I. Bukharin (1926): *Put' k sotsializmu i rabochi-krestyanskisoynz*, Moscow and Leningrad, 3rd edn.
N. I. Bukharin (1927): *K desyatiletiyu oktyabrskoi revolyutsii*, Moscow.
N. I. Bukharin and Ye. A. Preobrazhensky (1919): *Azbuka kommunizma*, Petrograd.
E. H. Carr (1971): *Foundations of a Planned Economy*, vol. 2, London.
C. Castoriadis (1973): *La Société bureaucratique*, Paris.
Yu. Chernyak (1975): *Sistemnyi analiz v upravlenii ekonomikoi*, Moscow.
S. F. Cohen (1974): *Bukharin and the Bolshevik Revolution*, London.
J.-M. Collette (1968): *Politique d'investissement et calcul économique: l'expérience soviétique*, Paris.
C. Cross (1968): *The Observer* Supplement, 25 August 1968, London.
R. Dahrendorf (1957): *Soziale Klassen und Klassenkonflikt*, Stuttgart.
R. B. Day (1973): *Leon Trotsky and the Politics of Economic Isolation*, Cambridge.
I. Deutscher (1964): *The Age of Permanent Revolution: a Trotsky Anthology*, New York.
M. Djilas (1957): *The New Class*, London.
M. Ellman (1971): *Soviet Planning Today*, Cambridge.
A. Erlich (1961): *The Soviet Industrialisation Debate*, Harvard.
N. Fedorenko (1964): *Planirovaniye i ekonomiko-matematicheskiye metody*, Moscow.
N. Fedorenko (ed.) (1969): *Optimal'noye planirovaniye*, Moscow.
J. Gacs and M. Lacko (1973): *Economics of Planning*, no. 1–2, 1973.
A. Galich (1974): *General'naya repetitsiya*, Frankfurt.
E. Gellner (1974): *The Times Literary Supplement*, October 1974.
A. Gerschenkron (1974): 'Figures of speech in the social sciences', *Proceedings of the American Philosophical Society*, October 1974.

J. Goldmann (1964): *Economics of Planning*, no. 2, 1964, Oslo.

D. Granick (1975): *Enterprise Guidance in Eastern Europe: a Comparison of Four Socialist Economies*, Princeton, NJ.

H. J. Habakkuk and M. M. Postan (eds) (1965): *Cambridge Economic History of Europe*, vol. 6, Cambridge.

S. Heitman (ed.) (1967): *Put' k sotsializmu v Rossii* (a selection of Bukharin's works), New York.

S. Heitman (1969): *Bukharin, A Bibliography with Annotations*, Stanford, Calif.

B. Higgins (1959): *Economic Development*, New York.

J. A. Hobson (1902): *Imperialism: a Study*, London.

I. Howe (1976): *Essential Works of Socialism*, New Haven.

L. Kantorovich (1964): *The Best Use of Economic Resources*, Oxford.

L. Kantorovich and V. Makarov (1965): in *Primeneniye matematiki v ekonomicheskikh issledovaniyakh*, Moscow.

A. Katsenellenboigen, Yu. Ovsienko and E. Fayerman (1966): *Metodologicheskiye voprosy optimal'nogo planirovaniya*, Moscow.

T. S. Khachaturov (1976): *Methods of Long-term Planning and Forecasting*, London.

P. Knirsch (1959): *Die ökonomische Anschauungen Nikolai Bucharins*, Berlin.

J. Kornai (1971): *Anti-equilibrium* (English translation), Amsterdam.

M. Lacko (1975): *Acta Oeconomica*, vol. 15, no. 3–4.

D. Lane (1976): *The Socialist Industrial State*, London.

C. Lefort (1971): *Eléments d'une critique de la bureaucratie*, Geneva.

V. I. Lenin (various dates): *Polnoye sobraniye sochineniy*, 5th edn, Moscow. *Collected Works*: English translation of 4th edn, Moscow. Quotations from 5th edn are translated by the author.

A. Lindbeck (1971): *The Economics of the New Left*, New York.

R. Lipsey (1973): *Introduction to Positive Economics*, London.

G. Lisichkin (1966): *Plan i rynok*, Moscow.

B. J. Loasby (1976): *Choice, Complexity and Ignorance*, London.

R. Löwenthal (1976): *Social Research*, Summer 1976, New York.

E. Maiminas (1971): *Printsipy planirovaniya v ekonomike*, Moscow.

R. Medvedev (1972): *Kniga o sovetskoi demokratii*, Amsterdam. Published as *On Socialist Democracy*, London (1975).

V. Nemchinov (ed.) (1964): *The Use of Mathematics in Economics*, Edinburgh.

A. Nove (1969): 'Internal economies', *Economic Journal*, vol. 79, December 1969.

A. Nove (1973): *Efficiency Criteria for Nationalised Industries*, London.

A. Nove (1977): *The Soviet Economic System*, London.

A. Nove and J. A. Newth (1967): *The Soviet Middle East*, London.

D. P. O'Brien (1976): *Economic Journal*, September, 1976.

A. Pashkov (1958): *Ekonomicheskii zakon preimushchestvennogo rosta proizvodstva sredstv proizvodstva*, Moscow.

L. Pasinetti (1965): in *Study Week on the Econometric Approach to Development Planning*, Pontificia Academia Scientiarum, Scripta Varia 28, Amsterdam.

V. I. Perevedentsev (1966): *Migratsiya naseleniya i trudovye problemy Sibiri*, Novosibirsk.

T. Podolski (1972): *Socialist Banking and Monetary Control*, Cambridge.

V. Pugachev (1968): *Optimizatsiya planirovaniya*, Moscow.

A. Pushkin (1887): *Sobranie sochinenii*, St Petersburg.

P. C. Roberts (1971): *Alienation and the Soviet Economy*, Albuquerque.

242 *Political Economy and Soviet Socialism*

P. A. Samuelson, 'Understanding the Marxian notion of exploitation', *Journal of Economic Literature*, June 1971.

R. Selucky (1974): 'Marx and self-management', *Critique*, no. 3, 1974.

P. Sweezy (1972): *Monthly Review*, vol. 23, no. 9, 1972.

N. Spulber and I. Horowitz (1976): *Quantitative Economic Policy and Planning*, New York.

L. Terekhov (1968): *Ekonomiko-matematicheskiye metody*, Moscow.

H. H. Ticktin (1973): 'Towards a political economy of the USSR', *Critique*, no. 1, 1973.

L. Trotsky (1937): *The Revolution Betrayed*, London.

L. Trotsky (1964), see Deutscher (1964).

M. Tugan-Baranovsky (1934): *Russkaya fabrika*, Moscow, 6th edn.

N. Valentinov (1971): *NEP i krizis partii posle smerti Lenina*, Stanford.

P. Wiles (1963): *Political Economy of Communism*, Oxford.

P. Wiles (1977): *Economic Institutions Compared*, Oxford.

O. Williamson (1975): *Markets and Hierarchies*, London.

L. N. Yurovsky (1928): *Denezhnaya politika sovetskoi vlasti*, Moscow.

A. Zauberman (1975): *The Mathematical Revolution in Soviet Economics*, London.

A. Zinoviev (1976): *Ziyayushchiye vysoty* ('Yawning Depths'), Lausanne.

Index

abundance 121-2
accident 89-90
accounting 76, 77; prices 102
accumulation 68-71, 97
adventurism 51-2
Aganbegyan, A. G. 143, 147, 161
agriculture 166-77; backwardness of 37, 47; changes in 177; climate and 171, 176; diseconomies of scale in 171; farm sizes 171; food distribution 173; fertilisers and 171; investment in 173; labour problems in 172; livestock herds 174-5; mechanisation of 49, 172-3; organisation of 176-7; output 173; party attitude to 177; performance of Soviet 170-7, 225; private allotments 172; productivity in 38, 169; Russian capitalism and 66; smallholders in 170; state farms 171
Alexander II 35
alienation 233
aristocracy, the 5-6, 25; their dependence on the Tsar 29
army officers 9-10
art 90
Augustinovics, Maria 155, 232
Ausch, S. 141
authority, and authoritarianism 223; attitudes to 6-8; tradition of in Russia 199-200
autonomous organisations 24-5, 196; weakness of 8

Bazarov, V. 135
Belotserkovsky, Vadim 238
Benkendorff, Count 5
Berdyaev, Nikolai 27
Bettelheim, Charles 122-31 *passim*, 138, 140, 157, 164-5, 205, 208, 228-9
Birman, I. 145-6
black market 186
Blyumkin, Y. G. 52
Böhm-Bawerk, E. von 83, 90
Bogdanov, A. A. 85, 151
Bolsheviks 223, 227, 236, 238
Bonapartism 54, 58
Borzovshchina 203

bourgeoisie, Russian 95, 118-19, 127-8
boyars 3, 6
Boyarsky, A. 159-60
Brezhnev, Leonid 20, 127-8, 156, 158
Brus, Wlodimievz 1, 141, 157, 162
Bukharin, Nicolai I. 1, 81-99, 135, 200, 214; criticised by Lenin 84-5; his economic ideas 82-9, 115, 134; his social philosophy 89-91; his view of NEP 91-7; his warning against extremism 51; his writings on imperialism 71-2, 75; importance of 98-9; *Road to Socialism and the Worker-Peasant Alliance* 93; *Teoriya istoricheskogo materializma* 89-90; Trotsky and 43, 45, 46, 48
Bulgaria: agriculture in 166-7
bureaucracy 8-9, 129-30, 196; Communist Party and 56-7; elimination of 21; Lenin's view of 76; necessity for 199; recruitment to 198; subjectivism and 127; vested interests of 203-4; *see also* nomenklatura
Byulleten oppozitsii 43, 52

Campbell, R. W. 225
capital: constant and variable 68-71; for investment 109-10; surplus of 72, 73-4
capital output ratio 70
capitalism: imperialism and 71-5
capitalism, Russian 227; Lenin's view of 65-6; serfdom and 32
Carr, E. H. 203
caste 214
Castoriadis, C. 205-6, 207
Catherine II 31
censorship 222
Central Asia 18
centralised planning 41; alternatives to 156-7; bureaucracy and 201-2; consumer demand and 105, 187; effect of growth on 137; imbalances in 183; inconsistencies in 156; Lenin's view of 80; microeconomic decisions and 141-2; non-price information and 143;